Best wishes
Martin Plaut

Happy Reading!

# Promise and Despair

*The First Struggle
for a Non-Racial South Africa*

GW00506573

Martin Plaut

JACANA

First published in southern Africa by Jacana Media (Pty) Ltd in 2016

10 Orange Street
Sunnyside
Auckland Park 2092
South Africa
+2711 628 3200
www.jacana.co.za

ISBN 978-1-4314-2375-0

Cover design by publicide
All photos from the author's personal collection, except:
    National Library of Scotland: p. 81
    National Library of South Africa: pp. 62, 66, 94, 124, 172, 173
    University of London, kind permission of Sol Plaatje Educational Trust: p. 191
Set in Sabon 10.2/13.87pt
Printed and bound by ABC Press, Cape Town
Job no. 002469

Also available as an e-book:
d-PDF 978-1-4314-2393-4
ePUB 978-1-4314-2394-1
mobi file 978-1-4314-2395-8

See a complete list of Jacana titles at www.jacana.co.za

*In memory of Stephen Ellis (1953–2015),*
*author, scholar and activist,*
*one of the greatest Africanists of his generation*

# Contents

# Preface

Just over a century ago, a remarkable constellation of men and women came together to fight for a common cause. Their aim was to defend the Cape's non-racial franchise that had, since 1853, allowed men of all races who had sufficient income or property to vote. Africans, Coloureds and Indians had never had this right in the Free State and the Transvaal. In Natal so many obstacles had been placed in their way that few ever gained the franchise. The black leaders hoped the Cape franchise would be extended to the rest of the country when the Union of South Africa was established in 1910. They were outraged when they learnt that this was not to be the case. Together with a handful of white supporters they appealed to the British government to reverse this decision, without success. But their campaign brought together radicals who went on to reshape their world: the pioneers of African nationalism, who established the African National Congress; Gandhi, the father of Indian nationalism; and Keir Hardie, the key figure in the early years of the British Labour Party.

Black South Africans had put their trust in Britain. Promises – some explicit, many implicit – given at the outbreak of the Anglo-Boer War had led many to hope that if they backed the British cause they would be rewarded. The Prime Minister, Lord Salisbury had promised in 1899 the time had passed when his government could ignore the 'treatment of these countless indigenous races of whose destiny I fear we have been too forgetful'. But by the time the conflict ended on 31 May 1902 the scene had changed utterly. The war had been the largest colonial conflict Britain ever fought. London had been required to draw on all the resources of its empire to defeat an enemy once dismissed as a rag-tag army of farmers. Britain had emerged victorious, but only just. Were they in any position to live up to the promises they had made of a better future for the black population?

South Africans found that the war had left so many elements unresolved that there was a rare fluidity in the politics of the four colonies. For a moment the world seemed young and much was possible. African aspirations met Afrikaner resurgence; Indian demands and Coloured hopes came up against white fears and indifference. All this took place within the overarching constraints of the British imperial system. This brief period – just over a decade – was the cauldron in which the noxious ingredients that would finally produce apartheid were broiled.

It was a time of extraordinary leaders. Some major figures are only dimly recalled today: giants like Dr Abdurahman, a leader of the Coloured community, who sat on the Cape Town City Council for 40 years. There was the pugnacious John Tengo Jabavu, editor, politician and Quaker, who engaged in a bitter feud with his quieter but resolute rival, the Reverend Walter Rubusana. Sol Plaatje, brilliant diarist, linguist and one of the founders of the African National Congress, strove to persuade a sceptical British public of the wrongs his people were enduring. These black leaders fought for that essential political right: the right to vote.

All South Africans – black and white – understood that the franchise was vitally important to their communities. They turned to London and the British Parliament to settle the question of who would be allowed to decide their country's future. In 1909, after years of debate in South Africa itself, opposing delegations made the long voyage to London to finally settle the issue. All gathered in the Imperial capital. If the vote was denied to the black population, it would be the first time this would be entrenched in a constitutional settlement within the British Empire. Everyone understood the significance of the choices they were making. As Labour's Keir Hardie declared at the end of the parliamentary debate, to leave Africans unrepresented in the new dispensation was like writing above the portals of the British Empire 'abandon hope all ye who enter here'.

Despite the strength of their arguments the British turned down their appeal. The Liberal government's decision was not simply a reflection of racism: the First World War was already on the horizon. The government's aim was to lock white South Africa into the British Empire and ensure Louis Botha's loyalty when the conflict finally erupted. It was a rational decision that paid handsome dividends when the war began, but for the majority of South Africans it had devastating consequences. The Union of South Africa emerged with the stain of racism as its birthmark.

I have long been fascinated by elements of this story, but there was much that I discovered that I was not ready for. The major movements – the mainly Coloured African Political Organisation and the South African Native National Congress (renamed the ANC) – worked much more closely together than I had anticipated and made real efforts to support one another. A genuine warmth was established between black South Africans and the early British Labour Party. And the powerful influence that women played in shaping the political process, despite being denied political rights, came as a surprise. Emily Hobhouse, the renowned campaigner for Boer lives, also played an extraordinary but vital role in Gandhi's final confrontation with Smuts. Betty Molteno gave help and encouragement to the black deputation in London. And Nokutela Dube, wife of the ANC's first president, extended friendship and assistance to their neighbour, Gandhi, and his community during their conflict with the white authorities.

In writing this, I have drawn on archives from Edinburgh to Cape Town; from Grahamstown to Washington. I am indebted to the historians who wrote so eloquently long before I even set out on this road, and to three in particular: André Odendaal, whose work on the founders of the ANC is unsurpassed; Gavin Lewis, for his excellent account of the history of the Coloured people; and Ramachandra Guha, for his eloquent portrayal of that most difficult of subjects: Gandhi.

I hope I have been able to take their insights and weave them together with the archival material I found to make a convincing and accessible account of this period, while also throwing light on the workings of the imperial system. One word of warning: I have referred to the South African Native National Congress as the African National Congress from its inception. I am aware that it changed its name to ANC in 1923, but I have used this name from the start, to avoid confusion. If this offends historians, I can only apologise.

# Acknowledgements

As ever, it is difficult to adequately acknowledge all the sources of assistance and support I have received, and I apologise in advance to anyone I have overlooked. I would like to acknowledge the support of all the archives and libraries that I consulted, but especially the assistance of the University of Cape Town and the British Library.

My first thanks go to Catherine Corder, whose insights and generous help with Betty Molteno provided me with material I would otherwise never have found. Chris Saunders and David Killingray were unstinting in their advice and helpful criticism. My late friend Robert Shell taught me how to value documents and Sandy Shell provided critical help and suggestions. I am also deeply indebted to the many historians who read and commented on my work, pointing me in the right direction: Andrew Whitehead, Brian Willan, Heather Hughes, Janet Remmington, Robert Molteno, Richard Rathbone, Shula Marks, Susie Newton-King, David Welsh, Herman Giliomee, Gwil Colenso, Neil Parsons, Vivian Bickford-Smith, E.S. Reddy and Peter Limb. My thanks to Tanya Barden for the work she did to find many of the illustrations and to Nancy Edwards for the illustrated maps.

My friends in my London writing group all read and discussed my chapters as they were written, providing useful feedback as I made gradual progress. Zina Rohan was among them; her painstaking comments and criticism were particularly helpful. Russell Martin was a model editor: meticulous and rigorous, but also wonderfully supportive. Finally, I must thank my wife, Gillian Black, for the intellectual contribution she has made to this book, as well as her love and assistance. Without her it would not only have been impossible to undertake this project, it would have been an inferior product.

All failings and mistakes are, of course, my own.

# 1

# Setting sail

A faint breeze floated across Cape Town harbour, just enough to stir the flags.[1] The sharp peaks of the Hottentots Holland, the mountains marking the edge of early settlement at the Cape, shimmered in the distance. It was 23 June 1909 and beneath the towering cliffs of Table Mountain the *Kenilworth Castle* moved gently on her moorings. One of the newest liners in the Union Castle fleet, she had been completed just five years earlier at the famous Belfast shipyard of Harland and Wolff.[2] Now she was taking aboard a group of men and their wives who would shape the future of South Africa.

The city they were about to leave was showing a new confidence and prosperity. While Cape Town had been a re-supply point for European powers on the way to the East for centuries, it really came into its own during the Anglo-Boer War, which had ended seven years earlier. As the capital of the Cape Colony and one of the main ports through which supplies travelled to support the British war effort, the city prospered as never before. New cranes had been bought for the harbour, which could barely keep pace as the tonnage of goods passing through the port trebled. It was an auspicious time to celebrate Cape Town's status and a brand-new civic building had been commissioned: a City Hall, constructed of golden Bath stone and replete with a neoclassical façade and ornate clock tower, was taking shape.

*(opp) The Cape Town docks, from which the delegations left for London in 1909 to finalise South Africa's constitution.*

*The departure of the 'Carisbrook Castle',*
*which took Generals Botha and Smuts to London in 1909.*

Now some of the Cape's leading citizens were aboard the *Kenilworth Castle*. They were a confident group of men. John X. Merriman, the tall, handsome Prime Minister of the Cape, was in discussion with his ally, the prominent liberal Afrikaner, J.W. Sauer. They were among the throng that congregated at the entrance to the saloon, exchanging greetings with a host of friends. Others had already departed on the *Briton*, the previous week's sailing, including London's representative in southern Africa, the High Commissioner, Lord Selborne, and the former Cape Prime Minister William (W.P.) Schreiner.[3] The rest of the deputation would follow later, as they arrived from upcountry. But for the moment all eyes were on the *Kenilworth Castle*.

'The crowd on board the steamer was an enormous one,' wrote the reporter from the *Cape Times*. 'The scene on the hurricane deck, where the ship's band played lively selections from "The Belle of New York", "The Orchid", and other favourite musical comedies, was one of extreme animation, the buzz of hurried conversation, as passengers and their friends made the most of the brief time available, being incessant. The ship was crowded below as well, large numbers of people being below in the saloon, in which a conspicuous object was some lovely bouquets of lovely flowers, exquisitely arranged, which had been sent down for Mrs Merriman.'

This illustrious gathering was about to sail for Britain to settle the burning question of the day: how to unite South Africa as one country. Their aim was to bring together the four colonies that Britain now controlled as a result of the war. That conflict, so bitterly fought, had left an uncertain future. The British had won by mobilising troops from across the Empire but, even then, only just. When peace finally came, everything was in flux. The country's mines and farms had to be rebuilt. English- and Afrikaans-speaking whites had to be reconciled. And – as whites saw it – blacks, some of whom had been armed to fight on either side, had to be put 'back in their place'. The solution suggested by London was Union: to bring together the four separate colonies. So the political leaders of the colonies had met in October 1908 to discuss their future in a National Convention: men from the old British possessions of the Cape and Natal, together with the Afrikaner-controlled territories of the Orange River Colony and the Transvaal. They represented whites – about a fifth of the total population – but saw this as no obstacle to thrashing out a proposed constitution for all the people of the new country.

It had been hard going over seven long months, but finally consensus had been achieved. Only whites would be allowed to vote in the proposed Union. And only men at that – this was, after all, 1909. A handful of 'suffragettes' had called for South African women to have the vote, but their views were easily brushed aside. The only exception was the Cape: the 'liberal Cape', as it became known. After much discussion it had been agreed that the Cape would retain the non-racial franchise it had enjoyed since the 1850s, even if women would still be excluded. It had taken an acrimonious debate, but finally all delegates had accepted that African and Coloured men would retain the right to vote they had exercised in the Cape, as long as they had sufficient property or wealth.[4]

A week after the *Kenilworth* sailed, her twin funnels belching smoke, her sister ship, the *Carisbrook Castle*, also left Cape Town for Southampton. 'A cold and somewhat fresh breeze was blowing in from the north-west,' noted the *Cape Times*. 'And though during the afternoon the sun shone brilliantly, overcoats were the order of the day on the Carisbrook's decks, and great lowering masses of grey clouds hung with threatening aspect over the summit of Table Mountain.'[5] On board were many of the remaining figures in the official, white delegation: men who had travelled south from the former Boer Republics. There was ex-President Steyn, from the Orange Free State, and Generals Botha and Smuts from the Transvaal. With them were the mining magnate and author Sir Percy FitzPatrick and F.R. Moor, the Prime Minister of Natal. They were off to London to seek the blessing of the Imperial Parliament for their plans. The omens were good, the British had been informed of every step of the discussions and there were no indications of major obstacles ahead. This was a moment of optimism and satisfaction, with the prospect of a bright future in a united, confident new country.

*　*　*

These white leaders were not the only South Africans travelling to London to shape the future of their country. Excluding the majority of South Africans from a say in their country's affairs had galvanised the black population as never before. For them the draft Union constitution represented nothing short of a catastrophe; the slamming shut of a door on their hopes for a better future. Long-cherished dreams that the Cape's non-racial vote would be extended to the rest of the country were about to be extinguished. So, for the first time in South African history a truly representative group of men had been assembled to fight for this precious right. Organising this deputation to lobby the British government had been a painfully difficult process. But now, finally, they were making their way to London, hoping to get justice from their imperial masters.

The African delegates included the brightest and best of their generation: the clergyman and author Walter Rubusana, the newspaper editor John Tengo Jabavu and the educationist John Dube among them. Some of these men would go on to become the founding fathers of the African National Congress (originally styled the South African Native National Congress) in just three years' time.[6] As he set out, Rubusana spelled out in cool, lucid terms just why they were so furious about the racism embedded in the draft constitution.[7]

'We could understand a man being excluded for want of education or property qualifications,' Dr Rubusana said. But the proposals being carried to London meant that the benefits of citizenship would be confined only to British subjects of European descent. This was a 'reflection on the whole [of our] race, throwing a man outside the political pale on the grounds of his colour. We have exhausted all constitutional means of bringing our grievances before the various South African Parliaments, and much as it is a painful thing for us to have to appeal to the Imperial Government, we think it is a duty we owe, not only to ourselves but to the good government of the country that we shall lay these matters before the Secretary of State for the Colonies, and the British public if necessary. We have to protect ourselves as well as posterity.'

The deputation included representatives of the Coloured community. Dr Abdullah Abdurahman, a powerful orator and a member of the Cape Town City Council, was making the journey with two other Coloured leaders. All the delegates knew they needed someone of real stature to lead them; someone who had the contacts and clout to stand up to the white South African politicians and whom the British would respect. They turned to one of the most liberal white men of this era, W.P. Schreiner. The former Prime Minister was a Cambridge graduate and a London-trained lawyer, with excellent contacts in Britain and South Africa.[8] He had a reputation for supporting black rights. Schreiner had given up a seat on the National Convention to defend the Zulu king, Dinuzulu kaCetshwayo, who had been on trial for his life.[9]

It had not been easy for Schreiner to accept the leadership of the delegation. He had already made enemies of many he counted as friends

*William Philip Schreiner, former Cape Prime Minister.*

for insisting that black rights should not be ignored in the future Union. Schreiner had intervened and spoken no fewer than 64 times during the final discussion on the constitution when it came before the Cape Parliament. His colleagues had ground their teeth in frustration.[10] But Schreiner was a determined man, who was not easily dissuaded from his chosen path. As a former Speaker of the Cape Parliament had said of him: 'You have ever been a champion of the unpopular and you are one of the few men in our day who are prepared to follow the true light at all costs.'[11]

The only major South African group not participating in the deputation led by Schreiner were the Indians. But travelling on board the *Kenilworth Castle* was a passenger whose name was already known across three continents and who would become even more famous in years to come: Mohandas Karamchand Gandhi. He had arrived in Natal in 1893 newly qualified as a lawyer. Gradually assuming the leadership of the Indian community, he had devised a means of challenging the colonial governments in the Transvaal and Natal for their unjust laws in a way that they were finding it difficult to resist. This was what he described as 'passive resistance' – the defiance of authority to obtain a just end, without the use of violence. It was a philosophy that would, in time, win Gandhi the title Mahatma, or 'great soul', and the leadership of the movement that brought India to independence, the Congress Party.

Gandhi sympathised with the Schreiner deputation and liaised with them, supporting them where he could, but he was going to London to fight for the rights of Indians in the Transvaal. It was not a journey Gandhi was making with any enthusiasm. He (like Smuts and Schreiner) was a London-trained lawyer who understood the obstacles he faced.[12] Gandhi had returned to the British capital in 1906 to plead for the cause of his people, with little success. It was therefore with some reluctance that he agreed to make the voyage once more. Despite this, Gandhi put on a brave face and Cape Town's Indian community had come in large numbers to see him off. A reception had been held on the promenade deck and Gandhi had been presented with impressive bouquets of flowers.

\*\*\*

As the passengers boarded the ship, an event took place that unsettled the calm of this winter's day. Up the gangplank strode a short, rather stout woman: W.P. Schreiner's sister Olive. She had not come to see off her brother – he had left a week earlier.[13] Not outwardly an impressive figure, Olive Schreiner was far more than just a sibling of a former Prime Minister of the Cape. Although she had lived most of her life in the isolation of small country towns deep in the Cape hinterland, her fame as a novelist had made her one of the most widely acknowledged and internationally recognised South Africans of her generation.[14] Olive had campaigned, as an English-speaking woman, for the Afrikaners during the Boer War: hardly a popular cause among her community. As a result, she had been ostracised and her views had been attacked. This had not deterred her. Olive was a leading feminist and a woman who would defend the rights of all her countrymen and women, irrespective of their race. Her stand had brought her wide recognition. Indeed, even after her brother W.P. had been in Britain for weeks fighting to change the draft constitution, a campaign that had been extensively covered by the press, a Welsh paper reported his return to Cape Town in September 1909, under the headline 'Olive Schreiner's Brother'.[15]

*Dr Abdullah Abdurahman*

Olive Schreiner was not accompanying the passengers on the *Kenilworth Castle*. She had come on board to wish the departing passengers bon voyage, but above all to make a political gesture. What she did next shocked polite white society, confirming their worst suspicions about her, and her reputation as a notorious 'negrophile'. Together with her elder sister Henrietta Stakesby-Lewis, Olive made a point of walking up to and openly greeting the Coloured deputation. The two women 'took the opportunity of wishing, through Dr Abdurahman, success to the deputation, which expected to be absent from the Cape for about three months,' wrote the *Cape Times* reporter. Olive had met the Doctor and his wife in April, and had written to him in the warmest terms, hoping that their 'brief acquaintance may ripen into sincere friendship'.[16] Now she was making good on her promise of support.

Olive Schreiner and Henrietta Stakesby-Lewis then proceeded to seek out and greet Gandhi. The journalist observed them engaging in 'earnest conversation' with the Indian leader. This was the first recorded meeting of Gandhi with Olive Schreiner, although he had known of her and her brother W.P. for some years. Gandhi immediately grasped the significance of her gesture and why it was that she had ruffled feathers by her public support of him. It left an indelible impression and he described the meeting in a letter from London to his friend and supporter Henry Polak.[17] 'Olive Schreiner and her sister, Mrs. Lewis, both came up to me when I left Cape Town, to shake hands. Dr. Abdurahman tells me that Mr. Sauer tackled her and she, in her own charming and yet refined manner, told Mr. Sauer that she merely wanted to shake hands with me. She performed this ceremony most heartily in the presence of a huge crowd and both the sisters were quite for a few minutes with us. Fancy the author of *Dreams* paying a tribute to passive resistance, but the whole Schreiner family, from what I have learnt through Dr. Abdurahman, seems to be perfectly exceptional.'

A handshake, brief murmurs of support and good wishes in the Cape Town sunshine hardly seem worthy of a mention. Yet this public gesture by Olive Schreiner was a powerful signal, even if those who witnessed it probably only partially recognised its significance. Olive Schreiner, in her support for the Boer cause, had looked beyond the interests of her own English-speaking community. In now making a point of greeting Abdurahman and Gandhi she signalled a shift in her loyalty. No longer were the Afrikaners the underdog; she would champion the black cause. Olive Schreiner had supported African rights for years but now she was publicly reaching across the racial divide.

Given Olive Schreiner's record as a radical thinker, it was perhaps hardly surprising that she was so determined to make such a public show of support. When discussions on the proposed Union were drawing to a close in the National Convention in October 1908, she had written at length to the editor of the *Transvaal Leader*.[18] The letter, later published as a book, argued passionately that a united South Africa should have a non-racial constitution. Although she called for a franchise based on educational attainment, she declared that the vote should be extended to all races.[19] 'I am of opinion that where the Federal franchise is concerned, no distinction of race or colour should be made between South Africans. All persons born in the country or permanently resident here should be one in the eye of the State.'

It was a brave stand and one that set Olive Schreiner apart from all but a handful of her white contemporaries. She had come to Cape Town in April 1909 to watch the debate on the constitution in the Cape Parliament, and was horrified by what she had seen. As the members rose to speak on the issue, she looked down from the gallery in disgust, as friends she had known and respected for years refused to make Union conditional on a vote for all South Africans, irrespective of their race. Her anger and frustration is captured in her letter to her brother William.[20] 'That scene in the house yesterday, was without any exception the most contemptible from the broad human stand-point I have ever seen in my life, which has been pretty long & varied. It seemed as though the curse of the serpent had fallen on them all – "on thy belly shall thou crawl & dust shalt thou eat". I hardly know what was the most awful thing Jameson's face, so much worse than it ever used to be, with even that with an uncomfortable leer on it, – or dear old [F.S.] Malan [a Cape liberal Afrikaner] looking like a lost soul – for he has a soul & a noble one! And as they squirmed & lied, & each one giving the other away, & all gave away principle, all the while there was Abdurahman's drawn dark intellectual face looking down at them. Men selling their souls & the future – & fate watching them. One sees strange things from that gallery!'

The debate caused Olive real anguish, and she was not alone in deploring the unfolding situation. A small band of whites, many of them women, took a similar stand. Betty Molteno (daughter of the first Prime Minister of the Cape, Sir John Molteno) and her partner, Alice Greene, were among them. So too were the Colenso family, who worked tirelessly for the Zulu people both in South Africa and Britain. British Quakers, like Helen Clark – a friend of Smuts who also became a supporter of John Tengo Jabavu – were part of this circle. When W.P. Schreiner and his colleagues arrived in Britain, it was to these men and women that they would turn for support.

All that lay ahead. At four o'clock warning bells sounded on the *Kenilworth Castle* and the ship prepared to sail. Anyone not making the voyage walked back onto the quay. Half an hour later the third bell was rung and the gangway hauled ashore. 'Under her own steam the Kenilworth slowly backed out into the open water, the ship's band on the hurricane deck playing "Auld Lang Syne" as the vessel slowly gathered way. The usual greetings were exchanged as the steamer got into position to steam out of the dock entrance, but at the time none of the delegates were visible on the deck, the only local celebrity to be seen was the Speaker [Sir James Molteno], who had selected an advantageous position on the boat deck just under the captain's bridge, from which he placidly surveyed the animated scene. By ten minutes to five the Kenilworth was well on her way to England.'

The reporter left the ship a little before it sailed, watching it steam out into the Atlantic. At a quarter to five the crowd gave the ship a final send-off, as it made its way through the heavy surge, on its way to England. It would be many months before the passengers returned from this momentous journey. Afrikaner leaders like Generals Botha and Smuts – who had fought the British so fiercely just seven years earlier – would receive a rapturous reception in London; welcomed in Parliament and honoured by King George V. For the African and Coloured deputation a much more painful path lay ahead. In Whitehall officials received them politely but coolly, and were impervious to their appeals for justice.

Gandhi was to suffer a similar fate. Despite this, all would be changed by their time in London and all would gain something before they returned to South Africa, even if it was not what they had expected.

The Africans would hold important meetings with fellow Africans living in the British capital; talks which helped pave the way for the founding of the African National Congress in 1912.[21] Dr Abdurahman, as leader of the Coloured community, found friendship with men of other races and returned to Cape Town strengthened in the conviction that a unified, non-racial opposition was possible. But it was perhaps Gandhi for whom the visit was most significant. While he engaged in weeks of lengthy and finally fruitless discussions with the British and with Smuts, he spent valuable hours in intense debate with London's Indian community. His intellectual wrestling match with the radical members of the Indian diaspora altered his perspective. On the voyage back to Cape Town Gandhi wrote a book that encapsulated his ideas; concepts that would play a major role in undermining, and finally ending, British India.

If the days spent in London left their mark on the South Africans, it had an important impact on the British as well. The infant Labour Party, founded in 1900, supported the Schreiner deputation throughout the lengthy parliamentary debates. The Labour Party's first leaders, Keir Hardie and Ramsay MacDonald, had both travelled to South Africa after the end of the Boer War. Drawing on what they had seen, they worked tirelessly with Schreiner and his colleagues to try to win the vote for all South Africans. Some Liberals also backed the deputation, but their party was in power and, when the final votes came, they supported their government. Their campaign helped preserve the independence of the states surrounding South Africa: Bechuanaland, Swaziland and Basutoland, but overall it was not a success. It did lay the groundwork for a relationship between Labour and black South Africans that was to last for many years, arguably presaging the campaign against apartheid fifty years hence.

The British Empire was the largest the world has ever seen. It is generally portrayed as a well-oiled machine transmitting policy and orders from London to the furthest corners of the earth. Local administrators took day-to-day decisions, while providing information and intelligence to London on which policy was based. This is only part of the story. By the early twentieth century British colonial subjects were coming to London to try to influence their imperial masters. Some came almost as equals.

The governments of Australia, Canada and New Zealand were no longer content simply to implement British orders. When it came to key issues these dominions backed each other in demanding control of their futures, and London listened. There was a real concern among British politicians and officials that their possessions might break away from the 'mother country'. The Anglo-Boer War had put paid to suggestions that such a breach with white colonials could be resisted by force. As Gandhi put it so aptly: 'The relations of the mother country with the colonies were in the nature of a silken tie which would snap with the slightest tension.'[22]

Powerful as they were, this was no longer just a relationship between white rulers in Britain and the Empire. Men like Gandhi knew how to use their imperial contacts to extraordinary effect. By skilfully mobilising his supporters in Britain and South Africa, and by galvanising popular opinion across India in 1913, Gandhi managed to force the Viceroy to intervene on his behalf with London and Pretoria. Even the King was finally drawn in to prevent a quarrel between parts of his Empire that was threatening imperial unity. Black South Africans, while not as skilful at mobilising popular opinion across the globe, found that they were also not without international support. Networks were being established across the black diaspora, connecting with and building upon supporters in the white community. These 'hands across the sea' provided support and encouragement as the movement for colonial freedom unfolded in the next fifty years. The 1909 deputation was an early example of a movement that would, in time, unravel the imperial order.

This book is a narrative, not a theoretical exposition, but it necessarily throws up some critical issues. The American scholar and activist W.E.B. Du Bois memorably remarked in 1903, at the very start of his book *The Souls of Black Folk*, that 'the problem of the Twentieth Century is the problem of the color-line'.[23] Although other pressing issues defined the century, he was largely right, as the movements against colonialism indicated. Yet as everyone who has grappled with this question knows, South Africa is rough terrain for theorists. Many have attempted to tackle the relationship between class and colour – among other variables.[24] I would suggest that race is situationally conditioned and frequently imposed from outside.[25] It is the slipperiest of concepts and varies over time as well as place. Afrikaners were – prior to and during the Anglo-Boer War – frequently treated with contempt by the British; little different from any other 'natives' the rulers in London fought across the Empire.

*The 'Kenilworth Castle' leaving Cape Town docks.*

Yet within seven years of the end of the conflict their leaders, including Botha and Smuts, were being revered and honoured by the King.

Some whites, of all nationalities, were ruthlessly racist about anyone of colour, while others treated everyone as equals. A section of convinced English imperialists stood for the equality of all people under the Crown, while the majority took quite the opposite point of view. Africans could – and did – make racist remarks and sneer at Indians. On occasion Gandhi treated Africans little differently from the most prejudiced white. Yet over time Gandhi learnt from the men and women he met, and was on excellent terms with leading members of the ANC when he finally left South Africa in 1914. This is a complex tale with no glib conclusion.

# 2

# South Africa's troubled century

Ask almost any South African when the vote was extended to black people and the answer will almost invariably be 1994. It was, they will tell you, the ending of apartheid and the election of Nelson Mandela as President that marked the birth of democracy. Suggestions that this is not the case are frequently met with incredulity. Inside and outside the country almost no one questions the assumption that 27 April 1994 marked the moment when the first non-racial election was ever held in South Africa. This is clearly incorrect.

In the Cape, from early in the nineteenth century, any man with sufficient property or income could vote.[1] For the best part of a century men of all races participated in the Cape's elections. The votes of Coloureds and Africans decided the outcomes of a number of parliamentary seats. Their support mattered and politicians, unsurprisingly, took their opinions and concerns seriously. In Natal similar provisions applied, but were so hedged around with restrictions that almost no one of colour ever managed to win this right.[2] By contrast, in the territories that became the Orange Free State and Transvaal, only white men were included in the franchise.

This chapter will look at how this came about, and how it was challenged by the African, Coloured and Indian communities, supported by a small number of white men and women. These developments took place against the background of unprecedented change. Between 1800 and 1900 the country was utterly transformed. The quiet refreshment station at Cape Town on the way to the Indies became a gateway to one of the richest regions on earth. Avarice and imperial competition brought South Africa onto the centre of the world stage – only to be ravaged by the Anglo-Boer War. Most black people sided with the British and were promised by the Imperial government that their concerns would be addressed. In 1902 Britain finally emerged victorious, master of the entire region. As London contemplated bringing its four colonies together in the Union of South Africa, one central question remained: who would get the vote and decide the political future of the country?

* * *

When the British took the Cape from the Dutch, first in 1795 and then more permanently in 1806, they inherited a sprawling, thinly populated pastoral settlement that depended on the labour of slaves and a rural workforce of indigenous Khoikhoi whose condition was akin to serfdom. In 1806 the entire population of the colony consisted of fewer than 80,000 people: 26,768 whites, 1,200 free blacks (manumitted slaves), 29,861 slaves and 20,426 Khoikhoi.

From early on the British made a determined effort to remodel this society by introducing principles of freedom and equality before the law. In 1807 the British government ended the slave trade and, finally, in 1833 outlawed the practice of slavery throughout the Empire. Under pressure from the humanitarian lobby in England, acting in concert with a local missionary campaign and some radical journalists, the government abolished the Khoikhoi's serf-like status by the promulgation of Ordinance 50 of 1828. According to the government's instructions, 'all Hottentots and other free persons of colour lawfully residing in the Colony are, and shall be, in most full and ample manner, entitled to all and every rights, privileges and benefits of the law to which any other of His Majesty's subjects are, or can be, entitled.'[3] This became known as the 'Hottentots' Magna Carta'. The equality of all people – black or white – appeared to be assured. As a result, when municipal boards were set up in the colony's towns and villages from 1836, any male resident who lived in property with a yearly rent of not less than £10 could vote for his town board. From the very beginning, therefore, people of colour were able to participate in local elections.

The principle of a non-racial franchise was to be entrenched when the Cape was granted representative government in 1853. Part of the reason, no doubt, lay in the desire to give propertied Khoikhoi a greater stake in the political system. In 1850 the Khoikhoi of the Kat River Settlement had risen in rebellion and, though the uprising was defeated, it did concentrate the minds of those colonial officials and politicians who were responsible for drawing up the constitution of 1853. As the Cape's Attorney General, William Porter, famously said: 'I would rather meet the Hottentot at the hustings voting for his representative than meet the Hottentot in the wilds with a gun on his shoulder.'[4] In terms of the constitution of 1853, any man who owned property worth at least £25 was entitled to vote for or stand in the Cape's Parliament.

These developments were not without criticism or opposition. Indeed, the abolition of slavery and the promulgation of Ordinance 50, and the accompanying extension of rights to the black population, were deeply resented by the white Dutch farmers of the Cape as undermining their way of life. Starting in 1834, thousands of these Boers set out on one of the most defining events of white South African history – the Great Trek. The Dutch who moved away from the Cape did so in the hope of leaving British control and British ways of ordering society behind them. In the interior of southern Africa they would carve out independent states for themselves, the South African (or Transvaal) Republic and the Orange Free State, whose constitutions enshrined the principle of no equality between white and black in either church or state.

Within the Cape, too, as the nineteenth century progressed, there was increasing white opposition to the non-racial franchise, especially as the Cape expanded, incorporating formerly independent African chiefdoms by war and conquest. Initially the Cape had attempted to assimilate the Xhosa into colonial society, funding schools, hospitals and roads and aiding missionary societies in their efforts to convert the 'heathen' Xhosa into Christians and educate them. One outcome of this was the development of a class of 'school people', who 'emerged as a distinct stratum of society in the Eastern Cape and started to make their voices heard'. This process accelerated and by 1882 the educated elite made up no less than a fifth of the total African population of such colonial towns as King William's Town.[5]

Among these 'school people' were the young leaders of the future. Walter Benson Rubusana, who would participate in the deputation to Britain in 1909, received his schooling at Lovedale College, the most famous of the Eastern Cape mission schools. Thomas Mapikela, who

*Daniel Dwanya, a law agent and representative of the new African elite, with the local magistrate and African headmen. He was to accompany the 1909 Schreiner delegation to London.*

travelled to London with him, was educated in Grahamstown.[6] Nor were they restricted to the Eastern Cape. Solomon Plaatje, who helped found the African National Congress in 1912, was taught by Elizabeth Westphal, a missionary's wife, on a mission station at Pniel, 17 miles west of Kimberley. She gave Plaatje private lessons, introducing her young pupil to Shakespeare and other English classics.[7] John Dube, who became the first president of the ANC, was sent from his home in 1881 to Adams College outside Durban. There he received a solid but rigorous education from American missionaries.[8] In a few decades the missionaries had produced a class of well-educated young men who had the skills and confidence to lead their people.

With education came new tastes and interests. The 'school people' sought fresh ideas and greater information. In 1862 *Indaba*, the first newspaper of substance aimed at Xhosa speakers, appeared; it was published monthly by Lovedale. One of its contributors was Tiyo Soga, educated at Glasgow University and the first African minister in the Presbyterian Church. Writing in the initial issue he described it as 'our national newspaper' and called on his people to use it to preserve their history: 'Why should we not revive and bring to light this great wealth of information?'[9] In 1870, to cater to this growing public, the principal of Lovedale, Dr James Stewart, began a monthly newspaper, the *Kaffir Express*, also known in the vernacular as *Isigidimi sama-Xosa*.[10]

The paper's English pages covered political and economic issues, including the Franco-German war and the discovery of diamonds. The Xhosa pages were written by the African students. Letters from across South Africa dealt with subjects from religion and education to traditional marriage practices and male circumcision. The paper soon had a small but influential readership: 800 subscribers at the end of the first year, 500 of whom were African. Copies of the paper were often read by groups, some of whom organised debates around the subjects raised in its pages.

Among the paper's earliest and most regular correspondents was a brilliant, but sometimes irascible, school teacher: John Tengo Jabavu. His letters to the paper urged Africans to mobilise politically, calling for the 'nation' to demand their rights. Jabavu declared that Africans should use their votes for the Cape Parliament wisely to support candidates sympathetic to their cause as well as backing candidates of their own.[11] He also understood the importance of fostering links, both nationally and internationally; conducting a long correspondence with the influential

Aborigines' Protection Society in London, which kept a watch on South Africa.

In 1881 Jabavu's contribution was recognised when James Stewart offered him the editorship of *Isigidimi*. It was an influential and powerful position, which Jabavu exploited to the full. Soon his was among the most important voices in African society, being read with care by the colonial authorities as well. As André Odendaal remarks: '*Isigidimi* became the recognised "mouthpiece of the nation", a forum for school people to swap ideas and keep in touch with each other across regional divides.'[12]

The paper was also associated with the emergence of new forms of organisation. The Native Educational Association was formed in the 1870s to represent teachers. Jabavu became its vice-president soon after arriving at Lovedale. Other organisations followed, among them Imbumba Yama Nyama (the South African Aborigines' Association), but although it initially had Jabavu's backing, he fell out with its leaders and the organisation went into decline.[13] Clearly, the support of an editor and his newspaper was an important ingredient for success; it was not the last time that Jabavu's support was to be a decisive factor in African politics.

The growing political consciousness of the new educated African elite came up against the strictures and mores of the Christian missions that had fostered them. As Jabavu developed his journalism, and the range of issues he was prepared to tackle in *Isigidimi*, the authorities at Lovedale became increasingly uneasy. Dr Stewart warned Jabavu about his criticism of the Prime Minister and Governor. The two men finally fell out over the editor's backing of a young liberal lawyer, James Rose-Innes, during parliamentary elections, and on 29 May 1884 Jabavu tendered his resignation.[14] But Jabavu refused to be silenced. With the support of Rose-Innes, his brother Richard and the merchant James Weir, he established a rival newspaper, *Imvo Zabantsundu* (Native Opinion), the first edition of which appeared on 3 November 1884.[15] Jabavu was to edit it for almost forty years, until his death in 1921. He turned *Imvo* into a national institution, serving an African public far beyond the Eastern Cape.

\* \* \*

In 1872 responsible government was granted to the Cape Colony, with the same franchise qualifications as before. This development helped stimulate a new political consciousness and the growth of political parties.

Educated African voters soon took advantage of this and in 1873 a group of 100 voters registered in the Queenstown district, accounting for over 10 per cent of the electorate in the constituency.[16] The following year a magistrate in the Eastern Cape declared that Africans were 'beginning to understand that a man with a vote is of more importance than one who does not possess that advantage'.[17] During the 1880s Africans in the Eastern Cape made strenuous attempts to assert themselves electorally. Their leaders called on them to become enfranchised and began co-ordinating their political activities.

In 1884, before he resigned as editor, Jabavu used *Isigidimi* to mobilise votes for candidates who were prepared to promote African interests. Writing in support of James Rose-Innes, Jabavu declared that he was an ideal candidate for Africans to support, since 'he hates the way we are treated'.[18] With the backing of the African electorate Rose-Innes was elected in a race ahead of six other candidates. Two years later Jabavu once again campaigned for candidates of his choice. The result was a triumph, with Javavu able to claim that white liberals were returned 'in every contest we interested ourselves in'.[19] This was something of an exaggeration, but African voters had clearly become a force to be reckoned with. By 1886 Africans made up 43 per cent of the vote in six constituencies of the Eastern Cape.[20] This was recognised – particularly by the defeated candidates – who attacked the missionaries for manipulating elections by encouraging African voters and called for Africans to be removed from the voters' roll.[21] It was to be a theme that white politicians would return to time and again in the years ahead.

For the newly enfranchised, the newspaper and the ballot box were proving an effective means of having their voices heard. This view, turning away from the military conflicts of old, was reflected in a poem by Isaac Wauchope, clerk and interpreter in the Port Elizabeth magistrate's court:[22]

Your cattle are gone, my countrymen!
Go rescue them! Go rescue them!
Leave the breechloader alone
And turn to the pen.
Take paper and ink,
For that is your shield.
Your rights are going!
So pick up your pen.

Load it, load it with ink.
Sit on a chair.
Repair not to Hoho [a natural stronghold],
But fire with your pen.

Stung by the reverses they had suffered at the hands of black voters, many white politicians continued to press for the franchise to be tightened. The Afrikaner Bond, representing white farming interests, was at the forefront of the campaign. In September 1887 the Parliamentary Voters Registration Act was passed by the Cape Parliament. The Act extended the vote to the newly incorporated territories of the Transkei, but at the same time determined that land held under communal or tribal title was not to be counted as part of the property franchise qualification. For Africans this was a great blow and the Act became known as *Tung' umlomo*, or the 'sewing up of the mouth'.[23]

Jabavu launched a vigorous campaign against these restrictions. Using his newspaper and touring the Eastern Cape, he was instrumental in bringing about the first regional conference of African organisations. Held in King William's Town in October 1886, the conference took two important decisions. A Union of Native Vigilance Associations was formed, to be co-ordinated through *Imvo* with Jabavu as secretary-general.[24] Secondly, it was decided that a four-man delegation should be sent to England as soon as practicable to petition the Imperial Parliament. In the end, the idea of a delegation was dropped because of the opposition of some African leaders, as well as some white 'friends of the natives', among them Jabavu's mentor, James Rose-Innes.[25] Instead, attention was focused on the Afrikaner Bond's attempts to remove Africans from the electoral register. African groups hired lawyers to defend their rights and had considerable success.[26] But despite these efforts the Voters Registration Act resulted in some 20,000 voters, or a quarter of the electorate, being struck off the list.[27] This was a real setback but it did not mean the African vote was eclipsed. The general election of 1888 saw several seats decided in favour of liberal candidates who were supported by African voters. Encouraged by this success, Africans continued to press for their enrolment, and by 1891 had succeeded in bringing their voting numbers back up to the previous level.

The mining magnate Cecil Rhodes, who became Cape Prime Minister in 1890, was determined to further reduce the African vote. As early as

June 1887, in a speech in Parliament Rhodes had declared: 'The native is to be treated as a child and denied the franchise. We must adopt a system of despotism, such as works in India, in our relations with the barbarism of South Africa.'[28] In 1892 the Cape Parliament passed the Franchise and Ballot Act, which substantially raised the property and income requirement for the vote, from £25 to £75, and also introduced an educational qualification.[29] This again eroded the rights of Africans and Coloureds as well as poor whites.[30] Jabavu once more used his newspaper to organise opposition.

These developments were by no means restricted to the Eastern Cape. The discovery of diamonds in Kimberley in 1866, and then gold on the Witwatersrand in 1886, transformed southern Africa. Tens of thousands flocked to seek their fortunes – many of them Africans. Missionaries followed, providing education and ministering to the 'school people' who had arrived from the Cape and Natal. Social societies, sports clubs and embryonic forms of political organisation were established in Kimberley. Similar moves were taken on the Witwatersrand goldfields. Here they became enmeshed in the development of the 'Ethiopian' or African-controlled churches. A significant step in this process occurred when Charlotte Manye, then a young Xhosa woman studying at university in the United States, introduced leading figures in the independent church movement, including James Dwane, to the African Methodist Episcopal Church.[31] Dwane travelled to America and was appointed the AME's general superintendent in South Africa. Soon the church had 10,000 members in 73 congregations throughout South Africa. In the territories outside the Cape where Africans were denied political rights, these churches became what André Odendaal describes as 'the primary vehicle for political expression'.[32]

By the last decade of the nineteenth century African political move-ments had developed a national dimension, with links across South Africa. With the growth of the mining metropolises of Kimberley and Johannesburg, Africans had moved there in large numbers to work, not only as labourers on the mines but as clergymen, teachers, lawyers, clerks and artisans. Of this educated stratum, many had come from the Eastern Cape, bringing their new ideas and organisations with them. In a short time, personal, professional and political networks began to ramify across what was to become South Africa and draw Africans of different regions and languages together. These networks laid the ground for the

*John Tengo Jabavu.*                    *Dr Walter Benson Rubusana.*

founding of a single, national political organisation for African people –
the South African Native National Congress, later renamed the African
National Congress – in 1912.

These developments were not a seamless, easy progression towards
African unity. Beneath the surface lay real tensions, one of which would
take some twenty years to heal. It was a personal, ethnic and political
fracture which begins with tensions between the Xhosa and the Mfengu
(once called the Fingo). The origin of the Mfengu remains controversial.
Conventionally they have been portrayed as a group closely related to
the Zulu, who fled during Shaka's great wars – the *Mfecane*. They settled
among the Xhosa, with their name (amaFeng) meaning 'wanderers' or
'suppliants'. A section of the Xhosa – according to Mfengu tradition
– oppressed and enslaved the Mfengu, who then sided with the British
colonial authorities in return for land and support.[33] Their status as
outsiders made the Mfengu receptive to Christianity and Western
education, and gradually they became prosperous peasant farmers.

Jabavu was among the most prominent of the Mfengu. His main
rival was Walter Rubusana, a Xhosa, who had become an influential
minister in the Congregational Church.[34] The division between them
was exacerbated by these ethnic tensions, and first became evident in the
early 1890s when a group of Africans in the Eastern Cape called for the
formation of a new movement to represent their interests. Although a
lively debate took place in the pages of *Imvo*, Jabavu dissociated himself

from these plans. Despite lacking Jabavu's support, a meeting went ahead on 30 and 31 December 1891 and as a result the South African Native Congress was founded, bringing together many educated men, including Walter Rubusana.[35] Although it initially made little impact, the Congress decided to found its own newspaper, *Izwi Labantu* (The Voice of the People) in November 1897, with the financial support of Cecil Rhodes.

For the first time Jabavu, who had hitherto been almost the sole voice of African opinion, had a real fight on his hands. He responded by reviving a moribund body, Imbumba (The Union), which had been founded more than a decade previously. In the same month that the Congress was inaugurated, he held a conference for his Union. As Odendaal colourfully explains, this introduced a 'second bull' into Eastern Cape politics, 'with distinct patterns on its hide'.[36] By the late 1890s, with war between Britain and the Boer Republics looming on the horizon, African politics fell into two camps. On the one side was Jabavu, with the Union, backed mainly by Mfengu. On the other side stood men like Rubusana and the Congress, supported by the Xhosa. There was no rigid division between the camps, but the differences were nonetheless real. As the founding fathers of the ANC put it, one of the chief aims of their movement was to put an end to what they referred to as 'the aberrations of the Xhosa-Fingo feud'.[37]

*  *  *

At the turn of the twentieth century, the Coloured community represented less than a tenth of the population of the four territories that made up South Africa. Like their African compatriots, Coloured voters in the Cape gained confidence in their electoral rights and began to organise themselves politically. At the same time they were aware that they represented only a small fraction of the population, who had to find a way of living with their more numerous fellow citizens. Should they support white politicians aligned with pro-British parties? At times the English had been more liberal than the Afrikaners, but supporting them might mean backing the arch-imperialist, Cecil Rhodes.[38] Or should they instead support the Dutch Afrikaners, who had formed the Afrikaner Bond in 1883 to represent the interests of farmers?[39] After all, many Coloured people spoke Afrikaans as their first language and shared the Afrikaner's Calvinist Christianity.[40] Many also had a common ancestry, even if whites frequently wished to obscure this. Perhaps the emerging African political movements were the

*Meetings at the Stone, in District Six, Cape Town, were important in the early development of Coloured political consciousness.*

real allies of Coloureds. Or would the Coloured people best be served by developing parties of their own? All of these options were attempted down the years, with varying degrees of success. Which path to pursue was to divide the Coloured leadership too.

Like all British subjects in the Cape, Coloured men had gained the right to vote when representative government was granted to the colony in 1853. As we have seen, it was not long before white politicians began challenging the rights of Coloureds and Africans to vote. The passage of the Franchise and Ballot Act, which raised the property qualification from £25 to £75 in 1892, met with an angry response from Coloured voters.[41] There was particularly strong opposition to the Act from men who had gone to Kimberley to seek work. They formed the first Coloured political organisation, the Coloured People's Association, in that year to fight the measure.[42]

Cecil Rhodes had been behind this attempt to rig the franchise, yet he, like other white politicians, was aware that the black vote could swing an election. Faced with a tough electoral contest in 1899, and concerned that his party might lose, Rhodes pulled out all the stops.[43] Although the campaign itself is now long forgotten, one speech that Rhodes made while out electioneering was to echo down the years. Previously, Rhodes had called for equal rights for all *whites* in South Africa. Coloured men from the Kimberley area wrote to Rhodes querying his stand, and asked whether he would support *their* rights as well.[44] Speaking near Kimberley, Rhodes replied: "'The coloured men have been asking me to-day about it,' he told the audience. "I said to them 'You consider that you should have equal rights also.' They replied 'Yes.' I said, 'Then I will alter it if you like to equal rights for every civilised man south of the Zambesi.'" (*Loud cheers*).'[45] Rhodes defined a 'civilised man' as a man, white or black, 'who has sufficient education to write his name, has some property, or works. In fact is not a loafer.'[46]

In the political discourse of the day, the idea of votes for *all* 'civilised men', regardless of race, became a much-quoted phrase. It was a promise that Coloured and African politicians came to treasure. For English-speaking whites, as well as a section of the British public, the promise of 'votes for all civilised men' became the test of their liberalism and the cornerstone of their attitude towards the franchise. At this time few politicians, black or white, called for a universal franchise, irrespective of educational status or property. For many Coloureds the idea that citizenship would be so defined as to include them was very attractive. As the Anglo-Boer War loomed, they believed that their security would best be served by supporting the British cause that Rhodes championed.

\*\*\*

The Indian population had arrived in South Africa as indentured labourers to work on the sugar plantations of Natal from and after 1860.[47] Most intended to return home, but, as migrant communities often do, they gradually put down roots. The majority lived in Natal and by 1891 their numbers in the colony had grown to 46,788.[48] By this time the indentured labourers had been joined by others – merchants and professionals – who decided to settle in the country.

On 24 May 1893 a 23-year-old London-trained lawyer arrived from Bombay: Mohandas Gandhi. He had come at the request of a business-man, Dada Abdulla, who needed legal advice to try to settle a dispute his firm was having with Abdulla's cousin.[49] The business in question was in the Transvaal, and Gandhi soon had a taste of South African racism, when he was thrown out of the first-class compartment on a train, despite having a valid ticket. It was not to be his last. Despite the problems he faced, and although he was a diffident performer in court, Gandhi managed to win the case in early 1894.

By May that year he was attending a farewell dinner the community had thrown for him in Durban, on his way back to India, when the conversation turned to a new topic.[50] Natal whites had formed an Anti-Asiatic League a year earlier. They drew up plans to deprive Indians of the right to vote, which, in theory and subject to property qualifications, they possessed under the constitution of the Natal colony. The real motivation of the League may well have been economic: Indian traders were successfully competing with Natal whites, who considered them a threat. There were more than 10,000 whites on the voters' roll. Fewer than 200 Indians were rich enough to own immovable property worth over £50 or pay rent in excess of £10, but the League argued that whites in Natal were in danger of being 'swamped' by the Asians.

Gandhi's farewell dinner turned into what he later described as a 'working committee' to plan resistance to these attempts to end the Indian's right to the franchise. As a result Gandhi remained in South Africa, soon becoming a prominent figure on the political scene.

During the second half of 1894 Gandhi drafted letters to the authorities and collected more than 8,000 signatures for a petition to Lord Ripon, the Colonial Secretary, who had previously been the Viceroy of India. He also began mobilising support in Britain by writing to the first Indian to be elected to the British Parliament, Dadabhai Naoroji. Despite Gandhi's pleas, a Franchise Amendment Bill was passed overwhelmingly by the Natal legislature. Henceforth, no further Asians would be added to the voters' list. Lord Ripon, on being told of this, asked that the legislation be modified, since it excluded 'Asiatics solely upon the grounds of race'. He argued that such laws might cause disturbances in India and pointed out that if the Imperial Parliament could accommodate men like Naoroji, why should Natal not come up with an alternative solution? Ripon suggested that this might involve a higher property qualification or a longer length of residence.[51] The Governor replied from Natal that the legislature was determined to stick by the proposal and would continue passing the law until it was accepted.

By 1897 the whites had found a means of getting round Lord Ripon's objections. The Act was passed including a clause denying the vote to people whose countries of origin did not have 'representative institutions founded on the Parliamentary franchise'.[52] The franchise for Asians was thus limited to those who had been registered prior to 1893. After that date Asians could not acquire franchise rights for parliamentary elections, although they retained municipal voting rights.[53] Although there was no mention of race in the legislation, Indians were effectively excluded. It was what one historian described as 'a mere disingenuous device for maintaining a political colour bar without saying so'.[54] By 1907 there were 23,686 registered voters in Natal of whom 23,480 were white, 150 Indian, 50 Coloured and just 6 African.[55]

In his campaigning Gandhi's position was essentially that as members of the Empire the Indians had the same rights as any other subjects of the Crown.[56] It was not a fanciful suggestion. Gandhi, like many Indians, relied on Queen Victoria's Proclamation of 1858, a year after the Indian Mutiny.[57] This assured Indians that the Crown and the Empire were 'bound to the natives of our Indian territories by the same obligations of duty which bind us to all our other subjects, and those obligations, by the blessing of Almighty God, we shall faithfully and conscientiously fulfil ... And it is our further will that, so far as may be, our subjects, of whatever race or creed, be freely and impartially admitted to offices in our service, the duties of which they may be qualified, by their education, ability and integrity, duly to discharge.'

Despite this pledge, and despite appeals by Naoroji to the British government on the basis of its promise, the Natal laws were allowed to stand.[58] Although the Indian community had met with this setback, the campaign was not without its rewards. Resistance to the Franchise Amendment Bill led to the founding of the Natal Indian Congress in August 1894. Gandhi was appointed its secretary, and with this the lawyer had made his first real step into the world of politics. The campaign also had the hallmarks of all Gandhi's work in the years to come: a skilful use of a mixture of public and private persuasion and an unrivalled understanding of the international nature of Imperial politics. He had thought nothing of going right to the top: approaching the Colonial Secretary and using a British MP of Indian origin to assist his cause. Gandhi had also become among the best-known Indians in Natal and a leader of the movement in the colony.

In 1894 Gandhi was asked to intervene in a case in the Transvaal. Thousands of Indian traders, who had made their homes there, were facing having their businesses pushed to the margins of the towns by a law designed to forbid the purchasing of property by 'so-called Coolies,

*Indian stalls in Marshall Square, Johannesburg.*

Arabs, Malays and Mohammedan subjects of the Turkish Empire'.[59] The traders protested to the Transvaal government – to no avail – and then took their grievances, as British subjects, to London. The Chief Justice of the Free State was asked to adjudicate. He ruled in 1895 that 'every European nation of European origin has an absolute and indefeasible right to exclude alien elements which it considers dangerous to its development and existence, and more especially Asiatic elements, from settling within its territory'.[60] Gandhi appealed against the ruling, but lost his case.[61]

Shortly thereafter the Anglo-Boer War broke out and thousands of Indians fled from the Transvaal since, as British subjects, they were identified with the enemy. There was some discussion within the Indian community as to whether they should support the British, as this might result in further hostility from the Boers. Gandhi argued that it was time to show that they were loyal servants of the Queen. By the first week in 1900 he had recruited 500 Indians to an ambulance corps that he had established. The Indian community, like the Coloureds and Africans, had decided to side with the British in the war. That conflict, and its consequences, would be a defining moment in the history of southern Africa.

# 3

# Scorched earth and broken promises

In October 1899 the war that had been threatening to break out between Britain and the Boer Republics for some years finally erupted. Essentially it was fought over the vast wealth of the Witwatersrand gold mines and to establish British control over the entire region. As Joseph Chamberlain, the Secretary of State for the Colonies and a prime instigator of the war, remarked prior to its outbreak: 'Our strength in South Africa and our existence as a great power in the world are involved.'

To put the South African war in context, it represented the largest conflict Britain fought in the century between the defeat of Napoleon and the First World War.[1] Even the Crimean War had required fewer than half the number of soldiers sent to fight the Boers. Before British victory, of a sort, was achieved in 1902, the Empire had to pour more than 450,000 troops into South Africa. London had been forced to come to terms with the limitations of its power and authority. The war was certainly a monumentally uneven contest. On the one side stood Britain and all its possessions. On the other side stood the two Boer Republics, whose total population was tiny by comparison, even if its exact size was a matter of some conjecture.[2] Despite this, at the outbreak of the war the two Boer Republics could field some 50,000 well-armed and well-provisioned men, while the British had barely 20,000 troops at their immediate disposal.[3]

Britain was used to dealing with poorly armed and disciplined native militia. They were not ready to face the Boer Republics, which were armed with some of the most modern weapons available, carefully purchased just prior to the outbreak of hostilities. These included German Mauser rifles and modern, rapid-firing artillery.[4] There was another factor that had to be taken into account: Boer morale. Francis Younghusband, special correspondent for *The Times*, who visited the Transvaal, wrote a perceptive description of the Boers. '[They were] excellent pioneers, with marvellous powers of physical endurance; a brave self-reliant people, with high military aptitude; peace loving, yet ever ready to defend their independence; slow to move, but bitter and obstinate when roused, suspicious but credulous, and sensitive to ridicule and criticism; genial, hospitable and affectionate in their family relationship; a large-hearted people, and as a result of their stern life, possessed of a broad common sense not always attained by more highly educated nations, yet at the same time a people who, from their tendency to shirk the competition of modern life and from the effect of their surroundings, deficient in honesty and veracity, ignorant, unprogressive and in most important respects two centuries behind other European nations.'[5]

By comparison, the British army was deficient in tactics, leadership and manpower. Most soldiers joined in their late teens, drawn from the urban slums created by the Industrial Revolution. They were badly nourished. Before the war began the minimum height requirement for a soldier was 5 foot 3 inches. By the end of 1901 the minimum height requirement had decreased to 5 feet, yet a third of the men still fell below this standard.[6]

Within weeks the Boers had routed their enemies, driving deep into the British colonies of Natal and the Cape. With the moral backing of London's enemies in Paris and Berlin, and supported by volunteers from as far afield as Russia and Ireland, the Boers seemed in a powerful position. But Britain overcame its hesitant first moves and began mobilising its forces. Drawing on its vast imperial resources it mobilised soldiers from Australia, Canada, New Zealand and India. Gradually the weight of numbers, together with fresh tactics, told on the Boers. On 18 May 1900 the siege of Mafeking, which had lasted 217 days, and which almost reduced its inhabitants to starvation, was finally lifted, to immense British relief. There were wild celebrations in London. Then, in March 1900 Bloemfontein was occupied and finally, on 5 June, President Kruger's capital, Pretoria, fell. The Boer forces were close to disintegration and the conflict all but at an end. On 30 May 1900 Sir Alfred Milner, the British High Commissioner in southern Africa, wrote jubilantly to a friend, declaring the war was over. 'I have saved the British position in South Africa and have knocked the bottom out of "the great Afrikaner nation" forever and ever.'[7] He could hardly have been more wrong.

Deprived of the cities, the Boers adopted guerrilla tactics. Commandos fanned out across the open veld, attacking British lines of communication. In retaliation, the British burnt their farms to the ground. In the Orange Free State alone, 600 farms were destroyed within the first six months of 1900.[8] The scenes were heartbreaking. Captain Phillips of the Rimington Guides, a unit recruited from among English-speaking South Africans, provided a moving description of what took place: 'The worst moment is when you first come to the house. The people thought we had called for refreshments, and one of the women went to get milk. Then we had to tell them that we had come to burn the place down. I simply didn't know which way to look … We can't exterminate the Dutch or seriously reduce their numbers. We can do enough to make hatred of English and thirst for revenge the first duty of every Dutchman, and we can't effectively reduce the numbers of men who will carry that duty out. Of course it is not a question of the war only. It is a question of governing the country afterwards.'[9] Having destroyed their homes, the British consigned the Boer women and children to concentration camps, in which they languished. By the time the war ended these notorious camps housed 154,000 Boers, together with their African servants who had been interned with them. The camps became a byword for oppression.[10]

It was an Englishwoman, Emily Hobhouse, whose visits to South Africa in December 1900 and May 1901 provided evidence that was so shocking that it changed the tide of British public opinion towards the war. Her campaign against conditions in the camps led to the appointment in late 1901 of the Ladies Commission, which reported back on what they had found.[11] The Liberal Party, then in opposition, had been opposed to the war from the start, but had muted its criticism for fear of being branded unpatriotic. As reports of the concentration camps filtered back to England, the party's position changed. On 14 June the Liberal leader of the opposition, Henry Campbell-Bannerman, gave a speech attacking the government for using the 'methods of barbarism' in prosecuting the war.[12]

Despite the steely determination of the Boers, by early 1902 it appeared that they had finally lost the war. The British commander,

*The concentration camps left a bitter legacy among white Afrikaners.*

General Kitchener, had devised strategies to cope with the Boer incursions deep behind their lines. Eight thousand blockhouses strung out along roads and railway lines were built, crisscrossing the country. Kitchener conducted vast sweeps, pinning the Boer commandos into pockets of territory. Under unrelenting pressure Boer fighters became exhausted and dispirited, learning that their farms had been torched and their families put into the camps. Men gradually drifted away from their commandos and some went over to their British foes. By the end of the war, five thousand Boers had joined the British (more than a quarter of the Afrikaners then in the field), and Boer leaders feared that their forces might surrender en masse.[13]

\*\*\*

The time had finally come to sue for peace. The Boers appeared broken and the Empire seemed to have triumphed. The reality was rather more complex. For a start, the two sides were further apart than this simple narrative of victor and vanquished suggests. Preliminary peace talks had been held in Middelburg in March 1901, but had proved inconclusive. Yet even during these initial discussions attempts had been made to accommodate Boer concerns about the future of Africans in their territories. London wanted to ensure that Africans in the Transvaal and Orange Free State were given civil rights, although the government knew it had to tread carefully. Considering the terms to be offered to the Boers, the Colonial Secretary, Joseph Chamberlain, telegraphed Sir Alfred Milner, the High Commissioner, on 6 March, saying that the African franchise in the Transvaal and Orange Free State would be among his list of conditions for self-government.[14] But he added that the vote would only be given *after* the colonies gained a form of representative government. In other words, London would not impose a non-racial franchise on the Transvaal before it regained self-government. 'And if then given [the franchise] will be so limited as to secure the just predominance of the white races, but the legal position of Kaffirs will be similar to that which they hold in the Cape Colony ... We cannot consent to purchase peace by leaving the coloured population in the position in which they stood before the war, with not even the ordinary civil rights which the Government of the Cape Colony has long conceded to them.'

Lord Kitchener, as military commander, transmitted this offer to his opposite number, General Louis Botha, on 7 March 1901. In a letter describing his meeting with Botha, Kitchener recorded: 'the Boer General accepted the British Commander-in-Chief's proposal to leave the question of a native franchise to be settled by a future representative government.'[15] This was probably the first intimation to the Boers of the position the British would adopt on the franchise. Kitchener was concerned that an insistence on the 'native franchise' would make peace doubtful. 'I was amazed that the Govt. were not more anxious for peace,' he wrote to his confidante, Lady Cranborne.[16] Milner was also more cautious than Chamberlain. In the middle of the war he wrote to Chamberlain warning him against 'the fatal doctrine' that the Imperial government could 'deal with the native question regardless of colonial sentiment'.[17] Milner cautioned against extending the Cape franchise to the whole of South Africa, especially as few Africans would qualify for the vote given their poor education and poverty. 'It would be very unfortunate to raise the question of native voters. There would be practically none in the Transvaal, and for the sake of a theory it would be unwise to start with a conflict with the Whites. The Cape experience is not encouraging. If necessary the thing could possibly be brought about *sub silentio*.'[18]

*General Louis Botha during the Anglo-Boer War.*

Despite these concessions the talks failed, the war continued, and it was a year before another attempt was made at negotiations. In March 1902 both sides agreed to further negotiations. Boer leaders gathered in the Transvaal town of Vereeniging to consider terms. En route, Jan Smuts, the former State Attorney, who had been transformed by the war into a tough, resolute guerrilla fighter and general, held a significant meeting with Kitchener. The British commander, who had so ruthlessly prosecuted the war, was by this stage convinced of the need to strike a deal with the Boers. Indeed, he had already informed William Brodrick, the Secretary of State for War, that the enemy believed Britain was finding the going difficult, and was being financially crippled by the conflict. On 24 January 1902 Kitchener wrote: 'The Boers are being continually told that if they keep the war going a little longer, England will be financially ruined and have to stop.'[19] This was not far from the truth.

The meeting between Kitchener and Smuts was a turning point, for it addressed key issues that now separated the two sides, among them the question of the African franchise. Smuts's biographer W.K. Hancock describes the critical meeting between the two men at Kroonstad on 4 May: 'According to the notes that Smuts wrote down in his little brown notebook Kitchener gave a fair report of the negotiations up to date and a blunt statement of his own views – which were not in every case the views of his colleague Milner or of the British government.

1. Natives to be disarmed and no franchise until after self-government.
2. Surrender with honour; retention of weapons under permits; as regards horses burghers will be treated with "generosity".
3. No chance of immediate self government, no chance whatever.'

It is striking that the question of the franchise was the very first item on Smuts's list. The war had *not* been fought about 'native rights'. Yet Smuts had considered for some time that the franchise was a critical element in any settlement. In January 1902 he wrote a tract aimed at winning European support.[20] In it he denounced the British for what they had done to his people, but then had this to say: 'The war between the white races will run its course and pass away and may, if followed by a statesmanlike settlement, one day only be remembered as a great thunderstorm, which purified the atmosphere of the sub-continent. But the native question will never pass away; it will become more difficult as time goes on, and the day may come when the evils and horrors of this war will appear as nothing in comparison with its after effects produced on the native mind.'

Under the Middelburg peace proposals of March 1901, it had been suggested that the question of a 'native franchise' in the Boer Republics would be left on one side until the states were granted representative government. Milner's original draft treaty of May 1902 still seemed to suggest that Africans would *eventually* acquire the vote.[21] The actual words were: 'The Franchise will not be given to Natives until after the Introduction of Self-Government.' This went further than the terms offered at Middelburg, but as the negotiations at Vereeniging proceeded, London softened its position. At Smuts's insistence the British abandoned the proposal that Africans should ultimately gain the vote in the Transvaal and the Orange Free State.

Hancock comments: 'If the article remained unaltered the principle of votes for Natives would have been written into the treaty. Smuts made one or two shots at tinkering with the article but in the end he rewrote it completely: "The question of granting the Franchise to Natives will not be decided until after the introduction of self-government." This form of words left it completely open whether or not Natives would be given any voting rights at all. When Kitchener, Milner and the British government accepted the new article they threw away their country's case on what remained from that day to this [1962] the most crucial issue of South African politics.' Smuts, ever the lawyer, had understood the implication of the change, and was determined to force it through. His formulation became Clause 9 of the Treaty of Vereeniging. As his biographer notes wryly: 'Surrender was not all on the Boer side.'[22]

British resolve had simply ebbed away. In reporting to the King, the Prime Minister, Lord Salisbury, revealed that the question of the black franchise had been discussed in cabinet and they had decided to avoid a quarrel with the Boers.[23] The King was told that a breakdown in negotiations over this issue was considered more serious 'than the danger to which the natives would be exposed by the maintained supremacy of the Boers'. When peace was finally signed, Milner called its articles 'terms of surrender'; Kitchener called them 'terms of peace'; Botha, 'a treaty'.[24] In retrospect it would seem that Botha was right.

On 31 May 1902, after much debate, the peace terms were finally put to the assembled Boer leaders. Some argued strongly that they should continue fighting, but in the end most were won round. Of the 60 who were present, all but six – three from the Transvaal and three from the Orange Free State – voted for the motion. The two secretaries who were recording the event wrote: 'As the members of the Governments of the now late republics stood up, as men stupefied, to leave the apartment, Lord Kitchener rose and, going up to each of them, offered his hand, saying "We are good friends now." General De la Rey broke the Boer silence, remarking, "We are a bloody cheerful-looking lot of British subjects!"'[25]

*\*\**

If the Boers were divided and uncertain about the peace, so too were the British. Milner was furious that the Boers had been offered terms he considered too lenient.[26] He believed that Kitchener had not supported him and that the Boers had been on the point of surrender. In London there was overall relief that such a lengthy and costly conflict was finally over. Yet the question of the 'native franchise' created some pause for thought among officials in the Colonial Office.[27] The mandarins concluded: 'the native franchise ... is the only point worth hesitating about. As clause 9 stands the native will never have the franchise.' The Permanent Secretary,

PUNCH, OR THE LONDON CHARIVARI.—April 24, 1901.

**"PAY! PAY! PAY!"**

Master John Bull. "I 've put a lot of pennies into this machine, and I haven't got anything out. But "—(with determination)—"I 'm going on till I DO!"

[In consequence of the South African War expenditure, Master John Bull has to meet a deficit of fifty-five millions.]

*British public frustration mounted at the growing costs of the Anglo-Boer War.*

Sir Montague Ommaney, declared: 'Clause 9 seems to me to want nothing except the omission of the word "after".' Certainly the word 'after' was critical, and for precisely that reason Smuts had insisted that it should be retained, if peace was to be achieved.

Joseph Chamberlain, the Colonial Secretary, was also distinctly uneasy about the wording. He had, as we shall see, made statements during the war implying a better future for Africans in return for their support. In May 1902 Chamberlain raised the issue of the clause with Milner, pointing out that if it stood as drafted, there would be a permanent disenfranchisement of black people.[28] Milner replied bluntly: 'Clause 9. Yes. That was the object of the clause. Clause suggested by you would defeat that object. It would be better to leave out clause altogether than propose such a change. While averse in principle to all pledges, there is much to be said for leaving question of political rights of natives to be settled by colonists themselves.' With some reluctance, Chamberlain gave way. This was the end of the matter.

Why were Boers offered such relatively generous terms, and why were Milner and Kitchener incapable of striking a tougher bargain? In reality, although the Boers were battered and bloodied, they had not been defeated. Despite their terrible state, the Boers could still have mustered their forces and fought on. General Kitchener understood this, even if Milner did not. The war had been costly and was continuing to eat away at British reserves; it absorbed far more resources than anyone had foreseen. The final price of the conflict was in excess of £200 million.[29] This is the equivalent of £20 billion in today's money.[30] The expenditure deepened, even if it did not cause, an Edwardian financial crisis. In September 1901 the Chancellor of the Exchequer, Michael Hicks Beach, had to go to cabinet to warn that mounting war expenditure might shortly necessitate an unpopular increase in taxation and called for 'iron discipline' from his fellow ministers in their planned expenditure.[31] Financial constraints and the willingness of the Boers to continue resistance had forced Britain into an unsatisfactory peace.

There was also strong pressure from outside the government, not least from the opposition Liberal Party, which had questioned the war from the start.[32] Kitchener himself had drawn Smuts aside during the negotiations and intimated to him that the Liberals would soon be likely to replace the Unionists in government, and that if he accepted the peace terms, relations between Pretoria and London should improve under a new administration.[33] Smuts took Kitchener's advice and peace was concluded, but the war left South Africa terribly scarred. The losses among the Boer forces stood at over 7,000, while between 18,000 and 28,000 Boer women and children had died in the concentration camps.[34] Hardly a farm remained unscathed: their roofs destroyed, their windows and doors burnt for firewood, and livestock butchered. It was a bitter peace indeed, but the fate of the African and Coloured populations was more bitter still.

\* \* \*

When war was declared between Britain and the two Boer Republics, there was an understanding between them that this would be a 'white man's war' in which black people would not be involved. Under the Boers the African population had few, if any, rights. Yet they had, from time to time, been required to fight alongside their white masters. The Boers had 'excluded blacks from their state and church, but not from the vitally important institution, the commando, though the Africans that went along were unarmed and served as mere auxiliaries'.[35] Yet the idea that black South Africans would remain as unarmed auxiliaries would soon change, with both sides coming to rely on African and Coloured troops, as well as Indian non-combatants.

When the conflict erupted, the reaction of most black people was one of overwhelming support for the Crown. The Natal Native Congress was typical. At its founding meeting on 1 June 1900 it adopted several resolutions, pledging loyalty to 'our beloved Queen' before thanking the Colonial Secretary, Joseph Chamberlain, and his South African representative, Alfred Milner, for their position on the Republics.[36] They called on the British government to safeguard African rights and provide a degree of direct African representation in the legislatures of the South African territories.

It is not difficult to see why they took this stand. Not only had the Boers generally treated them harshly, but even before the war the British had held out the promise of a better life. Chamberlain himself made this clear in the House of Commons in October 1899.[37] He pointed out that when Britain took over the Transvaal in 1881, 'we undertook the protection of the natives of the Transvaal. Those natives had been our subjects. They were the majority of the inhabitants, and we retroceded them to the Transvaal, the natives whom we had promised to protect. How have we kept our promise? Sir, the treatment of the natives of the

Transvaal has been disgraceful; it has been brutal; it has been unworthy of a civilized Power.' A few months later the Prime Minister, Lord Salisbury, said that there must be no doubt that, following victory, 'due precautions will be taken for the philanthropic and kindly and improving treatment of these countless indigenous races of whose destiny I fear we have been too forgetful'.[38]

A more honest assessment of the dilemmas Britain faced in attempting to deal with (and, if possible, satisfy) its black *and* its white subjects was given by Milner in a frank private letter to his friend Herbert Asquith in 1897.[39] It was written shortly after Milner had taken up his responsibilities in South Africa. The letter, which has frequently been misquoted, contains a truly memorable phrase: 'You have only to sacrifice "the nigger" absolutely and the game is easy.'[40] The phrase is almost always taken out of context. Milner was in fact describing the problems confronting him in South Africa. His instructions required him to restore relations between the 'Dutch and English' while at the same time securing for the 'native' what was described as 'adequate & sufficient protection against oppression & wrong'. Milner, who had travelled widely across southern Africa, made it clear that these dual aims were incompatible.

In his letter Milner explained that it would be extremely difficult to achieve the one at the same time as the other. He lamented how badly black people were being treated and how hard it would be to live up to Britain's promises and responsibilities. It was in this context that he deployed the 'nigger' phrase. It was written in inverted commas: clearly not a position he shared. 'It seems to me', Milner confided to Asquith, 'we are equally bound to secure the good treatment of the natives in the Transvaal, where we specially, solemnly promised them protection, when we gave back the country to the Boers & inserted a provision in the Convention [of 1884] giving us the fullest right to intervene in their behalf.' Achieving this objective without further alienating the Afrikaners was to prove impossible, and the black population would discover this soon after the guns had fallen silent. In the meantime they generally backed Britain and British war aims.

In theory, the British as well as the Boers rejected the idea that Africans, or even Coloureds or Indians, would play a role in their dispute. The Cape government maintained that arming Africans would create an unfavourable effect on the African population, a stand that was endorsed by the British government.[41] This did not exclude their use as labourers or transport employees, but Africans were not meant to be armed or to participate in the conflict.

When the going got tough, however, it became a very different story. In April and May 1900, during the siege of Mafeking, Colonel Baden-Powell, who was leading the defence, ran out of troops. He had little option but to turn to Africans who had been recruited to dig trenches and act as spies. The Colonel armed 300 Africans, called them the 'Black Watch', and gave them the task of manning sections of the perimeter.[42] When his opposite number, General Cronje, discovered what had happened, he was furious. 'It is understood that you have armed Bastards, Fingoes and Barolong against us,' he wrote in a letter to Baden-Powell. 'In this you have committed an enormous act of wickedness ... reconsider the matter, even if it costs you the loss of Mafeking ... disarm your blacks and thereby act the part of a white man in a white man's war.'[43]

Even before the war broke out, the black population of Mafeking were convinced that they could not escape the conflict. Sol Plaatje, whose diary vividly recorded life during the siege, explained how the Barolong refused to accept assurances that this would be an exclusively 'white man's war'. 'We remember how chief Montshiwa and his councillor Joshua Molema went round the Magistrate's chair,' Plaatje later recalled, 'and, crouching behind him, said: "Let us say, for the sake of argument, that your assurances are genuine, and that when trouble begins we hide behind your back like this, and, rifle in hand, you do all the fighting because you are white; let us say, further, that some Dutchmen appear on the scene and they outnumber and shoot you: what would be our course of action then? Are we to run home, put on skirts and hoist the white flag?" Chief Motshegare pulled off his coat, undid his shirt front and baring his shoulder showing an old bullet scar, received in the Boer–Barolong war prior to the British occupation of Bechuanaland, he said: "Until you satisfy me that His Majesty's white troops are impervious to bullets, I am going to defend my own wife and children. I have got my rifle at home and all I want is ammunition."'[44]

In reality blacks had played a part in British defences from the start of the war. The Cape Mounted Rifles, sent to protect the Transkei and East Griqualand, was supported by a Native Affairs Department police force of some 600 men, which contained both African and white policemen.[45] Soon it became clear that such measures would not be sufficient. During the early days of the war the Prime Minister of the Cape, W.P. Schreiner, was resolutely opposed to any African participation. As the threat of Boer attacks into the Cape grew, his attitude changed. He relented, allowing the Transkeian forces to 'defend themselves and their districts against actual invasion'.[46] Milner, as High Commissioner, wrote forcefully that this step was only to be taken as a last resort. 'What I think about arming Natives is, when we have said "Don't do it until absolutely necessary" we have said all we can, without unduly interfering with the discretion of the man-on-the-spot.'[47] By December 1899 African levies were being raised all along the borders of the Cape by magistrates for their defence.

Lord Kitchener, who took over as Commander-in-Chief at the end of 1900, had fewer scruples about using black troops. At the same time, he was less than keen to advertise the fact. The Secretary of State for War, William Brodrick, asked for the numbers being deployed, but Kitchener was not forthcoming.[48] When pressed, he finally conceded that 10,053 blacks had been armed. They were used extensively as scouts, guides, dispatch riders, sentries and guards along the vast lines of Kitchener's blockhouses. This figure is almost certainly a gross underestimate. A further 5,000 to 6,000 men – mostly Coloured – were used as town guards in the Cape alone.[49] Some estimates put the total number of blacks who fought for the British as high as 30,000.[50]

\*\*\*

If the British had, somewhat reluctantly, turned to black soldiers to bolster their army, so had the Boers. This was by no means the first occasion on which Boers had relied on Africans to do their fighting. At the time of the Great Trek black servants, 'Fingoes' and Bushmen did much of the skirmishing.[51] When the Boer War came, Lieutenant Charles Massey, an intelligence officer with the Grenadier Guards, accumulated 'evidence of both armed and unarmed natives among our adversaries in the [Cape] colony'.[52] Boer commandos had been observed and 'all had some natives armed, and on horseback, wearing slouch hats and other Boer clothes ... I have always believed what was said of the Boers and their abhorrence of blacks, but now I know better.'

Senior Boer commanders strenuously denied that this ever took place. In early 1902 Smuts assured the strongly pro-Boer British journalist W.T. Stead: 'The leaders of the Boers have steadfastly refused to make use of coloured assistance in the course of the present war. Offers of such assistance were courteously refused by the government of the South

African Republic, who always tried to make it perfectly clear to the Natives that the war did not concern them and would not affect them so long as they remained quiet ... The only instance in the whole war in which the Boers made use of armed Kaffirs happened at the siege of Mafeking when an incompetent Boer officer, without the knowledge of the Government or the Commandant-General, put a number of armed Natives into some forts.'[53] But the evidence, assiduously collected by historians like Bill Nasson, points firmly in the opposite direction.

What Bill Nasson describes as 'fighting retainers' (or *agterryers*, in Afrikaans) were widely deployed. Some were captured and interrogated by the British. As one British officer put it: 'I talked to some of the Boer prisoners and found that there were Coloured men among the Boers, half Dutch, half Native. Also, a goodly number of Kaffirs. The Boers claimed they were only employing black men for digging, driving oxen, etc., but we know that some regularly used rifles.'[54] Another British officer remarked on the camaraderie between the Boers and their African compatriots: 'I was very surprised at their familiarity with their black comrades ... they laugh, talk, eat and joke with them like equals.'[55] Perhaps the exigencies of war had brought together and united bands of men who had come to rely on each other for their lives, and bonds had been formed that cut across the old enmities.

The role of these 'black Boers' is captured in this British ditty:[56]

Tommy, Tommy, watch your back
There are dusky wolves in cunning Piet's pack
Sometimes nowhere to be seen
Sometimes up and shooting clean
They're stealthy lads, stealthy and brave
In darkness they're awake
Duck, duck, that bullet isn't fake.

\* \* \*

The death toll in the war was terrible.[57] Africans suffered some of the most severe losses. No one bothered to keep accurate records of the 'black Boers' who were swept up into the concentration camps – the farm workers and their families who had been captured during the burning of Boer farms. At least 115,700 Africans were interned.[58] Their accommodation and food were even worse than that offered to the whites. White adults struggled to survive while on rations worth 9d a day; Africans were given food worth half that sum.[59] Recent research suggests that some 18,000 of the African inmates of the camps perished.[60]

There is evidence the Boers executed large numbers of Africans for helping the British either as dispatch riders or armed scouts. Kitchener wrote to Brodrick, saying that 'Cold-blooded murders of natives by Boers are frequent'.[61] Other stories circulated of Africans having been killed, although the reason for their deaths was not recorded. There is not an authoritative toll of the numbers of Africans or Coloureds who died serving either the British or the Boers in battle. This account by Canon Farmer, a British missionary in the Transvaal, will have to suffice as their memorial: 'Of all who have suffered by the war, those who have endured most & will receive least sympathy, are the Natives in the country places of the Transvaal ... they have welcomed British columns & when these columns have marched on they have been compelled to flee from the Boers, abandon most of their cattle & stuff & take refuge in the towns or fortified places, or be killed. I have been asking after my people & this account I get of them all ... For instance, at Modderfontein, one of my strongest centres of Church work in the Transvaal, there was placed a garrison of 200 [white] men. The Natives – all of whom I knew – were there in their village: the Boers under Smuts captured this post last month & when afterwards a column visited the place they found the bodies of all the Kaffirs murdered and unburied. I should be sorry to say anything that is unfair about the Boers. They look upon the Kaffirs as dogs & killing of them as hardly a crime.'[62]

The hope and expectation of black people that they would be rewarded for their loyalty to Britain following victory soon evaporated. Africans had welcomed the British as liberators as they advanced through the Transvaal and Orange Free State. They believed that they would be treated as British subjects, equal to whites in the eyes of their new masters, but they misjudged the intentions of the victors.[63] 'Expecting that an English victory would signal their liberation from oppressive conditions, throngs of workers burned their passes when British soldiers first appeared on the Rand. In the countryside, Africans generally thought that the war had freed them from their former landlords, whose lands would fall into their possession.' The British authorities soon dispelled these hopes, though not without resistance.

Africans in the Transvaal who had moved onto deserted Boer farms, believing they could recover their aboriginal land, were soon disabused of this notion. British troops and police were sent to evict them.[64] An African commentator wrote: 'One strong incentive reason impelling the Natives of the New Colonies to put themselves at the disposal of His Majesty's troops in the late war was that the British Government, led by their known and proverbial sense of justice and equality, would, in the act of general settlement, have the position of the black races upon the land fully considered, and at the conclusion of the war the whole land would revert to the British Nation, when it would be a timely moment, they thought, for the English to show an act of sympathy towards those who had been despoiled of their land and liberties. Alas! This was not the case. The black races in these colonies feel today that their last state is worse than their first.'[65]

Much the same happened in the Cape. Coloured workers were initially unwilling to work for Dutch farmers after the war.[66] 'Why do you want to be called *baas* [master],' they told their former employers. 'Why are you back here? Why should we work for you?' In June 1902, when popular discontent boiled over, British troops were called on to put down the unrest.[67]

The war had – as Rudyard Kipling put it – taught the British 'no end of a lesson'.[68] With the conflict over, London had to deal with a restive black population to whom they had made clear commitments. At the same time Britain had to cut a deal with the whites whom they had scarcely managed to conquer. It was an unenviable task. Peace would prove almost as difficult as war, and testing times lay ahead.

# 4

# From war to Union

Britain might have appeared supremely confident at the start of the twentieth century. After all, it had just won a lengthy and costly war against the Boers. Imperial dominion was at its zenith, stretching across the globe. From a handful of buildings in Whitehall, its statesmen and civil servants ruled nearly a quarter of the world. The *St James Gazette* of 1901 conveyed a sense of awe and some disbelief at the extent of the British domain: 'One continent, a hundred peninsulas, five hundred promontories, a thousand lakes, two thousand rivers, ten thousand islands.'[1]

Yet London's rule was less than absolute. The officials understood just how fragile their powers might prove to be. The threat was not only from their traditional European rivals or from the rising powers of the United States or Japan. The white colonies that Britain had so carefully nurtured were beginning to emerge as self-confident nations. They were being transformed from colonies ruled from Whitehall into dominions, with the right of self-government within the Empire. These white dominions were prepared to pursue their own policies, as well as the opportunities for co-operation between themselves, even if this meant sometimes working against British policies. Australia, Canada, Newfoundland and New Zealand were asserting their interests. As the new Union of South Africa came into being, the white politicians of the dominions saw it as a potential ally in their dealings with Britain.

With the Anglo-Boer War at an end, the British had four rather different colonies on their hands in southern Africa. London needed to find a way of dealing with these possessions: getting the mines on their feet again, reviving the war-ravaged farms, bringing about a single system of administration and then leading South Africa towards Union. When the British Colonial Secretary, Joseph Chamberlain, visited the country in February 1903 he told a meeting that they should 'make preparations for the ultimate federation of South Africa which is destined, I hope in the near future, to establish a new nation under the British flag, who shall be "daughter in her mother's house and mistress in her own"'.[2]

\* \* \*

The immediate challenge in the Transvaal and Orange Free State was immense: reconstruction after the devastation of war. There was also the larger need to establish a unified system of laws and regulations to govern the whole of South Africa. This meant facing the question of race. Should different rules apply to whites, Africans, Coloureds and Indians, or should they all be regarded simply as British citizens?

The task of dealing with this issue fell to Lord Milner, High Commissioner of South Africa and Governor of the two former Boer Republics. A brilliant scholar and administrator, Milner had prosecuted the war against the Boers ruthlessly. He had clashed with the military commander, Lord Kitchener, whom he criticised for failing to obtain an unconditional surrender. Although German-born, Milner was a strong anglophile. Assisted by youthful Oxford graduates who became known as the Milner Kindergarten, he set about attempting to turn South Africa into a state in which the English were predominant. But his plan to 'swamp' the Afrikaners came to naught, since he could not persuade a sufficiently large number of British families to migrate.[3]

The failure to anglicise the country was a severe setback for Milner. He worried that South Africa might, in the long run, leave the Empire, and said as much in a private letter to his successor, Lord Selborne.[4] Afrikaner leaders were not to be trusted, he wrote. All had the same ideal of 'a separate Afrikander nation and State, comprising, no doubt men of other races, who are ready to be "afrikanderized," but essentially autochthonous, isolated and un-British.'[5] In the same letter Milner accepted that he had misjudged the depth of racism of both English- and Afrikaans-speaking whites. He now believed that the provisions of the Treaty of Vereeniging which allowed the question of the franchise to be decided *after* the Transvaal and Free State were given self-government had been a mistake.[6]

If South Africa was to be rebuilt, it was essential to get the mines working as quickly as possible so that they could generate taxes for government and provide jobs for the unemployed. To secure the cheap labour that the mines required, Chinese labourers were imported to supplement the African recruits. By July 1906 the gold mines were employing some 17,500 whites, 102,000 Africans and 53,000 Chinese.[7] But the introduction of the Chinese indentured labourers stirred up a storm of controversy. In South Africa the policy was virulently opposed by organised labour, black and white. African and Coloured communities also voiced their opposition.[8] In Britain the Liberal Party criticised the conditions under which the Chinese were imported, describing them as 'akin to slavery'.[9]

The use of the Chinese was also contentious in the rest of the Empire, but for very different reasons. There was an outcry among white political leaders in the dominions who opposed the measure on racial grounds. There was much international comment about what was described as the 'Asiatic Invasion of the Transvaal'.[10] The Australian Prime Minister, Alfred Deakin, joined the New Zealand Prime Minister, Richard Seddon, in an official protest. The Cape Colony and Newfoundland passed special Chinese Exclusion Acts.

In the Colonial Office, Charles Lucas, a senior civil servant, worried about the consequences for Imperial unity. In a paper entitled *The Self-Governing Dominions and Coloured Immigration*, Lucas noted that the introduction of Chinese labour in the Transvaal had undoubtedly served to strengthen 'the bias against coloured immigration in the self-governing Dominions'.[11] Lucas's concerns about the position of non-Europeans in the dominions had been strengthened by the victory of the Japanese over the Russians in 1905. The Japanese navy, armed with the latest warships sold to them by the British, had inflicted a dramatic and quite unexpected defeat on a major European power. 'The rise of Japan', Lucas concluded, 'has given the Eastern races a new status which has been won by force and not conceded as a matter of grace.'[12] The Japanese victory had led to 'native peoples' around the world believing that the day of unchallenged European rule might be coming to an end. The Johannesburg *Rand Daily Mail* published a letter signed by an African, declaring that, with the victory of the Japanese over the Russians, the time had come for full racial equality.[13]

Charles Pearson, an Oxford historian who made his home in Australia, had pointed out the dangers associated with the rising power of 'Eastern races' as early as 1893. His book *National Life and Character: A Forecast* starkly described the future that confronted the white race.[14] He foresaw that 'the day will come, and perhaps not far distant, when the European observer will see the globe girdled with a continuous zone of the black and yellow races, no longer too weak for aggression or under tutelage, but independent, or practically so, in government, monopolising the trade of their own regions, and circumscribing the industry of the European … We shall wake to find ourselves elbowed and hustled, and perhaps even thrust aside by peoples whom we looked down upon as servile, and thought of as bound always to minister to our needs.'[15] Pearson's work was acclaimed and avidly read: in London by Prime Minister Gladstone and in Washington by President Roosevelt. Pearson's ideas were even more warmly received in the dominions. In Australia politicians saw his book as a call to arms.[16] The Australians, looking to the southern states of the United States for guidance, drew up a constitution for their new federation with a view to preserving the country for Europeans – the 'White Australia' policy.

Back in London, civil servants like Charles Lucas would certainly have been aware of Pearson's writing. Lucas pointed out in his document that even in countries like the United States, where whites were predominant, racism and segregationist policies continued to grow in popularity and there was no move towards a more 'liberal treatment of the coloured races'.[17] 'As far as can be judged', he wrote, 'this policy of excluding the coloured races has come to stay and to grow. It derives its strength from being based on a natural antagonism, from receiving the solid support of all the working classes, and from being presented, with a strong element of truth, as conducive to the interests of the Empire through maintaining the purity of the race.'

Yet the conundrums this posed for the multiracial Empire that Lucas was helping to administer were immediately clear. It was an issue that men like Gandhi had seen for years: the Imperial promise of equality under the Crown came up against the racism of the white colonists, who were determined to maintain their rule, even if they were in a minority. Lucas's lengthy survey of race relations and race legislation across the Empire in July 1908 came to a clear conclusion: the white colonials were racists and were unlikely to change their views.[18] They displayed, he said, 'little or no inclination to differentiate between coloured men who are British subjects and coloured men who are not'. 'The danger of it is obvious,' Lucas declared.[19] 'We may conceivably have to choose between our self-governing Dominions and the Japanese alliance; we may conceivably have to choose at some future date between India and the self-governing Dominions; and the matter is now, and will always be, one which may give cause or pretext for complaints against us by the United States, and for attempts at interference on the part of the United States in our relations with the Dominions.'

Here was the nub of the issue: London was increasingly concerned that the unity of the Imperial project might be imperilled. Its dominions were up in arms about some of its policies. How would the British make the choice between India – the 'jewel in the crown' – and its natural allies in Australia, New Zealand and Canada? Even its most recently subjected people – the Afrikaners – were suspected of harbouring insurrectionary thoughts. Would the white, self-governing nations in the end break their ties with the mother country and form alliances of their own or, worse still, link up with the United States? A tour of the Pacific by the American fleet – to show the Japanese just who was really in charge – had been rapturously welcomed in Australia. Tens of thousands greeted the warships as they sailed into Auckland harbour – a tenth of New Zealand's entire population.[20] The Americans were giving just the kind of reassurance of white supremacy that the dominions sought. Why was London so hesitant to provide it?

For the moment these were just stirrings of colonial nationalisms of which London was beginning to be aware. They were to grow in importance and play a significant role in deciding the constitution of the proposed Union of South Africa. As the drive to Union gathered pace, white politicians became frequent visitors to London and got to know and understand their opposite numbers in Britain and in the other dominions. When South Africa's new Union constitution finally came before the Imperial Parliament for ratification, the British government had to decide on its attitude towards the competing claims of black and white South Africans. In particular, London had to face the issue of who should get the vote.

\* \* \*

In December 1905 the Conservative Prime Minister, Arthur Balfour, having suffered a series of by-election defeats, was forced to hold a general election. The Liberals, out of power for a decade, seemed to be on the brink of victory. Jan Smuts saw his chance, and set off to London, determined to try to win self-government for the Transvaal from the new administration.[21] He thought it was vital to act before policy towards his country was established. Smuts believed he had to remind the British of the promises they had made in the Treaty of Vereeniging, that whites would be able to determine their own fate.

Smuts arrived in London on 6 January 1906, but it was not until the last week in January that the new Liberal government was ready to receive him. Smuts had produced a draft memorandum, *On Points in Reference to the Transvaal Constitution*, which he presented to all concerned. He managed to see Winston Churchill, his old foe from the Boer War days, who had been given the position of Under Secretary at the Colonial Office. The meeting was less than successful. Churchill told him he would read his memo and that he looked forward to a settlement 'fair to both parties in South Africa'. He wished Smuts a pleasant journey home, but promised nothing, leaving the South African deeply depressed. Churchill's rejection of Smuts should not cause much surprise. The Colonial Office of this era had little time for the citizens of its Empire, black or white: Smuts was dismissed by civil servants as 'cunning' and clearly not to be trusted.[22] The mandarins should not have underestimated him.

Almost ready to pack his bags and go home, Smuts decided on one last throw of the dice. He sought a final meeting with the newly elected Liberal Prime Minister, Sir Henry Campbell-Bannerman. Years later Smuts recalled their meeting on 7 February 1906.[23] 'My mission failed with the rest, as it was humanly speaking bound to fail. What an audacious, what an unprecedented request mine was – practically for the restoration of the country to the Boers five years after they had been beaten to the ground in one of the hardest and most lengthy struggles in British warfare. I put a simple case before him that night in 10 Downing Street. It was in substance: Do you want friends or enemies? You can have the Boers for friends, and they have proved what quality their friendship means. I pledge the friendship of my colleagues and myself if you wish it. You can choose to make them enemies, and possibly have another Ireland on your hands. If you do believe in liberty, it is also their faith and their religion. I used no arguments, but simply spoke to him as

## UNITED SOUTH AFRICA.

[The Act of Union is about to be presented, for sanction, to the British Parliament.]

*With the Anglo-Boer War at an end, peace arrived and, with it, a cautious reconciliation between Boer and Brit.*

man to man, and appealed only to the human aspect, which I felt would weigh deeply with him. He was a cautious Scot, and said nothing to me, but yet I left that room that night a happy man. My intuition told me that the thing had been done.'

Smuts was right. On 8 February 1906, Campbell-Bannerman held a cabinet meeting and overcame the doubts of his colleagues by arguing that the time had come to trust their former enemies, the Boers. Smuts had won self-government for the Transvaal.[24] He retained a deep affection for Campbell-Bannerman all his life: a portrait of the British Prime Minister hung in Smuts's study to the end of his days.

That year the Transvaal was granted self-government, to be followed in 1907 by the Orange Free State. Just five years after the end of Britain's most costly colonial conflict, London had given away a good deal of the control over the former Boer Republics that it had fought so hard to achieve. Yet the decision paid almost immediate dividends for the British. In his first speech as Prime Minister of the Transvaal, Louis Botha promised: 'British interests would be absolutely safe in the hands of the new Cabinet.'[25] He went on to say that the Transvaal was 'actuated by motives of deep gratitude, because the King and the British Government and people had trusted the Transvaal people in a manner unequalled in history by the grant of a free Constitution. Was it possible for the Boers ever to forget such generosity?' As a mark of reconciliation the Transvaal bought and presented to King Edward the largest diamond yet discovered – the 3,106-carat Cullinan – for inclusion in the Crown jewels.[26] The gem was, in reality, an extravagant bribe in return for a loan. After some hesitation, and at the prompting of Churchill, London decided it would allow the King to accept the gift. The Transvaal, so long a thorn in British flesh, was becoming an integral part of the Imperial system.

Now that they were self-governing colonies, the Transvaal and Orange Free State could set about determining how they should rule their African, Coloured and Indian subjects. At the same time Britain was determined to bring all its colonies together in a new Union of South Africa. A formula for 'native policy' was needed that would suit them all. John X. Merriman, a leading Cape liberal and, from 1908, the Cape's Prime Minister, began a dialogue with Smuts in the Transvaal. The subject of their debate was the franchise for the envisaged Union. Merriman sought to have the Cape's qualified, but non-racial, franchise extended to the whole of South Africa. In the larger scheme of things his interchange with Smuts went a long way to deciding the issue. On 16 March 1906 Merriman wrote to Smuts, saying: 'God forbid I should advocate a general enfranchisement of the Native barbarian. All I think is required for *our* safety is that we shall not deny him the franchise on the account of colour. We can then snap our fingers at Exeter Hall [synonymous with the liberal missionary movement] and Downing Street, and experience teaches me that there is no surer bulwark for all the legitimate rights of any class or colour than representation in Parliament.'[27]

Later that month Merriman wrote to Smuts again, urging that Africans should be given the vote, although he believed there should be a high qualification for voters. Once more, Merriman made his argument in terms of the security of whites. 'In the Native case we are fettered by the notion which all of us entertain that the Native is a schepsel [creature]. But he is a human being, though an undeveloped one, and my contention is that the only safe way of management is to give him a chance to acquire political rights if he shows himself fit to manage them. Therefore I confess I dread what you call manhood suffrage. In my humble opinion this is a country for a high franchise and for a property qualification.'[28]

Smuts refused to accept this argument, insisting that there should be a whites-only franchise for the Union.[29] He pointed out that it was simply impossible to suggest to large numbers of whites that they should be deprived of a vote they currently enjoyed by introducing a property or income qualification. Whites as a whole, and Afrikaners in particular, regarded the franchise as their right and would not abandon it.[30] 'We have had to go in for manhood suffrage, not only because it existed among burghers before the war, and seems a democratic principle ... but also because even the low franchise of Milner's constitution resulted in the disenfranchisement of some 10,000 bywoners [tenant farmers or squatters] and grown-up sons on farms, the loss of whom we cannot afford.'

For a white politician this was an unarguable case. Smuts could not go to members of his own electorate and suggest that they be deprived of this right so that a small number of wealthy, educated Africans could be given the vote. The alternative was to propose a universal franchise, without qualifications of any kind. In the early 1900s that was simply inconceivable for almost all whites.[31] Although Merriman continued to put the argument, he made no progress. In February 1908 Merriman wrote to Smuts once more, suggesting that the Cape might keep its non-racial franchise, while the other provinces retained a racial franchise. At the same time he called for the Cape arrangement to be safeguarded against amendment by insisting that change could only be agreed on by a two-thirds majority in the Union Parliament.[32] On this basis the two men reached an agreement, whose terms were to become the foundation for the Union franchise.

\* \* \*

While whites were moving towards reconciliation, black people were wondering what their position would be in the two newly conquered colonies. They had, after all, been given promises both prior to and during the war. A Coloured delegation, for instance, had been to see Milner in 1901 and were informed that their hope that a non-racial constitution would be extended to the former Boer Republics was a reasonable one, which he supported, since 'it was not race or colour, but civilisation which was the test of a man's capacity for civil rights'.[33] What would Britain now deliver?

After the war, black people began to receive a rather different message. Milner's policy was that they were to be ruled well and justly, but by whites. Immediately after the war he declared that in his view the white race was, as he put it, 'many, many steps above the black man', which the latter would 'take centuries to climb'.[34] Afrikaners found considerable reassurance from his views. Many whites in the Transvaal and Orange Free State complained that Africans had become 'uppity' during the war, since most had backed the British and anticipated a better life once the conflict was over. According to Louis Botha, 'Kaffirs looked down upon the [conquered] Boers', regarding themselves as their equals under British rule.[35] But Africans were soon left in no doubt that this was not the case.

In 1903 a South African Native Affairs Commission was established by Britain to provide a 'common understanding' on the question of 'native policy' for the whole region. African leaders from all four colonies went to great lengths to make representations to the commission. Most argued for an extension of the Cape franchise across the whole country. Their arguments carried little weight with the commissioners. When the final report was written, the commission came out against the Cape solution. According to the report, giving Africans the vote was 'sure to create an intolerable situation and is an unwise and dangerous thing ... pregnant with danger'.[36] African political aspirations needed to be catered for, but without giving real power 'in an aggressive sense, or weakening in any way the unchallenged supremacy and authority of the ruling race'.

Much the same conclusion was reached by a committee established in 1906 to look at the most appropriate constitutions for the Transvaal and Orange River colonies, which were about to be granted self-government. Led by Sir J. West Ridgeway, it decided that the question of the African franchise would be left to the new self-governing colonies. The committee said that it did not believe that black people could 'ever be placed on an equality with the white population in the matter of the franchise'.[37] This conclusion was reached despite a massive petition from Africans in the Transvaal, signed by 46 chiefs and 25,738 others.

Although most African opposition to white dominance took the form of petitions and well-mannered deputations, black resistance had not quite been snuffed out. In February 1906 the Bambatha rebellion erupted in Natal over the imposition of a poll tax on all adult African men in the colony. The uprising was put down with immense savagery. Gandhi, who organised a team of voluntary stretcher-bearers, commented, 'This was no war but a man-hunt.'[38] The British Labour Party leader, Keir Hardie, kept informed of what was taking place in Natal by the Colenso family, raised the question of the treatment of Africans during the rebellion in the House of Commons on several occasions, demanding to know why the army was taking no prisoners.[39]

The Liberal government came under considerable pressure to intervene in Natal, but the Colonial Secretary, Lord Elgin, with Churchill as his Under Secretary, felt this was impossible.[40] Churchill sent strongly worded telegrams to the government of Natal, but when its members threatened to resign en masse, Britain was forced to back down. Churchill complained privately of the 'disgusting butchery of natives', and what he described as miscarriages of justice that revealed 'the kind of tyranny against which these unfortunate Zulus have been struggling'.[41] But Elgin refused to act, responding, 'Where there are small white communities in the midst of large coloured populations, the former are liable to panics, and the vindictiveness which accompanies panics. But that does not mean the Government is tyrannous.'

The position that Liberals took on this question is explained, at least in part, by the angry protests from the Australian government. The Australian Prime Minister, Alfred Deakin, sent off a stiff cable to the Colonial Office about what he termed 'imperial interference' in the affairs of a colony.[42] The new Premier of Natal, Charles Smythe, wrote to Deakin, thanking him for his support and expressing his hope that 'the people in Downing Street will recognize that Colonies enjoying Responsible Government must be allowed to manage their own affairs'.[43] Churchill summed up the response of the British government in the Colonial Office's files by observing, 'This is a complete surrender.'[44]

By 1907 it was clear that Britain would press ahead with the union of the four colonies. In May the following year the question of African rights was debated in the House of Commons, at the initiative of the radical Liberal MPs Percy Alden and Charles Dilke.[45] Alden moved a motion: 'That this House, recognising signs of a growing opinion on the part of the self-governing Colonies of South Africa in favour of safeguarding the rights and future of the natives in any scheme of political unification or federation, expresses its confidence that His Majesty's Government will welcome the adoption of provisions calculated to render possible the ultimate inclusion of the whole of British South Africa in federal union.'[46] Speaking for the government Colonel John Seely, Under Secretary for the Colonies, made a strong speech in favour of extending the franchise to Africans.[47] 'The Cape Colony has adopted the franchise', he told the House, 'and ... the franchise is the key to the situation. There are many things pressing for solution – native land, native education, native rights of every kind. But given the franchise, these things will solve themselves, and without it we shall labour in vain.'

Seely was right in his analysis, but deluded in believing this could be implemented without riding roughshod over white opinion. Lord Selborne, as High Commissioner in South Africa, wrote to the Secretary of State commenting that Seely's views were 'founded on a complete misapprehension'.[48] No minister in either of the former Boer Republics would accept Africans being given the vote. And, as Selborne informed London, he regretted to say that they reflected the views of their constituents in taking this position. The British quietly capitulated.

* * *

This was the background to the National Convention, which convened in Durban in October 1908, bringing together politicians from the Cape, Transvaal, Natal and the Orange River Colony, as well as Rhodesia. Their aim was to draw up a constitution for the proposed Union.[49]

Only white men were invited to consider the future of their country; women and all other racial groups were excluded. This was in some ways anomalous. After all, qualified black men had enjoyed the vote in the Cape since the 1850s and – as long as they had sufficient property, income and education – continued to do so. In 1909 there were 14,388 Coloured and 6,633 African voters in the Cape.[50] Between them they made up 14.8 per cent of the electorate. In Natal, too, a handful of African, Coloured and Indian men had the right to vote, although this right was so constrained by hurdles that it was almost theoretical.[51] In the Transvaal and Orange River Colony only white men could vote.

Although Britain kept the closest watch on the discussions in the Convention, with almost daily dispatches being sent to London, the Colonial Secretary did not interfere, unless requested to do so. In October 1908 the chairman of the Convention, Sir Henry de Villiers, went to see the High Commissioner, Lord Selborne, to ask him what position London would take in relation to the franchise and to the possible incorporation of the Protectorates of Swaziland, Basutoland and Bechuanaland into the Union.[52]

Selborne explained this in a lengthy letter to Sir Henry, in which he spelt out Britain's responsibilities to the Protectorates. 'The obligations of His Majesty's Government to the tribes inhabiting Basutoland and the Bechuanaland Protectorate are obligations of the greatest possible weight. These tribes surrendered themselves under the dominion of Queen Victoria of their own free will, and they have been the loyal subjects of King Edward ever since.' Swaziland was not quite the same, but in any case all these peoples would be 'very loath' to be transferred to South Africa – something the white politicians were pressing for. Despite this, Britain was prepared to allow the transfer to take place, but only if the general question of the franchise was satisfactorily settled. 'The conditions of transfer of the Protectorates, which His Majesty's Government would think it necessary to discuss with the National Convention through me, must necessarily be affected by the decision of the National Convention on the general subject of the native franchise for South Africa.' In other words, no vote for black people would mean no transfer of the Protectorates.

John X. Merriman and others from the Cape had told the delegates that they had a special responsibility to protect the political rights of Cape Africans, who had enjoyed the franchise for more than half a century.

PUNCH, OR THE LONDON CHARIVARI.—August 8, 1906.

**PULLING TOGETHER.**

Baby Boer } "HERE, I SAY, DRINK FAIR!"
Baby Briton }

*Disputes between Boer and Brit over the proposed
constitution for the Union of South Africa.*

Their arguments cut little ice with the other colonies. Botha would not accept any extension of the 'native franchise' to the Transvaal, and said that if this was insisted upon there would be no Union. So, reluctantly, Merriman settled for maintaining the Cape's existing voting system, without extending it to the rest of the country. Instead he insisted that this compromise was entrenched in the constitution. When Sir Henry de Villiers sought the guidance of Lord Selborne, he replied that the British government expected to come under 'strong and urgent appeals' in the British Parliament if the vote was not given to black South Africans.

At the same time Selborne accepted that the British were under what he called a 'very difficult position' because of the terms of the Treaty of Vereeniging. He concluded that as long as the rights of Cape Africans and Coloureds were preserved and adequately protected, Britain would not insist on the franchise being extended to the rest of the country.[53]

Indeed, Selborne pointed out: 'Mr Merriman's amendment [entrenching Cape rights] cuts both ways. If it succeeds in making the franchise secure to the Cape natives, it will also make it practically impossible at any time to extend the franchise to any of the natives of the Transvaal, Natal or the Orange River Colony.' He also said he did not think the British government would object to 'only persons of European descent' being eligible to stand for Parliament. This position became the basis of the final agreement. Africans and Coloured people would retain most of their voting rights in the Cape, but would not receive them in any other part of the Union. It was 'a compromise between the Cape and the northern colonies'.[54]

In a covering letter to the Colonial Secretary, Lord Crewe, Selborne made plain his personal belief, which he felt 'strongly' and which he had shared in private with the delegates to the Convention.[55] This was that the franchise was a matter of 'justice and expediency', which would require 'giving the vote to such natives as have raised themselves to the level of the white man's civilization, and specially insisting on the very strong claims to consideration possessed by the coloured people'. But this was just Selborne's personal view, and neither he nor the British government forced them on the Convention.

*  *  *

All this was, of course, going on behind closed doors and among whites. What was urgently needed was for black South Africans to make their voices heard, and at this critical moment there was something of a failure of leadership. Theo Schreiner, brother of Olive and W.P. Schreiner, suggested in the African press that a united appeal should be made to the Convention and the British government to protect black rights. The time had come, he argued, for Africans to come together, 'sinking all petty jealousies and ignoring dividing lines in view of the importance of the crisis'.[56] His appeal was largely ignored. Africans believed that guarding their rights was the responsibility of their elected Cape politicians and the Imperial government. Tengo Jabavu declared: 'The Cape Africans are in a different position altogether. Their civil rights are not doubted by anyone.'[57] His newspaper came out against any form of protest against the Convention by Africans.

Among the Coloured population the response was largely articulated by and through the African Political Organisation, or APO. The party had been founded in 1902 to promote 'unity between the coloured races';

*The APO's national conference held in Johannesburg in 1912: with
(second row, centre) Dr Abdurahman and (on his left) Matt Fredericks.*

to defend Coloured people's social, political and civil rights; and 'get
all coloured men who are qualified to vote on the electoral register'.
The APO had been an almost instant success. By 1903 it could boast
a thousand members and 15 branches, and it appointed a full-time
secretary, Matthew Fredericks.[58] Although fewer than 15,000 Coloureds
were registered voters (just 3.7 per cent of the electorate in the Cape), in
several constituencies they made up more than a fifth of the voters. At the
APO's 1905 conference it was decided to elect Dr Abdullah Abdurahman
as president.[59] From then until his death in 1940, Abdurahman led the
organisation, making an indelible mark on Coloured and Cape politics.

Trained in Britain, Dr Abdurahman was a medical doctor, who came
from a well-respected Cape Town Muslim family. He had returned from
his training in Glasgow with a white British wife. In 1904 he was the first
black man elected to the Cape Town City Council, representing District
Six.[60] Dr Abdurahman told his supporters in 1905 that his main goal was
to extend the Cape's non-racial franchise to the former Boer Republics.

When a draft constitution for the self-government of the Transvaal
and Orange River Colony was being considered, the APO called for the
adoption of the Cape franchise. The organisation drew up a petition to
the King, on behalf of the 'Coloured British Subjects', which emphasised
the success of the Cape's non-racial franchise.[61] They went on to argue
that Clause 9 of the Treaty of Vereeniging, dealing with the franchise,

only applied to 'aboriginal natives, and not to ... coloured subjects'. If Coloureds were prevented from exercising their democratic rights in the Transvaal and the Orange River Colony, it would be a betrayal of their loyalty and their rights as British subjects. Consequently, when the West Ridgeway Committee decided to treat Coloureds in the same way as Africans in its proposals for self-government in the former Republics, the APO was spurred to action. The party decided to draw up a fresh appeal and dispatched Abdurahman and Matt Fredericks to London in 1906 to present it to the British Parliament.[62] Among other things, the petition urged that the franchise be granted in the Transvaal and Orange River Colony 'to all British subjects other than Natives'.[63]

In London the APO delegates managed to meet the Colonial Secretary, Lord Elgin. Dr Abdurahman pressed Elgin to 'stipulate that Britain would extend the franchise to all races if the new colonies failed to do so within a year of obtaining self-government', but to no avail.[64] He then drew up a letter to Parliament making much the same point. Abdurahman also sent a copy of the petition to Keir Hardie, the leader of the newly established Labour Party, explaining just how important the franchise was to the Coloured people.[65] These efforts similarly came to naught. All the same, the APO had managed to make its voice heard and, by contacting Keir Hardie, had managed to establish an important link that could be exploited in the future.

When eventually granted, the Transvaal and the Orange River Colony constitutions gave the vote to all white males over the age of 21, but to no one else. The failure was a severe setback for the APO. Deeply angered by the British government's behaviour, Dr Abdurahman went to his party's conference to denounce the way in which they had been treated.[66] It was apparent that neither the British nor white South Africans were prepared to see the Coloured people as very different from Africans. The policy of racial differentiation that the APO had attempted to follow had failed. The party then changed tack and developed a greater openness towards the African population. With the prospect of Union between the four British colonies now on the horizon, Dr Abdurahman sought allies from among the African people. He backed the idea of holding a convention in the Eastern Cape involving both Africans and Coloureds to thrash out a joint policy that would ensure the retention and extension of the Cape's non-racial franchise.

Even before the National Convention had ended its debates, Africans in Free State began mobilising their forces, with a proposal for a conference of their own uniting Africans from throughout South Africa. Protests were led by *Izwi* and *Imvo*. Regional conferences were held in all the colonies, except Natal, in preparation for a national gathering.

When the product of the National Convention was finally revealed it proved, of course, deeply unsatisfactory for the majority of South Africans. The APO organised what it called a 'monster meeting' in the Cape Town City Hall on 5 March 1909, where the draft constitution was denounced by Dr Abdurahman as 'wicked and unjust'. Africans shared these concerns. On 24 and 25 March 1909 Walter Rubusana and other African leaders held a South African Native Convention in Bloemfontein to discuss the draft Act. Dr Abdurahman wrote to *Izwi* stating that he had advised all APO branches to attend, 'for it matters not who initiates the movement so long as we attain our object'.[67] It was at this Native Convention that the decision was taken to call on W.P. Schreiner for assistance and to send a deputation to London to petition the British government, should their final appeals to South African whites proved fruitless. This was indeed the case. In May 1909 the National Convention approved the draft constitution unaltered. The white politicians dispatched it to London for ratification and sent a delegation to accompany the draft with strict instructions that it should be passed by the British Parliament without amendment.[68]

For black South Africans, London remained the last hope. The British people, the APO declared, would 'never be dragooned into bartering away the glorious reputation won by their ancestors as lovers of freedom and asserters of the rights of humanity'.[69] With these stirring words the APO selected Dr Abdurahman, Matt Fredericks and D.J. Lenders to join the delegation of Coloureds and Africans that was being convened by W.P. Schreiner.

\* \* \*

What of the Indian community in South Africa? In the early 1900s their concerns seemed to be focused on their civil rights rather than the franchise. In these years M.K. Gandhi became closely involved with the position of the small Indian community in the Transvaal.[70] One of his key demands was the right of Indians to travel to and from, reside within and trade in the colony. After all, Gandhi argued, they were members of the British Empire, so why should they not enjoy the same rights as any white person? But their access to the Transvaal was strongly resisted by the white businessmen, who saw Asian traders as a threat. In August 1906 fresh legislation was drawn up requiring all Indians to re-register with the authorities. The certificates they were to be given would have to be carried at all times and produced on demand. This was, in effect, a pass law.[71] Gandhi travelled to Pretoria to see the Colonial Secretary, Patrick Duncan, but Duncan refused to withdraw the legislation. Gandhi informed him that the Indian community would defy the ruling.

As the campaign developed, it became clear to Gandhi that he needed to take the fight to London in person, if he was to make progress. In 1906 he did just this, bringing with him a Muslim, Haji Ojer Ally, so that his protests could not be dismissed as being solely supported by the Hindu population. Once in the British capital Gandhi turned once more to influential Indians for advice and support. He contacted Mancherjee Bhownagree, the MP for Bethnal Green North East. With his help Gandhi managed to secure a meeting with Lord Elgin, Colonial Secretary in the newly appointed Liberal government, and his deputy, Winston Churchill.

The meeting with Churchill took place on 27 November. Churchill said the legislation could be halted, but warned that the Transvaal would very soon be self-governing and could then make its own laws. Gandhi said he accepted that whites were in charge in the Transvaal; however, 'we do feel that we are entitled to all the other ordinary rights that a British subject should enjoy.'[72] Churchill promised to do what he could, and the government duly blocked the legislation restricting Indian rights. Gandhi left Britain well pleased, having apparently secured a victory. He also set up the South African British India Committee. Consisting of Gandhi's Indian and English supporters, it would continue lobbying on his behalf.[73] But his triumph was short-lived. On 1 January 1907 the Transvaal received self-government. Just as Churchill had predicted, the new government reintroduced the measure, making it compulsory for all Indian males above the age of eight to be registered and have their fingerprints taken. Gandhi said the law would spell 'absolute ruin for the Indians of South Africa'. He argued that it was 'better to die than submit to such a law' and called for the campaign to be intensified.[74] In April 1907 Gandhi held an hour-long meeting with Smuts, by this time Transvaal's Colonial Secretary. Smuts listened politely but said that compulsory registration was required because there was 'strong evidence' of the 'unlawful infiltration' of Indians into the colony. There was also

*M.K. Gandhi (second on the left) with other leaders of the passive resistance campaign, 1907, outside his offices in Johannesburg.*

an exchange of letters between the two men, but to no avail. It was at this point that Gandhi launched his *satyagraha* (or non-violent resistance) movement, which would land him, and his associates, in jail. This was no easy step for a lawyer to take, but it was one that Gandhi was prepared to take to defend his community.

During all of the campaigns, there is no suggestion that Gandhi raised the question of the franchise. Even though he had fought hard to try to prevent Indians from losing the vote in Natal in the 1890s, Gandhi himself had failed to register on three different occasions.[75] In subsequent years he did not include the right to vote among the demands he made on the authorities, South African or British. For someone so keen to assert the rights of his community, this would, at first glance, appear somewhat odd. It may be that Gandhi believed that so few Indians would qualify for the right that it was not worth striving for. In any case, the wider human rights of his community were so curtailed that the vote was, in his view, of little importance.

This approach can be seen in an article in Gandhi's paper, *Indian Opinion*, in February 1909: 'The proposed Union has dangerous implications for Indians and other Coloured races,' he wrote. 'They will be left with no voting rights anywhere, and care has been taken to provide in the report that they should be deprived of whatever little measure of such rights they enjoy in the Cape. But franchise is a mere trifle. Where we are not allowed even standing room, voting rights can be of little avail ... Therefore, we have to educate ourselves and win freedom for ourselves by our own efforts. Till that is done, the franchise, in our opinion, will have no value.'[76] This stance ignored the benefits the vote had brought to communities in the Cape and may have been the result of ignorance. Gandhi had only limited contact with most Africans, and little with Africans in the Cape. He did not therefore know of the benefits they derived from the franchise – including the respect they had won from some white politicians, both English and Afrikaans.

Gandhi's lack of interest in the franchise was perhaps reinforced by the attitude of the Indian community in South Africa itself. Most had arrived in the country as indentured labourers. They were gradually joined by merchants and traders. A good many had, at first, seen themselves as temporary residents who would in time return home, and some did so.[77] Gandhi certainly did not intend to make the country his home and always planned to spend his life in India. He assiduously maintained his links with his mother country. It also meant that his ties to South Africa were relatively weak. But by the early years of the twentieth century the attitude of the community appears to have changed. Indians had been in South Africa for decades; many had known no other country. In 1911 a Colonial Born Indian Association was formed.[78] Indians had put down roots and saw themselves as South Africans. For them the vote had become as important as it was to any other group. But whatever the reason, while Africans and Coloureds made representations to the National Convention, calling for black people to be enfranchised, there are few indications that the Indian community did.

\*\*\*

The intransigence of the white politicians had, unwittingly, united the black opposition. By drawing up a constitution that for the most part excluded black South Africans, they had brought together African and Coloured parties from across the political spectrum. Even the difficult relations that had hitherto existed between Rubusana and Jabavu had been smoothed over. Both men participated in the Schreiner deputation, which included representatives of the African, Coloured and white communities. This was the first time unity had been achieved on such a significant scale. Only the Indians remained aloof, sending instead a delegation led by Gandhi to lobby for their civil rights, but not for the right to vote.

Having said this, there was still dissent within the Coloured community.

*F.Z.S. Peregrino.*

John Tobin, a founding member of the APO, opposed the deputation, arguing that the previous mission in 1906 had been a complete waste of money.[79] Tobin was supported in his opposition to the deputation by F.Z.S. Peregrino, a Ghanaian who had moved to Britain and the United States, before settling in the Cape in November 1900. Peregrino founded and edited the *South African Spectator*, which was aimed at a black readership. While always wishing to advance black rights, Peregrino was a conservative, stressing the need to avoid confrontation.[80] Rather, he believed that grievances should be laid before the relevant authorities. Peregrino was an influential and respected voice in Cape politics, even though he did not join the APO. He was also a well-connected Pan-Africanist, with links to black leaders across the English-speaking world. But there was another side to Peregrino, which is little known.[81] A series of letters from Peregrino exist which show him to have repeatedly contacted white officials, denouncing several African and Coloured politicians close to him, including Tobin, Abdurahman and Jabavu. Quite why he did this is not clear, since there is no evidence that he received financial reward for his efforts.

When the Schreiner deputation was about to sail, Peregrino and Tobin decided to act. Although they had not always seen eye to eye on every issue themselves, they joined forces to try to derail the appeal to London. They went to see the liberal Cape Afrikaner, Jan Hofmeyr, presenting him with a 'humble tribute'.[82] Hofmeyr, as leader of the Afrikaner Bond, had persuaded the Cape Town branch of his party to condemn the colour bar clauses in the draft Act. Hofmeyr thanked them, reiterating his support for a qualified non-racial franchise, as long as it did not endanger white rule. But Hofmeyr warned Tobin and Peregrino that given the hostility of many white politicians, the survival of the Cape franchise 'greatly depended on the moderation and wisdom of which your and other representative bodies of your people may give proof in their acts and utterances in connection with the draft Constitution and the National Convention'.

With this warning ringing in their ears, Tobin and Peregrino viewed the whirlwind of activities around the London deputation with alarm. They attacked the Schreiner deputation, arguing that 'agitation' might worsen the plight of black people and rejecting 'any scheme whereby an appeal shall be made to any party outside South Africa on behalf of our people for the redress of such grievances.'[83] Hofmeyr was presented with a statement forcefully laying out their position. This was widely circulated. The *Cape Times* published it in full under the heading 'Mr. Hofmeyr's Mandate: A Coloured Deputation: Deprecates Appeal to England'.[84] Claiming to speak on behalf of Coloured people, they rejected appeals to the British, instead expressing 'confidence and trust in our friends in South Africa who have consistently and steadily defended our cause, and whose efforts will, we believe, ultimately be crowned with success'.

The APO was furious. Matt Fredericks wrote a letter denouncing their approach to Hofmeyr, and declaring that Peregrino and Tobin were 'self-appointed' and did not represent the community.[85] But the protest was in vain. Hofmeyr had already sailed and was soon making sure the authorities were aware of Tobin and Peregrino's statement. Writing to them from London, Hofmeyr explained that their resolution had been put to good effect.[86] 'I had the pleasure of handing a copy to Lord Crewe [Secretary of State for the Colonies] of the address with which you honoured me on the eve of my departure for England,' Hofmeyr explained. Hofmeyr said that Lord Crewe had appeared to sympathise with their stand, and promised to provide a written reply. When Crewe did respond, he said the government had taken note of their views.

The Tobin–Peregrino denunciation was very damaging. *The Times* carried an article in which Schreiner was described as 'claiming a right to express the views of the South African natives'.[87] This the paper disputed, reporting that 'A large section of the coloured people definitely repudiate him'. As soon as he arrived on British soil, Schreiner found himself on the back foot, having to defend himself against allegations that he did not truly represent the views of the black community. His former ally, John X. Merriman, also attacked Schreiner. Interviewed on board the *Kenilworth Castle*, Merriman referred to Schreiner's position as 'entirely inexplicable'.[88] Speaking to *The Times*, the Prime Minister said that 'the agitation can have nothing but the worst possible effect ... I think Mr Schreiner's present mission is one of the most unkind things ever done to the natives.' It was hardly the reception that Schreiner, Abdurahman and the others might have hoped for.

The next few weeks in Britain would be vital for the future of South Africa. The constitution of the proposed Union would be settled. So, too, would the country's role in the Imperial system, with plans being made to include South Africa in Britain's defences. On the shoulders of the African and Coloured politicians rested the hopes and fears of their communities. So much money had been raised to send them: what if they failed? The white politicians were leaving with the clear instruction from the National Convention: to veto any major alteration to the constitution. Much was at stake and much would be decided before any of them saw the shores of Cape Town once more.

# 5

# London: Friends and allies

On Saturday, 4 July, W.P. Schreiner walked down the gangplank of the mail steamer *Briton* at Southampton.[1] Schreiner was accompanied by his wife, Frances, better known as Fanny. She was sister of the former President of the Orange Free State, Francis William Reitz. The voyage must have seen some fascinating interchanges: Lord Selborne – the High Commissioner – was on board, as was Sir Henry de Villiers, who had presided over the National Convention. Schreiner was well known to them all. While his companions were travelling to London to obtain a British blessing for the draft constitution, Schreiner was seeking to overturn the very compromises they had so carefully negotiated. There must have been some delicate moments.

Their arrival in Southampton marked the start of Schreiner's appeal to the British Parliament and public; his deputation's attempt to try to reverse the setbacks they had suffered during the writing of the constitution. It was an extremely ambitious project: asking the Imperial Parliament to override the decisions endorsed by the National Convention. While Schreiner and the deputation were not opposed to Union, their aim was nothing short of a rewriting of key elements of the draft. They wanted to extend the Cape's non-racial franchise to the rest of the country, to allow black South Africans to stand for Parliament, and to keep the Protectorates – Swaziland, Basutoland and Bechuanaland – out of the South African fold. If they were to be successful they would require powerful British supporters.

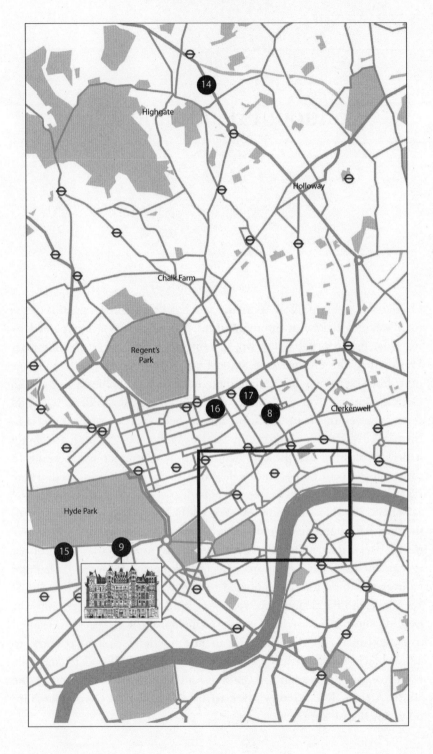

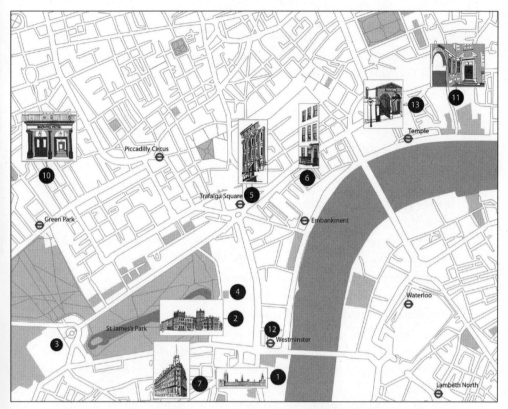

*Maps of London showing the main sites associated with the South African delegations of 1909.*

**LEGEND**

1. Houses of Parliament
2. Foreign Office, India Office and Colonial Office
3. Buckingham Palace
4. 10 Downing Street

**Schreiner Delegation**

5. Morley's Hotel (Schreiner)
6. Buckingham Temperance Hotel (Jabavu)
7. Westminster Palace Hotel (Gandhi)
8. Joseph Gerrans

**Official delegation**

9. Hyde Park Hotel (Smuts)
10. Brown's Hotel (Merriman)

11. South African British India Committee
12. British India Committee
13. Exeter Hall
14. India House
15. Imperial Institute
16. Alfred Mangena
17. Betty Molteno

\* \* \*

Schreiner was a shrewd lawyer and politician. He would have had plenty of time during the voyage to consider just how to frame his argument. As soon as they landed he gave an interview to the Reuters news agency, which was widely reported. 'I have come to England to do what I can to try and get the blots removed from the Act,' Schreiner told the reporter, 'which makes it no Act of Union, but rather an Act of Separation between the minority and the majority of the people of South Africa. True union must consider all elements, but here the principal element is not merely not considered but from our point of view is dealt with in an actually insulting way. The coloured inhabitants of South Africa are barred from the opportunity to rise and evolve naturally, which is the right of every man in a free country. We do not base our movement upon the doctrine of the equality of all men, but upon the doctrine of the right to freedom of opportunity – equality of opportunity.'

Schreiner had spent sufficient time in Britain to understand how to appeal to the imperial instincts of its political class. 'The principles of justice which are associated in our minds with Great Britain and her expansive policy', he argued, 'are violated in the proposed Act of Union. We do not dream that the Union is to be wrecked if Great Britain resolves that injustice, which is apparent, is to be removed. We know that the incentives towards union are so strong that none of the parties to the Convention would dream of rejecting it merely because the offensive exclusion of persons of non-European descent from political opportunity might be removed or because the position of inhabitants of Cape Colony should be placed upon a foundation of absolute security against future attack.'

Reuters also interviewed Sir Henry de Villiers in Southampton. He was left to argue that the position of black South Africans would not be undermined, but Sir Henry was hardly convincing. 'The status of natives as a whole will be immeasurably improved by the Union, so that if their position is somewhat lowered in the Cape Colony it will be vastly improved in the other colonies.' Sir Henry had little in the way of evidence to support this assertion, but tried to suggest that the transformation of the colonies into provinces – each with its own legislative council – would offer black people some form of representation. 'In the Cape there is nothing to prevent any coloured man or native from being elected for the provincial council [under the proposed Constitution],' he said. 'Of course, in the other South African parliaments, they have not a vote, and consequently are not entitled to be elected to provincial councils. In Natal there are such restrictions that very few natives can vote; but I repeat, as a whole, the position has improved.' It was rather lame: hardly the ringing endorsement of a carefully drafted constitution for a brand-new country. But Sir Henry and the official delegation did not really have to win the intellectual debate, important though this was. They had the support of their own colonial parliaments in South Africa and the cautious support of the British authorities. If all else failed, they always had a trump card: the threat of walking away from the Union that London so clearly desired.

The British government and Lord Crewe, the Colonial Secretary, had agonised for months about how to square an awkward circle: their promises given to black South Africans of a better life, made before and during the Anglo-Boer War, with their need to placate the whites who were so resistant to black advancement. At the same time Lord Crewe knew that the British Parliament was well aware of the issues. A number of Liberal and Labour MPs were determined to hold the government to account and stand up for black rights. Although the table was stacked against Schreiner and his colleagues, they were not without British allies.

The Schreiners set about establishing themselves in London. Ahead of them lay a gruelling marathon of meetings. They chose a base that was perfectly suited to their purpose. It was Morley's Hotel, on Trafalgar Square, within easy walking distance of Whitehall and the Houses of Parliament. Built in 1832, it was not quite in the class of Claridge's. Nonetheless it was a well-appointed, comfortable establishment, which took up the entire east side of the square, where the South African High Commission is now situated.[2] James Joyce was evidently impressed when he visited the hotel in 1893: 'Morley's Hotel proved indeed to be a ruddy spot; brilliant, in my recollection, is the coffee-room fire, the hospitable mahogany, the sense that in the stupendous city this, at any rate for the hour, was a shelter and a point of view.'[3]

The rest of the deputation arrived by various ships and gradually assembled in London. They included the Congregational Church minister and president of the South African Native Convention, Walter Rubusana. There was the influential editor of the Xhosa-language *Imvo Zabantsundu*, John Tengo Jabavu, who was also president of the Cape Native Convention. Thomas Mapikela represented Africans from the Orange River Colony. John Dube, the Zulu teacher and preacher, backed the deputation but rather covertly. Pressure exerted by the Natal authorities meant that his work with the deputation had to be kept from the public. The Africans were joined by Dr Abdullah Abdurahman, president of the African Political Organisation, as well as two of the organisation's senior members: Matthew Fredericks, its general secretary, and the vice-president and well-known cricketer, Daniel Lenders. One other white participated: he was Joseph Gerrans of Mafeking, who had been asked to speak on behalf of the Tswana chiefs of the Bechuanaland Protectorate.[4]

Some members of the deputation found hotels as close as possible to the Schreiners and Parliament, even if they were not as smart.[5] Others stayed at boarding houses or private addresses.[6] Between them these nine men represented the vast majority of South Africa's people. Gandhi, who was not part of the deputation, gave them encouragement and support. His mission was to try to win rights for Transvaal Indians with his colleague, Hajee Habib. They stayed at the well-appointed Westminster Palace Hotel on Victoria Street, within sight of Westminster Abbey and the Houses of Parliament.[7]

\*\*\*

As we have seen, the Schreiner deputation had been undermined by the attacks on its credibility even before they departed from Cape Town. Yet these were the least of their problems. The hurdles they faced once they had arrived in London were far more challenging. The British had, in reality, already decided that they would back the draft constitution in its current form and that no major amendment would be allowed. The long campaign by men like Smuts, Botha and Merriman had paid off and London was now firmly on their side. The official deputation, to which they and the other senior white politicians belonged, would be royally treated: every courtesy would be extended to them and their welcome would be warm and heartfelt.

How different the reception of the black deputation. They had had to pay for their own passage to Britain, find their own accommodation and make their own contacts with potential supporters. Yet Schreiner and his colleagues were not without friends and allies and they believed, rightly, that they had a fighting chance to influence the outcome. Their potential support came in four categories. First, there were the Liberal members of

*Morley's Hotel on Trafalgar Square, at which W.P. Schreiner and his family stayed in 1909, is today the site of the South African High Commission.*

Parliament. The second group were the socialist MPs from the emerging Labour Party. Some, like Keir Hardie and Ramsay MacDonald, had been involved in South African affairs since the Boer War and were well aware of the situation. The third group included the Aborigines' Protection Society and the Anti-Slavery Society (with which the former merged in 1909). These movements had a long history of fighting for 'native' rights in South Africa and were natural friends of the deputation. Finally, there was a heterogeneous group of British men and women who rallied to Schreiner's cause. Some were old friends of his, going back to his days at Cambridge University. Others were liberal imperialists or radicals, like the unorthodox but influential journalist William Thomas Stead, whose *Review of Reviews* was widely read.

Sir Charles Dilke was the most influential, active and vocal supporter of the deputation. A highly principled, radical Liberal MP, Dilke had caused considerable controversy in 1871 when he criticised the British monarchy and called for a republican form of government – a position he later renounced. He was widely regarded as among the country's leading authorities on the Empire and international relations.[8] His promising career had been blighted by an affair with the wife of a fellow MP, a scandal that became the cause célèbre of the 1880s. Dilke managed to salvage his reputation and, despite the gossip, he remained an influential figure in the House of Commons until his death in January 1911. Dilke was also on excellent terms with the Labour Party – the other potential source of support for Schreiner's deputation. Dilke had written that the emergence of Labour was 'The triumph of the principles to which I have devoted my life', since it would confront the more reactionary tendencies within British politics.[9]

Dilke was just the kind of man Schreiner would warm to: an independent-minded politician who had excellent connections throughout the British establishment. The two families had been in contact for some time. In September 1892 Olive Schreiner wrote to her brother, offering an introduction to Dilke when W.P. travelled to Britain.[10] Dilke had also taken an interest in South African 'native' rights for several years. In 1906 he placed the subject on the agenda of a group of like-minded MPs who were part of a Radical Committee in the House of Commons.[11] In February of that year Dilke urged the British government to clarify its policy towards the black population in the wake of the Boer War, in a letter he sent to the Prime Minister and in a parliamentary debate.[12] The motion he put forward declared that 'in any settlement of South African affairs this House desires a recognition of Imperial responsibility for the protection of all races excluded from equal political rights, the safeguarding of all immigrants against servile labour, and the guarantee to the native populations of at least their existing status, with the unbroken possession of their liberties in Basutoland, Bechuanaland, and other tribal countries and reservations'.[13] Although Dilke did not participate in the 1906 debate, he wrote: 'I am proud to have planned this letter and drawn up the motion for [Sir William Pollard] Byles [a radical Liberal MP who had opposed the Boer War] so that it was carried unanimously by the House.'[14] The resolution was important: it laid down guidelines for the Colonial Office to follow. Having the unanimous support of Parliament, it carried considerable weight.

Dilke did speak in later debates. In 1909 he told the House of Commons that the colour bar in South Africa's draft constitution was detrimental to the purpose of Empire. Including a racial exclusion was, in his view, the 'most momentous' imperial decision ever taken by Parliament. Arguing that it was Britain's duty to prevent racial domination, he suggested that the 'whole fabric' of Empire would collapse if the principle of permanent white supremacy was constitutionally enshrined.[15] As Dilke's biographer commented: 'His misgivings were well-founded. Never before had Britain made race a criterion for political participation.'[16]

Schreiner and Dilke began discussing the draft constitution well before the deputation set sail from Cape Town. On 16 February 1909 Dilke replied to a letter from Schreiner, saying that he had taken the issue of the Protectorates (Bechuanaland, Swaziland and Basutoland) to the Radical Committee in the House of Commons.[17] The Committee supported Schreiner's objections to the incorporation of these territories into South Africa but – Dilke pointed out – there was a problem. The Colonial Office was having to deal with the issue with some care, he said, because of the stand that Louis Botha could adopt. 'Botha might take steps which would place them in a great difficulty, both political and imperial, as Botha could get even more general support from the Dominions by telegram than Natal did when the Colonial Office interfered in the matter of the shooting of prisoners in the first so-called rebellion of those of the last three years.' The incident in Natal that Dilke was referring to was the Bambatha Rebellion of 1906, when the dominions united in refusing to accept London's interference – particularly in questions of race relations.[18]

From Dilke's letter to Schreiner in February 1909 it is clear that this lesson had not been forgotten. Indeed, the Colonial Office had tried hard to try to provide a coherent and unified policy towards 'native' populations across the Empire. As noted in chapter 3, Charles Lucas, a senior civil servant, had taken considerable trouble to detail the rights of citizens of different races across the Empire two years previously.[19] In his view the aim across all territories should be equality. 'It seems to me that the ultimate object to be aimed at, and avowedly aimed at, however far off it may be, is ordinary citizenship for all colours alike under whatever is the government of the country, and the making of laws for the benefit of natives by a Colonial Legislature in which they are represented, just as one class and another in this country is legislated for by a Parliament representing all classes. In other words, that the natives should be an integral part of the community, and that they should be legislated for rather as a class than as a race. This object may appear to be almost unattainable in a part of the world like South Africa, where there is responsible government and where coloured voters would, if coloured men were all equal citizens with the whites, swamp the whites.'[20]

Before arriving at his conclusion, Lucas went through all the problems facing equal citizenship in South Africa. 'Mr Rhodes proclaimed his belief in this ideal of equal citizenship irrespective of colour, and Mr

Schreiner lately avowed sympathy with the same object; *nor can I see any other final solution, though there may be and are intermediate stages of citizenship short of absolute equality.*'[21] Colonel John Seely, Under Secretary of State for the Colonies, highlighted this point in the margin of his copy of the report, adding a question mark. Although Colonial Office officials might back equal citizenship, senior politicians were apparently not as convinced.

There is one other point that it is important to note about Dilke: he was a Liberal and, although he could be critical of government policy, he was still loyal to his party, which was now in power. Hence he wrote to Seely on 26 May 1909, shortly before the South Africans arrived in London, laying out in detail his plans for how he might raise his concerns about the draft constitution.[22] Dilke explained that he would back Schreiner's argument that 'native affairs' could not simply be left to the local whites, but made it clear he would do so in a manner that would not embarrass the government. This explains, in part, the absence of Dilke from the floor of the House of Commons when the constitution was finally debated.

The Labour Party had also offered its support prior to the deputation's arrival. The party's general secretary, Ramsay MacDonald, had written to Schreiner, saying: 'I have just heard you are on your way here to take part in discussions connected with the new constitution for South Africa. I hope you will let me know when you get to London, and tell me where you are, as I might get together a few M.P.s, who are interested in the constitutional position of the natives, to discuss matters with you before any step has been openly taken.'[23] It was no surprise that Labour took this position. Senior party members, including MacDonald, had been actively involved in South Africa well before Labour was even founded as a party in 1900.[24]

Labour's leader, Keir Hardie, was well known as a 'Pro-Boer', opposing the British war effort against the Afrikaners during 1899–1902. Born and brought up in Scotland by his mother, a domestic servant, his early life had been marked by crushing poverty. Hardie was forced to go out to work at the age of seven and was down the coal mines at the age of ten. Self-taught, he had progressed through the trade union movement to become a leading socialist, while at the same time being an active Christian. In 1892 he took up a seat in the House of Commons, but refused to wear the stiff formal parliamentary dress of the day, preferring a tweed jacket

*Keir Hardie in his study, with the Union Jack salvaged from his disrupted meeting in Johannesburg. [National Library of Scotland]*

and Sherlock Holmes-style deerstalker cap. Having won a reputation as a doughty fighter for working-class causes, Hardie was the natural choice as leader of the Labour Party when trade unionists came together with representatives of the socialist societies to found the party in 1900.

When Olive Schreiner's husband, Samuel Cronwright-Schreiner, toured Britain in February 1900 to campaign for the Boer cause, Keir Hardie had welcomed him. The two men risked life and limb speaking at rowdy public meetings against British involvement in the conflict. For his part, MacDonald visited South Africa within a few months of the war ending, concluding that the whites were not to be trusted to control black affairs.[25] He had come to this view after meeting a wide range of men and women. 'Only on one South African matter might Downing Street advantageously interfere; I mean this native question. It is not safe to allow the people on the spot the sole decision on the native policy ... Sooner or later the country will have to face the problem of how to deal with the enormous native population, but I found nobody who had any very clear idea as to how that difficulty was to be met.' MacDonald went on to suggest that 'native policy' should be discussed at every Colonial Conference that London held to consider policy across the Empire.

*Keir Hardie (dressed in white) outside the Socialist Hall in Cape Town, 1908.*

In 1908 Hardie visited South Africa at the end of a round-the-world voyage. In the Transvaal he addressed packed public meetings in Johannesburg and Pretoria.[26] On both occasions he received a very rough ride and had to flee for his life, after urging white workers to make common cause with their black countrymen. As he fled, crowds sang about how they would hang him if given the chance. Leaving for Cape Town, Hardie took a day off to meet Olive Schreiner, to her great delight, and she gave him a letter of introduction to her brother, W.P. Once in Cape Town, Hardie again spoke in public. Cape Town's Trades and Labour Council and the Labour Representation Committee, almost certainly aware of the trouble his views had caused at his previous meetings, decided not to give Hardie a platform. It was left to the Social Democratic Federation to rise to the challenge. A meeting was arranged at the Social Democrats' Socialist Hall on the edge of District Six, followed by another at the Good Hope Hall, both of which were well attended. The Cape audience, more used to the non-racial message, was far more sympathetic and he had a warm reception.

\* \* \*

Prior to the Schreiner deputation's arrival, Dilke had taken steps to build alliances in Parliament. He gathered around him those who might support a challenge to the draft constitution and took them to see the

Colonial Secretary, Lord Crewe. The meeting, on 20 May 1909, was crucial. It was an off-the-record discussion between key activists and the government, and together they laid out the parameters for the debate in the months ahead. Hardie and MacDonald had come from Labour and they were joined by a number of Liberal MPs, including John Robertson and Percy Alden. In a letter to Schreiner, Dilke explained their approach.[27] The deputation had seen Lord Crewe privately, avoiding any publicity, because of the 'delicacy of the question affecting the future of the Protectorates', Dilke explained. The position of Bechuanaland, Basutoland and Swaziland appears to have dominated the discussions.[28] Dilke told Schreiner that they had based themselves on the resolution unanimously carried by the Commons on 13 May the previous year. They did so, he said, 'as Seely, the Under Secretary, who was present with Lord Crewe, had taken it as the base of Government policy'. This was the resolution calling for government action to safeguard 'the rights and future of the natives in any scheme of political unification or federation'.[29]

Dilke thought that the chiefs of the Bechuanaland Protectorate, 'who had friends in this country, could take care of themselves'.[30] The position of the Swazi was also 'satisfactory', but his real concern lay with the Basotho, who constituted a 'point of danger'. Dilke said he had evidence from South Africa that, if handled incorrectly, the Basotho 'were very likely to rise'. As we shall see, this chimed with the official estimation that the Basotho remained a considerable military threat.

Lord Crewe, replying to Dilke and his colleagues, said that he shared to a considerable extent some of the views they put forward, more particularly a strong feeling against the colour bar excluding Africans from Parliament.[31] The Colonial Secretary explained that he was willing to say as much in private, but not in public. He said that it was difficult to predict how far the South Africans could be expected to agree to amendments to this aspect of the draft constitution, especially since Australia maintained a colour bar, and in practice no African had ever taken a seat in any of the parliaments of the South African colonies.

When Dilke summed up what had taken place, he concluded that there was scope for making progress on the Protectorates.[32] At the same time Dilke warned Schreiner that they faced a major obstacle. This was what he termed the 'Natal question' – the argument that London should not interfere unnecessarily in the internal affairs of a colony. Just where the division of powers and responsibilities lay between the Colonial

Secretary and the local government was evidently a delicate question. 'The Natal precedent is terrible for us,' Dilke told Schreiner. As the Bambatha Rebellion had made clear, South Africa's whites, far from being cowed by a directive from London, were willing and able to seek support from the white self-governing dominions.[33] They had not been disappointed and had forced the British government to retreat in 1906. This united front established by the dominions against London's attempts to protect 'native rights' was clearly a major obstacle.

On a more positive note Dilke assured Schreiner that he was held in considerable regard by the British establishment. 'Everything you "do" on this side of the water aids us more powerfully than anything which could be done by any other man. The respect in which your name is held is such that every word is of the greatest value. A mere rumour of your views which were represented in an article by a gentleman who is, I believe, a friend of yours, in the current number of the *Socialist Review*, has caused the article to be eagerly read by the Secretary of State, the Under Secretary, and the permanent heads of the Colonial Office.'[34]

The article Dilke referred to was by F.G. Gardiner, an influential South African lawyer and later the Judge-President of the Cape. Gardiner had written a powerful defence of the Cape's non-racial franchise, and called for the elimination of the clause preventing any black man from standing for Parliament.[35] Gardiner said he was reluctantly appealing to the Imperial government to intervene, but argued that there was little alternative, since it was not about to be put before the South African people for endorsement. 'Why is this?' Gardiner asked rhetorically. 'Largely because the people who are vitally interested – the Cape natives and coloured men – might vote against the Constitution, and wreck this so-called Union of South Africa. Can one imagine a more unfair, a more unworthy argument?'

\*\*\*

Of the groups that came to Schreiner's aid, the backing of the Aborigines' Protection Society was the most certain and the most predictable. The Society had grown out of the public revulsion against the slave trade. After its founding in 1837 it spent the next seven decades lobbying the Colonial Office, colonial governors and British MPs and it kept up a series of well-informed public campaigns against abuses committed against many of the native populations that Britain ruled.

Over the years South Africa had been a central interest of the Aborigines' Protection Society, which had worked to expose the injustices perpetrated against the Zulu, Basotho, Griqua and the Tswana.[36] These campaigns frequently involved criticising the brutality with which the black population was treated by the Boers.[37] The Aborigines' Protection Society was divided over whether to support the Anglo-Boer War and at its 1901 annual meeting finally agreed on a general motion calling for 'constant vigilance' for the 'treatment of natives in that part of the world'.[38] It was Charles Dilke who had moved that motion.[39]

The Society had taken a firm stand on the question of the franchise. In 1900, while the war was still under way, its secretary, Henry Fox Bourne, had criticised the restrictions on the political rights of black people that existed in the Cape and Natal. 'In the Cape Colony the blacks have the same political and municipal franchise as the whites, and in Natal it [the right to vote] may be granted to them by favour of the Governor. But in both colonies the franchise is hampered by restrictions specially imposed with a view of keeping down the number of black voters.' Fox Bourne then complained that black people were 'expected to be loyal subjects' of the Queen, 'but not under the same conditions; to worship the same God, but not in the same churches and chapels; to be good citizens as their white neighbours, but only as those neighbours' menials and drudges'.[40]

As a well-known defender of 'native' peoples, the Society's activities were widely reported in newspapers across the Empire. It was highly regarded by black South Africans, who turned to it for support. In 1887 John Tengo Jabavu wrote to Fox Bourne, describing himself as 'writing from the depths of obscurity' and calling for the Society's assistance to prevent the passage of a law that would restrict the African franchise at the Cape.[41] 'We are marshalling local forces to defeat the measure,' Jabavu said; 'but, with a Dutch majority in the Cape parliament the battle will have to be fought out in England, and that by your useful Society.'

Other black activists from South Africa turned to the 'useful Society'. Alan Soga, the editor of *Izwi Labantu* (Voice of the People), asked Fox Bourne in 1906 for support in publishing a book in the United States, *The Problems of Black and White in South Africa*.[42] Although the book was prepared, sadly no copies have come to light. Keir Hardie wrote an introduction, which survives in the Society's archives.[43] 'Mr Soga was evidently aware', Hardie wrote, 'of the momentous issues affecting the whole population of British South Africa which would be involved in the granting of responsible government to the white residents in the Transvaal now on the eve of accomplishment.' The Labour leader also described the 'ruthless' campaign waged in Natal during the Bambatha Rebellion against the Africans, who rose after being 'goaded' by the whites. Soga's book, he said, 'makes timely appearance as a grave warning to the authorities in other parts of South Africa as well as in the Transvaal and Natal against continuance of lines of policy which the British government appears unable, even if it desires, to reverse'.

In 1906 Dr Abdurahman appealed to the Society for support before setting out from Cape Town for London to lobby the British for Coloured people to be granted the vote in the Transvaal, even if Africans were not.[44] This was, Abdurahman pointed out, in line with the promise Britain had given in the 1850s at the time representative government was being extended to the Cape. '[When], in answer to colonial demands for an exclusively white franchise, the Duke of Newcastle, the Secretary of State for War and the Colonies, declared it to be "the earnest desire of Her Majesty's Government that all her subjects at the Cape, without distinction of class or colour, should be united in one common bond of loyalty and common interest".' The Society took up the issue vigorously.[45]

These efforts to promote the cause of black South Africans were duly acknowledged by them. In November 1906 the Society's journal carried an extract from Soga's newspaper.[46] 'The Aborigines Protection Society is indefatigable in its exertions on behalf of the protection of the natives, and it is well that an expression of the gratitude of the people should be voiced in this public manner. That organisation, which is not popular with many colonists, is able to bring great pressure to bear with the British authorities in mitigating some of the needless severity which are a feature of the relations of black and white in several of our colonies, and for what the A.P.S. has accomplished in the past, and may be expected to do in the future, the natives of South Africa will be ever grateful.'

Given this history, the Society was a natural ally for Schreiner and the rest of his deputation. Yet the Society itself was really on its last legs. As its historian has noted, 'The powers of the Aborigines' Protection Society were waning, just as those of the Union of South Africa were waxing.'[47] In December 1908 it decided to merge with the Anti-Slavery Society.[48] This amalgamation took much of 1909 to organise and its members' attention was diverted from campaigning. A second blow was even more serious.[49] The death of Fox Bourne on 2 February 1909 robbed the

Society of its driving force, just as it was making the difficult transition to becoming part of a wider movement.

Despite its declining power, the Society was not without influence in high places, including Charles Dilke. He raised the question of South Africa and the Union constitution at the Society's meeting on 19 May 1909. 'I moved a resolution', he told Schreiner, 'on the three points – franchise, colour bar ineligibility, and Protectorates.'[50] These were the key issues that confronted the deputation. As Schreiner and his associates sailed towards London, friends like Dilke had already laid the foundations for a network of support and assistance. Certainly, they were going to need all the help they could get. There would be little time to organise a campaign, and the deputation was up against well-co-ordinated and well-resourced opposition: the combined weight of the political leadership of white South Africa and the British government.

# 6

# London: Campaigning for non-racialism

Once he had settled into Morley's Hotel, Schreiner began mobilising his forces. Most of the work inevitably fell onto his shoulders: he had been educated in England, his was the status as a former Premier and his were the contacts. What is clear from the archival record is that W.P. did all he could to involve the rest of the deputation in the discussions and negotiations, but that he was the channel through which most of the communications flowed.[1]

Schreiner wasted no time. On Monday, 5 July – just a day after arriving in Southampton – he launched his campaign. Over the next seven weeks Schreiner, supported by the rest of the deputation, attempted to win over the British government and public. It was a hectic, relentless 46 days of intense activity that would leave him exhausted and close to collapse. The key events came rapidly and the pressure was relentless. On 27 July the Bill was debated in the House of Lords and on 16 and 19 August it was before the House of Commons.

While this was under way, the British government was meeting with the official, white delegates. They were warmly welcomed and royally treated – not just because of their status as the official representatives of the people of South Africa, but because of the promise they held out of the formal inclusion of South Africa within the system of dominions. Former white British colonies, the dominions had evolved during the nineteenth century into semi-independent states under the British Crown. By 1900 they consisted of the Commonwealth of Australia, New Zealand, Canada and Newfoundland, and were about to be joined by the Union of South Africa.

But South Africa posed tricky questions. There was, of course, the franchise. But there was also the status of the Protectorates – the territories today known as Lesotho, Swaziland and Botswana. The South Africans, led by Louis Botha, were keen to have them incorporated into the Union, a fate their African leaders were determined to resist. All of these issues had to be settled before Britain's long-held ambition of incorporating a united South Africa within the Empire could be achieved.

\*\*\*

On Monday, 5 July, Schreiner wrote to Dilke accepting an invitation to lunch and informing Sir Charles that he was launching what he must have regarded as among his most potent weapons the following day. It was the petition he had brought from the Cape, signed by the good and the great.[2] 'You will read tomorrow in the papers an appeal', he told Sir Charles, 'on the subject which brings me to England. Its publication was arranged by an influential Committee in Cape Town.' The petition appeared in *The Times* and the *Manchester Guardian* and – since it was carried by the Reuters news agency – was picked up by newspapers in South Africa as well.[3]

The petition began: 'It is with a deep sense of responsibility that we, the undersigned citizens of Cape Colony, venture to present an appeal to the Parliament and Government of Great Britain and Ireland.'[4] While the authors declared that they were bound to accept the compromises hammered out during the National Convention, and would normally 'deprecate' interference in the purely domestic concerns of South Africa, they argued that the issues raised in the draft constitution were so serious that they had no option but to appeal to the Imperial Parliament. The issues were the familiar ones: the ban on anyone who was not of European descent standing for Parliament and the restrictions on the franchise. The petition was as eloquent and persuasive as possible and was designed to move the British public.[5]

'The essential principles of free government are in jeopardy: that constitutional freedom is endangered which is fully protected in Great Britain and elsewhere: and that well-established right of communities of civilised men freely to exercise the franchise without restrictions of race, creed or colour is threatened. The gravity of this inroad upon constitutional liberties is illustrated by the fact that those who would be deprived of these full citizen rights include ministers of religion, editors, teachers, doctors, public servants, clerks, landowners, traders and artisans – in a word, men of all sorts and conditions, who in their various spheres have won the respect of their fellow-citizens by their character, their ability, their loyalty, their public spirit, or their labours for the public weal.'

The appeal went on to argue that, if passed, the constitution would lead to a 'disastrous separation of the population of South Africa into more or less hostile camps'. It would undo Imperial and Cape policies which had been to 'raise those who are slowly emerging from the darkness of barbarism into the light of civilisation'. The petitioners pointed out the global implications of the constitution. 'Not only will the wave of discontent, moved by injustice, swell through the vast native populations of South Africa but we believe that throughout the Empire interested and anxious eyes are turned to see what will be the Act of the mother of Parliaments at this critical time. To regard this as a purely South African Question is to misunderstand and misconceive the whole idea which underlies the unity of the self-governing and independent, yet inter-dependent, communities which make up the Empire.'

The 21 signatories of the petition were as impressive as the wording. They included, of course, W.P. Schreiner and his brother Theophilus Lyndall, a well-known campaigner for black rights.[6] They were joined by Sir Gordon Sprigg, another former Premier of the Cape, who had succeeded Schreiner as Prime Minister in 1900. The Anglican Archbishop of Cape Town, William Carter, and a string of other dignitaries signed, among them the Rev. Ramsden Balmforth, who had helped persuade Schreiner to undertake the mission to London.

The appeal had to fight for space in other papers. This was, after all, the height of an Edwardian summer and the London public had other things on their minds. There was tennis at Wimbledon (H.A. Parker of New Zealand was defeated by a Canadian, R.B. Powell) and the Henley Regatta; the women's page of the London *Evening Standard* included a discussion of the advantages of parasols of hand-painted muslin and there was the grand summer sale at Selfridges to consider.[7] Nor was the South African Union very high up the agenda for the more serious-minded press. The debate over German naval construction was well under way. A series of articles began appearing in 1884, arguing that Britain's strength and international influence rested on her navy and calling for this to be substantially strengthened.[8] A British Navy League was established to support this cause and by 1908 their successful campaigning had built up a considerable head of steam. They called on the government to guarantee that orders for eight of the new Dreadnought class of battleships would be placed. This became embodied in a popular slogan, 'We want eight, and we won't wait!' As shall become clear, this had an important South African connection.

At the same time the Liberal government was also involved in the most serious constitutional confrontation between the House of Commons and the Lords. The hereditary peers were consistently blocking Liberal budgets, which sought to introduce a rudimentary system of welfare spending. David Lloyd George, the Chancellor of the Exchequer, memorably complained in July 1909 that 'a fully-equipped duke cost as much to keep up as two dreadnoughts'– but was 'much less easy to scrap'.[9] The titanic battle between the Commons and the Lords soaked up parliamentary time and energy and was only resolved (in favour of the Commons) in 1911, with the passing of the Parliament Act. As a result of these two major public issues, the news of South African Union did not receive as much coverage as might otherwise have been expected.

The Schreiner deputation's petition came as no surprise to the authorities in London. Sir Walter Hely-Hutchinson, the Governor of the Cape, had been informed of it by Merriman, as the Cape Prime Minister, nearly a month earlier.[10] Merriman, clearly infuriated by the initiative, pointed out that the preservation of the Cape franchise for 'natives' had been a compromise he had won at the National Convention from the other colonies after hard bargaining. But, he said, the price had been the 'disqualification for election to the Union Parliament'. He went on to say to the Cape Governor: 'However much this provision may be in conflict with liberal ideas, it is impossible to deny that it is the logical corollary of the exclusion of coloured people from the franchise in the three Colonies above named: and there is no doubt that without it Union would not have been agreed to.' Merriman claimed that the 'great bulk' of black people were satisfied with the compromise, and that it was only some 'educated Natives' who had decided to 'take up the cry that was raised for political purposes that their interests were being sacrificed and that they had been betrayed by the Cape representatives on the Convention'.

Merriman singled out Schreiner for personal attack. He described his former colleague as now acting as the champion of the 'natives' with the 'same vehemence with which not many years ago he denounced and scouted the notion that a coloured person should be admitted to Parliament'. Merriman predicted that if the Schreiner deputation succeeded in getting the Imperial Parliament to alter the draft Act, then Union itself would not go ahead. But if Schreiner failed, then black South Africans would believe they had been betrayed. His final sentence read: 'I venture to hope ... that my strictures upon this Deputation business will not be put down to anything beyond a sincere desire for the welfare of the natives which is, in my opinion, gravely jeopardised by this unfortunate attempt to create antagonism between black and white in South Africa.'

It was a damning critique, which found considerable resonance in Whitehall. By the time the South Africans had arrived in London, the Colonial Office and Lord Crewe were determined to support the draft constitution as the best compromise available. Lord Crewe set about convincing influential MPs of his position, as Schreiner soon discovered.

One of those Schreiner would have hoped to have on his side was a fellow South African (now resident in Britain), the Liberal MP Percy Molteno. The two men were old friends and Percy was a well-known supporter of African rights. He was also a personal friend of another member of the deputation, John Dube.[11] Yet Schreiner was to be sorely disappointed. We know all this from one of the most acute observers of what took place, Percy's extraordinary sister, Elizabeth Maria (Betty) Molteno.[12]

Percy and Betty were children of the Cape's first Prime Minister, John Molteno. Percy had made his home in Britain, becoming a Liberal MP in 1906. Betty spent time at Newnham College, Cambridge, before returning to South Africa to become a teacher at Collegiate Girls School in Port Elizabeth.[13] Rising to become its headmistress, she lost her position in 1899 for her 'Pro-Boer' views. She was an early feminist and strong supporter of black rights, a friend and confidante of black leaders, including John Dube and Gandhi. Betty was also someone who loved to be wherever events were unfolding and would travel to wherever she might observe what was taking place. Very well connected, she not only knew key women like Emily Hobhouse and Olive Schreiner, but was accepted in social gatherings with Smuts, Botha and Merriman. She had another trait that makes her a delight for any historian: she was an inveterate letter-writer. She corresponded with an extensive network of progressive friends and wrote long and passionate letters almost daily (and sometimes two or three times a day) to her partner, Alice Greene.[14] Her letters to Alice throw fascinating light on what was really transpiring in 1909 in London, to which she travelled from Geneva precisely to be 'where the action was'. While the men involved recorded their formal interactions, her letters provide an insight into their moods, their triumphs and failures.

Her first letter covering this period is dated 8 July 1909.[15] 'I called on the Schreiners yesterday afternoon', she wrote to Alice Greene, 'and found from Mrs S. that W.P. returned depressed from an interview with Percy – who will not aid him in any way or shape.' That Betty's brother Percy would not support Schreiner must have come as a cruel blow, but it was not inexplicable. Percy Molteno had written a series of letters to Merriman in 1908 calling for the racial bar to be excluded from the draft constitution. When this appeal failed, he decided to abandon such a fruitless approach and switched position, supporting the passage of the Bill, on the grounds that the draft was a delicate compromise between the four colonies and that any attempt to amend it in the House of Commons would wreck Union.[16] Percy Molteno had an important meeting with Lord Crewe around this time, which he mentioned in one of his letters. During their long discussion Percy found the Colonial Secretary taking 'a very just, sane, and sound view of affairs in South Africa'. Clearly Lord Crewe had won his Liberal colleague round, and Percy had decided that nothing further could be done to change the constitution. Hence W.P. Schreiner's fruitless meeting with Percy, whom he would otherwise have regarded as an important and well-informed ally. Betty's record of Schreiner's disappointment and depression so early on in the campaign (just two days after it was launched) was an ominous indicator of the battle that lay ahead.

\*\*\*

In the next six weeks Schreiner used the press to considerable effect, with regular interviews being published in Britain and South Africa. Other members of the deputation, including Jabavu, Gerrans and Abdurahman, also had their letters published; while the views of Rubusana, Jabavu and Abdurahman were quoted in the news columns. This media campaign

*The South African Native and Coloured People's Delegation of 1909: (front row, from left) Matt Fredericks, Dr A. Abdurahman, W.P. Schreiner, Walter Rubusana, Tengo Jabavu; (back row, from left) Thomas Mapikela, Joseph Gerrans, Daniel Dwanya, D.J. Lenders.*

was badly needed – and Schreiner knew it. 'The English people were like men asleep in a snowdrift regarding the South Africa question,' Schreiner complained to the *Cape Times*.[17] 'They must be awakened to a sense of their duty, otherwise the greatest blow ever struck at the Empire would be delivered.'

'Awakening' the British was no easy task. Schreiner's first attempt to get a letter published was rebuffed by *The Times* for its length. Basil Williams, a contemporary historian and biographer of Rhodes, wrote to Schreiner saying that he had expected to see his letter in the paper for some days, only to discover from a member of staff that it had been considered not urgent, put on one side and then considered too late.[18] *The Times* finally got round to publishing a shorter version of the letter from Schreiner on 27 July. By this time the debate in Parliament was about to begin – the second reading of the draft Act took place on the day the letter appeared.

Schreiner used the letter to remind readers of the fact that in the Cape Colony 'the full recognition of that principle of non-discrimination was established firmly nearly 60 years ago, when its Constitution was granted'.[19] Schreiner explained that these rights had been included in the Royal Instructions to the Governor when the Cape was first given self-government in 1853. This had directed the Governor 'not to propose or assent to any ordinance whatever, whereby persons not being of European birth or descent might be subjected or made liable to any disabilities or restrictions to which persons of European birth or descent would not also be subjected or made liable'. Schreiner pointed out that after exercising this right for all the subsequent years without difficulty, black people 'stand today alarmed, almost incredulous, at the prospect that the contrary doctrine' of racial discrimination should be applied to them. Black people were to be deprived of their right to stand for Parliament, no matter how highly educated or qualified they were. 'Will not the Mother of Parliaments still protect the majority of the people of the Cape Colony against injustice?' Schreiner asked, warning that 'my plea here is the honour and stability of the Empire, not merely the rights of certain subjects'.

It was a powerful argument. Delivered by an eminent, British-trained lawyer and a former colonial premier, it must have made uncomfortable reading in the Colonial Office. Despite this, the letter and the petition failed to change government policy, partly because the issues had already been so thoroughly discussed. A consensus had been arrived at earlier in the year and was unlikely to be altered. At the same time the setback reflected a weakness in the Schreiner strategy. Although the Archbishop of Cape Town, William Carter, was among the signatories of the petition, there is no indication that he had followed this up with letters to the head of the Anglican Church, the Archbishop of Canterbury, Randall Thomas Davidson. Davidson was, of course, an influential figure. Not only did he lead the Anglican faith worldwide, but he also sat in the House of Lords. His papers – stored at Lambeth Palace, just opposite the House of Commons – contain a number of letters from and about South Africa.[20]

Schreiner himself wrote to the Archbishop on 24 July from Morley's Hotel, enclosing a copy of the petition.[21] He mentioned that the Archbishop of Cape Town had signed the petition and said he had a letter of introduction from a friend: the brother of the theologian Walter Lock, Warden of Keble College, Oxford, and hence was 'emboldened' to address the Archbishop personally. Schreiner pointed out that black South Africans were being excluded from the proposed Union. 'I feel persuaded that we are trembling upon the brink of one of the most colossal mistakes ever made in regard to South Africa – the mistake of confusing the idea of Union of the European [destinies?] of our people with the idea of a real National Union under the flag. The great majority of the people cannot but regard the present proposals as tending towards Separation rather than towards Union. I speak in truth for millions in this matter – but have only the feeble voice of a crier in the wilderness.'

The appeal was eloquent but it lacked the authority that a similar letter from Archbishop Carter of Cape Town might have carried. Archbishop Davidson answered within four days, by which time the debate in the House of Lords had already taken place. It was hardly the reply Schreiner would have hoped for.[22] 'Before speaking in the House of Lords last night,' the Archbishop wrote, 'I took the opportunity of a good deal of conversation with those who, speaking generally, are on what I suppose may be called the side of the Natives in these matters, and I hope we have made it quite clear that we do not regard what has now taken place as betokening a permanent acquiescence on our side in arrangements which as we think fall so far short of those which will ultimately be practicable.' Schreiner replied on 28 July pressing his point, but there was little chance that the Archbishop – a very conservative figure – would change his mind.

In a letter to another British subject who had written to him on South Africa, Davidson explained that he had 'given a great deal of thought to this subject, and have had very full conversations with Lord Selborne, Lord Crewe, and many others about it, and have also heard from the Clergy who are specially interested in the Native question. The difficulties of the matter are not small, and I find that some of those who feel most strongly upon the Native question are equally keen that we should not do anything which might wreck the Bill as a whole.'[23] The 'threat' that the Bill might be defeated had apparently been the deciding factor in shaping the Archbishop's thinking.

* * *

While Schreiner was attempting to get his viewpoint published by *The Times* and then dealing with the consequences once it appeared, the rest of his deputation had not been idle. Joseph Gerrans – the other white member of the deputation – had written to the *Royal Cornwall Gazette*, in Truro.[24] As a local paper, it was not the most obvious of publications for the appeal; it was Gerrans's background that explained his choice. A former Cornishman, he had left Tregony to seek his fortune in South Africa. In the letter he appealed to the sense of justice of 'fellow Cornishmen and Britishers', pointing out that the plans to deprive black people of the vote was 'a heavy charge of dynamite placed at the base of a fabric [of society] which has taken nearly a century to erect and fired by their own hands'.

Gerrans was an interesting man. He had established himself in Mafeking in 1891, working for De Beers as a wagon-builder and blacksmith.[25] He became a town councillor and manufactured a gun – the *Wolf* – during the long siege of the town by the Boer forces.[26] Despite being wounded by an exploding shell during the siege, Gerrans was soon back at work.[27] His obituary in 1915 described him as 'a man of firm conviction [who] had a large sympathy for the native and coloured people who regarded him as a staunch friend'.[28]

Gerrans clearly had a good reputation among the Batswana. Paramount Chiefs Sebele of the Bakwena and Bathoen of the Ngwaketse recruited Gerrans to represent them on the deputation to London. The chiefs gave Gerrans letters of accreditation, which he sent to the Colonial Office. In his letter Chief Sebele said he had heard that Gerrans was 'going to England for your health. Knowing that you are always desirous to help the natives in any just cause, we desire you if possible to speak for us to the English people and ask them not to give us and our country over to the South African Government. We are still happy and well contented under the Imperial government and we have no desire to be under any other.'[29] Gerrans was not the only white to be asked to represent the Batswana. On 13 April 1909 Sol Plaatje, an interpreter for the British during the siege of Mafeking and later a founding member of the ANC, wrote to Schreiner on behalf of the Paramount Chief of the Barolong.[30] Addressing Schreiner as 'the fearless champion of the cause of the Natives', Plaatje asked him to 'pursue their objections [to Union] and to make them public'.

The chiefs had engaged in a lengthy campaign to remain under the British Crown and out of South African control as Union approached.[31] When the idea of incorporation was first mooted, the secretary to Chief Sebele wrote: 'We have found that the white settlers do not like the black people, neither do they appreciate to see them own land the wealth of which was given to us by God. They only desire to see destruction, hatred,

*The visit of Basotho chiefs to London, 1909.*

war, and poverty for the black people.'[32] When the Acting Resident Commissioner of the Bechuanaland Protectorate, Barry May, informed the Batswana of the likelihood that they would be included in the South African state, Sebele, as the most senior Paramount Chief, replied that he rejected the suggestion, pointing out that previous delegations had been sent to London to press this point. 'We wished to be under the direct control of the Imperial Government. I am under the King – King Edward. True, we may appear as useless people; nevertheless we have no desire for change.'[33]

As May reported it, Sebele was followed by Chief Bathoen, who held out his hand to the Acting Resident Commissioner to show a signet ring, engraved with a crocodile, the symbol of his people, and declared: 'A ring is a sign of an indissoluble bond. This ring was given to me by the late Queen Victoria ... as a proof that the promises made would never be broken and that the Bangwaketsi would for ever remain under the protection of Her Majesty.'[34] To strengthen their position they sent their own deputation to London, which was received by Lord Crewe on 15 February 1909.[35] The official reply was sympathetic and contained an assurance that no change would take place for some time.

The Batswana were not the only people of southern Africa resisting incorporation into the planned Union. The Swazi and the Basotho also made their feelings plain in petitions and deputations to the British, though they had not received any firm assurances to the contrary. But by 1908, other considerations were weighing on officials in Whitehall. A note from inside the Colonial Office, dated 2 July 1908, pointed out that Cape forces had been unable to put down a Basotho uprising in 1883 and that 'A Basuto rising of a very formidable character might easily take place as the result of handing of the Basuto to the Federal Government without their consent'.[36] The British estimated the Basotho had at their disposal between 60,000 and 80,000 troops.

A secret dispatch from General Methuen, Commander of British forces in South Africa, dated 6 November 1908, was candid about the threat. 'The leading feature of the Basutos as an enemy would be that every man would be mounted, and well mounted. Probably they would fight as mounted infantry, dismounting and using their rifles, but they are a nation of horsemen and quite capable of acting together in units.'[37] The Chief Magistrate at Matatiele in the Cape, just over the border from Basutoland, warned: 'I learnt from good sources that the Basuto Nation has determined in the event of Union government at any time endeavouring to force them to come under the Union they will resist if necessary with force of arms and that the tribes this side of the Berg [Drakensberg-Maloti] will join them.'[38] The Basotho therefore posed a real threat. The British believed they had no option but to keep a wary eye on them and take their views fully into account, if they didn't want another costly war in South Africa.[39]

The petitions and protestations, underlined by the Basotho military threat, caused the Colonial Office by late 1908 to decide against the immediate incorporation of the Protectorates into South Africa. At the same time their absorption at a later date was not ruled out, if the question of 'native consent' could be satisfactorily addressed. This position was communicated to the National Convention then drawing up the draft constitution on 25 October 1908.[40] The South African official delegation therefore understood, months before they arrived in London, that Swaziland, Bechuanaland and Basutoland would not be included in the planned Union. Botha, Smuts and the rest of the white delegation were not going to get their way on the expansion of South Africa's borders.

\* \* \*

If the white politicians were thwarted on this issue, they were accommodated on all others. They also received the warmest of receptions. Louis Botha dined with the King on 22 July. Agnes Merriman – the wife of the Cape Prime Minister – could hardly contain her delight:

'Botha dines with Lord Crewe on Tuesday and is to meet the King! he is quite the *favoured* Premier.'[41] The highlight of the visit came two days later. A formal lunch was held at Buckingham Palace hosted by the King and Queen, with Queen Alexandra wearing the Cullinan diamonds, so shrewdly given to the royal family by the Transvaal in 1905.[42] The lunch was attended by the Prime Minister, Herbert Asquith; the High Commissioner, Lord Selborne; and his predecessor, Lord Milner. All the South African official delegates were there – from Louis Botha and Jan Smuts of the Transvaal to the Cape's John X. Merriman and Marthinus Steyn of the Orange River Colony. With the band of the Scots Guards entertaining them in the splendour of Buckingham Palace, it must have been a glittering occasion.

The formal negotiations to settle the outstanding issues between the British government and the South African delegation began at 11:00 a.m. on 20 July at the Foreign Office. The official minutes of the meeting – marked Secret – are terse and to the point.[43] Lord Crewe opened the proceedings with a statement that left none of those present in any doubt about his intentions. There were two main questions to be decided: the exclusion of black South Africans from the franchise, except in the Cape, and the exclusion of non-Europeans from membership of Parliament. 'It is the fixed conviction of His Majesty's Government that these matters must be settled in South Africa itself,' the official recorded. 'It was of no use to express academic options, and His Majesty's Government feel that circumstances have not made it possible to adopt a different course than that adopted. His Majesty's Government were prepared to see the Bill through as it stands both as to Franchise and as to representation.'

The only questions that were debated in any detail concerned the Protectorates. A schedule had been drawn up allowing the three territories to be transferred to South Africa at an unspecified future date. Sir Henry de Villiers asked for the schedule to be dropped so that incorporation might take place immediately, but Lord Crewe said: 'He regarded the Schedule as a pledge, and was bound to press it as far as possible. He did not think it would be possible to get the Bill through Parliament without the Schedule.' Rather reluctantly, De Villiers backed down, saying that the delegates were prepared to 'abide by the Schedule as it stands'. One final appeal took place on the second and final day of the conference, when General Botha asked whether it would not be possible to have an 'early transfer' of Swaziland to South Africa, since, as he put it, 'two-thirds of the country were already allocated to white concessionaires'. Again, Lord Crewe resisted, saying he was 'unable to hold out the hope of an early change'. With that final flurry the conference was over. The British government and the South African delegates were fully in accord over the draft constitution. Only the parliamentary debates lay ahead.

Why was the British government quite so determined to reach a settlement with the white delegation? The answer lay far beyond South Africa's borders. The rumble of war was already a pressing issue for men like Lord Crewe. 'The business that has brought these distinguished visitors to London is twofold,' explained the *Daily Mail*, reporting the opening of the South African conference at the Foreign Office.[44] 'They have to consider with the Government the final form of the Act of Union, and later to discuss with the Imperial and Colonial authorities the important question of imperial defence.' While South Africans were naturally more concerned about the former (and commentators and historians still concentrate on the question of Union), the British were at least as worried about wider issues regarding the defence of the mother country and her Empire.

The background to the British position was to be found in two trends. The first was the growing strength of Germany, particularly on the seas. With the largest navy in the world, Britain had dominated the oceans for generations. It was the security on which the Empire rested. This was being challenged by the German Emperor Wilhelm II's desire to greatly expand his own fleet. The Emperor's plan was sparked off by the events that followed the failed raid by Rhodes's friend, Dr Jameson, on the Transvaal in January 1896.[45] The attack soured relations between Britain and the Transvaal government. Germany, which had interests in the region as well as around 15,000 German subjects in the Transvaal, decided to intervene.[46] When the Kaiser heard what had taken place he summoned his Chancellor, Foreign Minister and officers and drafted a telegram to Paul Kruger. The telegram sent the Emperor's congratulations to the Transvaal for having successfully fended off 'the armed bands which invaded your country ... and in maintaining the independence of the country against attack from without'.[47] Kaiser Wilhelm went further. He even discussed with his officials the possibility of sending troops to the Transvaal and turning it into a German protectorate.[48] The reaction from the British press and public was one of fury. 'England will concede nothing to menaces and will not lie down under insult,' stormed *The Times*. The windows of

German shops in London were smashed and German sailors attacked in the Thames docks.[49] German press reaction was equally furious, denouncing the British for their 'buccaneering' adventure.[50]

Sir Francis Bertie, Under Secretary at the Foreign Office, called in the German Ambassador. Sir Francis threatened that unless Germany desisted from interfering in the Transvaal, the Royal Navy would blockade the German coast and attack German shipping. 'A blockade of Hamburg and Bremen and the annihilation of German commerce on the high seas would be child's play for the English fleet,' Sir Francis told the ambassador.[51] The message was underlined by the halting and searching of the German ship *Bundesrat* in Delagoa Bay, on the pretext that it was carrying contraband for the Boers.[52]

The Kaiser took the threat very seriously indeed, ordering a programme of accelerated ship-building. The German navy was delighted. Rear Admiral Alfred von Tirpitz welcomed the telegram and its after-effect.[53] 'The incident may have its good side', he wrote to Germany's Navy Minister, 'and I think a much bigger row would actually have been useful to us ... to arouse our nation to build a fleet.' The indirect outcome of the Jameson Raid was the Anglo-German naval arms race. Both sides set about constructing naval vessels as rapidly as possible in an attempt to win a decisive global advantage.

By the early twentieth century British politicians were well aware that war with Germany was looming. The German historian John Röhl, drawing on newly discovered documents, has recently argued that the First World War was not the culmination of diplomatic blunders, but rather the result of deliberate German policy.[54] Berlin's aims – he suggests – amounted to the establishment of Germany as the pre-eminent European power. The plans called for France to be dismembered, with German farmers being settled on the coast facing Dover, and Britain losing India. British politicians faced an existential threat that they could not ignore, and turned to the Empire for assistance. 'Between 1904 and 1907 the great peripheral empires of Britain, France and Russia drew together in an effort to contain the rising power at the centre of the Continent,' Röhl concludes.

Officials and politicians across Britain's colonies and dominions certainly expressed a growing concern for the safety of the Empire. Foremost among these imperial civil servants was a group of South African-based Empire loyalists who had been brought together by Lord

*The Imperial Defence Conference, held from 29 July until 19 August 1909, which brought together senior politicians from the white dominions, was crucial in Britain's preparation for war with Germany.*

Milner.[55] This group, the so-called Milner Kindergarten, established a series of organisations and movements to strengthen the Empire with the aim of bringing order to what had, by the early 1900s, become an incoherent hotchpotch of territories under the British Crown. Some were self-governing dominions, others were colonies – and then there was India, with its Viceroy. Each had a different form of government and a different relationship with London. The movement known as the Round Table became a driving force behind the series of Imperial Conferences designed to regulate relations between London and its increasingly independent-minded offspring. An article in the very first issue of *The Round Table* in November 1910 focused on Anglo-German rivalry. 'The central fact in the international situation today is the antagonism between England and Germany,' wrote the editor, Philip Kerr, a member of the Milner Kindergarten. 'The solution to this rivalry between the great military power of Europe and the great sea power of the world is the most difficult problem which the Empire has to face.'[56]

Well before Union came about, South Africans were integrally involved in the series of Imperial Conferences. Louis Botha participated in the Imperial Conference in 1907 as the Prime Minister of the Transvaal, as did other white South African leaders. So just five years after the end of the Boer War, Botha was already playing an important role in shaping the establishment of an Imperial Secretariat.[57] Politicians like Botha were therefore already well known and respected in British government circles by the time they arrived in London in 1909. Another Imperial

Conference was scheduled for July 1909, to coincide with the visit to London of the South Africans. The white electorate in South Africa also publicly supported and understood these imperial aims. A meeting of the Cape Town branch of the Navy League held in June 1909 discussed the forthcoming conference and how the dominions might 'co-operate most effectively for the defence of the Empire'. The *Cape Times* reported: 'The South African delegates ought then to be able to say that as soon as South Africa is united, she will be ready to take her proper place in the general scheme.'[58]

Two conferences therefore took place in mid-1909: one to consider the details of the Bill to bring about the Union, involving just British and South African politicians. This was held on 20 and 21 July and was concluded without real difficulty. Apart from the issue of the Protectorates, over which Britain refused to give ground, it was really just a question of tidying up the draft. The second conference, to look at questions of Imperial defence, was much longer and – for the British – clearly a higher priority. It involved all the dominions and was held from 29 July until 19 August. It brought together senior politicians from Australia, Canada, Newfoundland (still a separate territory), New Zealand and the four South African self-governing colonies.[59] The South Africans were keen to participate, but made it clear that they were only attending 'for completeness' since they were not yet a dominion. They therefore insisted that they could not bind a future South African government by 'accepting the principles enunciated in the Imperial General Staff paper', which laid out how the forces of the Empire would collaborate in a time of war.[60]

The secret minutes of the conference provide an insight into what took place.[61] The naval expansion was the first topic on the agenda, with the British Prime Minister, Herbert Asquith, opening the proceedings by talking of Germany, Austria and France accelerating their construction of warships, and of the Dreadnought class of battleships in particular. Britain was to commence building eight new warships that year, and was looking to the Empire to play its part. Merriman pointed out that South Africa already paid a tax per head of the white population to help meet the costs of its naval defence. He told his colleagues that the Cape also shouldered another responsibility, which had been previously met by the British government – control over five million 'black people', who had in the past given London what he called 'a great deal of trouble'.

As the conference proceeded, the size of Germany's huge army was

*British Empire Club, inaugurated in the Guildhall on 29 July 1909, brought together white leaders who opposed the black franchise and W.P. Schreiner, who campaigned for it.*

discussed. Although, as the Secretary of War, Richard Haldane, put it, 'Nobody contemplates marching to Berlin nowadays, simply because it is out of the question', other theatres of war were considered. These might be Australia, Canada, South Africa or India. How might the dominions participate? Merriman dug his heels in. Rather testily, he explained that he had had the greatest difficulty in getting defence votes through the Cape Parliament over forty years and he was not about to pledge his troops to an unknown future war, far from home. 'Supposing you had a war in the Balkans, I feel absolutely certain the colonists would be very reluctant indeed to send a force to engage in that. Supposing that by any misfortune or mischance your alliance with Japan was to bring you into collision or conflict with the United States, if any such calamity was possible, do you suppose that any colonist would for a single moment send an expeditionary force to help an Eastern Power? Never!'[62]

Smuts, speaking for the Transvaal, questioned whether colonists would rally to the Empire's defence. 'It all depends on what is meant by "the general defence of the Empire",' he explained.[63] Agreeing with Merriman that 'for a long time … our probable enemy is the native', Smuts said he would resist the idea of a single Imperial General Staff, to which South African forces would be subservient. Instead, he preferred 'an Imperial Staff here at headquarters in England, and with general staffs in the self-governing Dominions, working in close association and with exchange of officers from time to time with the staffs in other parts of the British Empire'.[64]

Behind closed doors the British government was not getting its own way. Nonetheless, the implication was clear: the South Africans were prepared to play a significant part in British military planning, once Union was achieved. But there was a price to pay for this support: the white politicians demanded that they alone should settle their country's domestic issues. 'I understand the Dutch [Afrikaner] leaders have been impressing upon politicians in this country the wish of South Africa to be left alone to work out its own salvation,' reported *The Graphic*.[65] 'They have guaranteed they will play their part in the general scheme of Imperial Defence, more particularly since they have around them three European Powers whose policy may one day vitally affect them, but as regards all internal affairs they claim a free hand, and while they do not resent fair criticism, they will object to tactless and interested intervention on the part of the Home Government.'[66] It was a clear warning: keep away from 'native' policy or pay the price.

For his part, W.P. Schreiner, while a thorn in the side of the Colonial Office and the official South African delegation, was also an Empire loyalist. So by day he planned and manoeuvred to try to end the racism embedded in the draft constitution, and in the evenings he attended meetings designed to strengthen the Empire. Schreiner participated with the official South African delegates at a magnificent banquet held to mark the inauguration of the British Empire Club in the Guildhall in the City of London on 28 July.[67] He would no doubt have been among those who 'loudly cheered' when Smuts assured the gathering that 'Should the need arise, all the endurance and experience which has been gathered in South Africa will be at the disposal of the defence of South Africa and the Empire'.[68]

It is probably accurate to suggest that during his time in London Schreiner was, to use a modern idiom, 'in and against the state': he was working for it while attempting to transform it.[69] This extended to Schreiner's personal relations. W.P. and his wife received many invitations to stay at the country homes of England's great and good (some of whom he would have known from his university days, others from his time as

Cape Prime Minister). Schreiner also had a personal relationship with Lionel Earle, the Colonial Secretary's private secretary. Earle wrote to Schreiner on 8 July, saying that Lord Crewe was busy in the current week, but that it would give him 'real pleasure' to meet Schreiner in the following week.[70] Earle felt free to end his letter on a personal note, extending this invitation: 'I do hope that you and Mrs Schreiner and your daughter will be able to go down and see my Mother one day at Cobham; I know that it would give her very real pleasure.' The British establishment might do battle with W.P. during working hours, but it was by no means averse to welcoming him in the informal setting of a weekend retreat or an evening dinner party.

* * *

While Botha, Smuts, Merriman and the rest of the official delegation were in discussions with the Colonial Office and being entertained by the King, Schreiner was assembling his forces for the parliamentary debates. This would be the battleground on which the issue would be won or lost. As we have seen, his main ally was Sir Charles Dilke, whose standing as a radical Liberal with a reputation as an expert on international affairs and with close links to government was vitally important. During Schreiner's time in London the two men would conduct lengthy and detailed discussions over how best to proceed. Sometimes they met face to face. More frequently they exchanged notes several times a day, assessing the situation or contemplating some suggested amendment to be put before Parliament.[71]

What is apparent from the correspondence is Schreiner's determination, from the start, to involve the rest of his deputation in his attempts to persuade British politicians. The day after his initial letter to Dilke (5 July 1909) Schreiner wrote to Sir Charles again, saying, 'I should like you to meet them if you can make time.' He explained that his colleagues were important representatives of 'upwards of a million natives and coloured persons in Cape Colony and Natal alone, and their mission is also in a sense representative of the natives and coloured folk of the ORC [Orange River Colony] and Transvaal'.[72] Schreiner described Dr Abdurahman as 'a prominent Member of the Cape Town Corporation, Moslem, cultured and very able'. He said that Tengo Jabavu and Walter Rubusana, who were arriving in a few days, 'more particularly represent the natives of our Cape Colonial Eastern Province and Territories'. The following week

Schreiner introduced Sir Charles to Thomas Mapikela as 'a good man' who had been delegated to represent 'native and coloured' inhabitants of the Orange River Colony.[73] Schreiner continued: 'you might be able to aid me in obtaining an opportunity to introduce Mapikela to Lord Crewe under the authority of the letter which has been sent to me by those who have deputed him, and have extended to him a document in the nature of a petition which is of an important character'.

Schreiner's second line of support came from the Labour Party. When, on 7 July, Schreiner visited the House of Commons, the South African Press Agency carried this report from their London correspondent: 'The Hon. W.P. Schreiner spent two hours yesterday lobbying in connection to the passing of the draft South Africa Act of Union through the Imperial Parliament. He favourably interviewed Mr J.A.M. MacDonald, Liberal MP for the Falkirk Burghs; Mr Keir Hardie, the Labour Leader; Mr Arthur Henderson, Liberal member for the Barnard Castle division of Durham and prominent Trade Unionist; Sir Charles Dilke; Mr F.C. Mackarness, Newbury; and Mr J.M. Robertson, Liberal member for the Tyneside division of Northumberland, who came to South Africa in 1900 to investigate martial law in Cape Colony and Natal. These members have promised Mr Schreiner their support.'[74]

Schreiner did all he could to meet and influence the parliamentarians. Having the support of six MPs was a useful beginning, but there was a very long way to go if he and his deputation were to sway the majority of the 670 members of Parliament. On 13 July Betty Molteno wrote of meeting Schreiner at his hotel, 'looking handsome and much more cheerful and hopeful – he is seeing various Parliamentary groups – has seen Ramsay MacDonald who is arranging a meeting for him'.[75]

The next few weeks were a blur of activity. The letters to and from Schreiner register the broad range of organisations that he contacted and that came out in his support. Just over two weeks after the campaign had begun, the deputation had a formal meeting in Whitehall with Lord Crewe.[76] This took place on 22 July and Schreiner recorded the encounter in the cool, measured language of the day. This was probably an agreed statement issued by the Colonial Office, since it was reported in exactly these terms by Reuters and carried by *The Times*:

'The Right Hon. Secretary of State for the colonies this morning received at the Colonial Office the delegation on behalf of the native & coloured inhabitants of South Africa. Dr. A. Abdurahman, the Rev. W.

Rubusana, & Messrs. Mapikela, Lenders and Fredericks attended.

'They were accompanied and introduced by the Hon. W.P. Schreiner. They explained their object & the amendments for which they pressed in the proposed Act of Parliament to establish the Union of South Africa.

'The Secretary of State received them courteously & responded sympathetically, but without giving any assurance that the desired amendments would be made.'[77]

Support for the Schreiner delegation also came from the London-based South African Native Races Committee, which brought together a group of former missionaries and colonial administrators, who had published an influential book on conditions of black South Africans in 1909. They wrote to Schreiner assuring him of their backing and notified Lord Crewe in similar terms.[78] The committee was packed with men of influence. They included Sir Robert Hunter and the Rev. Canon Rawnsley (both founders of the National Trust) and several missionaries, including J.S. Moffat, Wardlaw Thompson and W.C. Willoughby, all of whom had extensive experience of southern Africa.

The Personal Rights Association (a forerunner of the organisation that is today Liberty) also backed the cause, petitioned Lord Crewe and reinforced the points made by Schreiner's deputation in the clearest terms. In very formal language they argued:

'That the erection of such a race barrier would be productive of evil results, not only in South Africa, but wherever the British flag flies over countries the inhabitants of which are mainly or partly of non-European race; and would mean the abrogation of a moral principle more permanently powerful for the maintenance of the British Empire, because more justificatory of British rule, than any support to be obtained by military or naval force.

'Wherefore your memorialists pray that your lordship, and His Majesty's Government generally, may tender such counsel to His Majesty the King as may result in the withdrawal of such provisions of the Draft Act for the Constitutional Union of the South African Colonies as would lessen the guarantees of personal and political freedom to those of His Majesty's subjects who differ in race and complexion from those of European origin.'[79]

Among Schreiner's strongest supporters were, of course, the Anti-Slavery and Aborigines' Protection Society, which took part in a meeting for MPs at the House of Commons on 13 July. This was arranged by Sir

Charles Dilke, who wrote to Schreiner saying he was pleased to do so – adding that he 'knew Dr Abdurahman well and should be glad to meet him again'.[80] This was followed by a larger, more widely attended public breakfast at the Westminster Palace Hotel, which took place on 27 July and which was well reported.[81] Sir Thomas Fowell Buxton, president of the Society, was in the chair. Opening the proceedings, he hoped South Africa would become what he called a 'real Union, not only of States, but of races'.[82] Schreiner then spoke, declaring that the proposals contained in the draft Bill were 'based on bad faith with the natives. They said that the rights given them sixty years ago should not be whittled away. It was true that they had in the Cape Colony the native franchise, but what they wanted to see was a real franchise without discrimination of race or colour.'

Dr Abdurahman was at the breakfast, as were Walter Rubusana, John Tengo Jabavu, Matt Fredericks, Daniel Lenders, John Dube, Alfred Mangena and Thomas Mapikela. It gave them an important opportunity to speak directly to the British public. Dr Abdurahman explained just how deeply he had been wounded by the inclusion of the words 'of European descent' for eligibility to stand as an MP. 'The people of England cannot expect coloured men to sit down quietly under that insult. The native and coloured population felt it very hard that the Imperial Parliament should now be asked to attach its seal to documents which would make them feel like outcasts and men without political and civil rights.'[83] For his part, Jabavu said that he 'doubted whether the people of this country realised the strength of sentiment upon this subject on the part of the natives'.[84] A resolution was adopted by the meeting, regretting that the Union did not provide for all races to participate in the proposed Parliament and that the native franchise of the Cape Colony was not adequately safeguarded.[85]

All in all, late July was a highwater mark for the deputation. Schreiner's letter was printed in *The Times* on the 27th. The following day *The Times* printed another letter, this time from Dr Abdurahman.[86] He pointed out that the Union abrogated assurances dating from the 1850s, and embodied in the Cape constitution, that all subjects would have equal rights. He attacked the assurances that their rights were secured by the requirement in the draft Act that the Constitution could only be changed by a two-thirds majority of a joint sitting of both Houses of Parliament. Dr Abdurahman quoted Botha and Smuts as having made statements in a public meeting on 24 February at which they pledged to end the native franchise, even in the Cape. Abdurahman quoted Smuts as saying, 'On the first occasion Parliament met it could be swept away. It was found necessary that there should be some check; perhaps it was no check at all. It has been put in there, but he did not think it meant much.'

Despite their access to Lord Crewe and their public support from an influential section of British society, the omens were not good. It was clear, even at this stage, that the campaign was not progressing well. The radical editor of the *Review of Reviews*, W.T. Stead, wrote to Schreiner explaining that he had held a 'long talk' with Louis Botha, Abraham Fischer (grandfather of Bram Fischer) and J.B.M. Hertzog 'on the question of the natives'. 'It is quite clear that they will accept no modification of the scheme in any form. The only new point that Botha made was that the Constitution really extends the rights of the natives inasmuch as it allows members elected by the Cape franchise, which includes blacks, to legislate for the whole South Africa, a privilege which blacks never before enjoyed.' Stead conceded that this was true, but he warned, 'that very fact may increase the temptation on the part of the other Colonies to disenfranchise the natives in Cape Colony'.[87]

Schreiner was well enough attuned to British society to know that the campaign was not making headway against such determined resistance. Outwardly he maintained a brave face, but with difficulty. Yet every time fate appeared to be against him, an unexpected piece of good fortune fell into place. Out of the blue he received a letter.[88] 'You will not remember me, so I will recall myself to you,' it read. 'I am Lady Edward Cecil. I used to see you at the Cape. I read with interest in the *Morning Post* and I wonder whether I can help you to get the positions (which are totally misunderstood) realised.'

A society beauty and daughter of an admiral, Lady Violet Cecil had married Edward Cecil in 1894, joining him in South Africa during the Boer War. He was sent to Mafeking, and was trapped in the town throughout the siege, serving as Baden-Powell's chief of staff. Lady Violet remained in Cape Town enjoying a social life and became acquainted with Lord Milner, who had a magnetic attraction for her, as he did for other women. Lady Violet would whisk him away from his official duties for private picnics on Table Mountain.[89] 'It was great fun,' she wrote, 'Sir Alfred being like a boy out of school – right away from Government House and its journalists and incessant interviews.' The two fell in love and Violet eventually married Milner in 1921, a dignified three years after Lord Cecil's death. Lady Violet was a true imperialist (she helped found the Victoria League in 1901 to promote Lord Milner's vision of Empire).[90] But she was also an egalitarian of sorts. For her the British Empire conferred rights as well as responsibilities, and this included the right to vote. Lady Violet wrote to Schreiner repeatedly, wishing him well and introducing him to various Liberal MPs, so that he might lobby them on behalf of 'your unrepresented blacks', as she put it.[91]

This was not a widely held opinion, but perhaps it was not as unusual as it might appear. It was shared by Sir Charles Bruce, a former colonial governor who campaigned for the rights of Indian immigrants in South Africa. He wrote from Fife in Scotland to the Archbishop of Canterbury just before the vote in the House of Lords.[92] His letter expresses the view perfectly and is worth quoting at some length.

'I assume that Your Grace is familiar with the terms of the Proclamation of Her late Majesty Queen Victoria to the Princes and People of India in the year 1858. In brief it declared equality of opportunity for all her Majesty's subjects in India without distinction of race, colour or creed. In the same year the Grondwet (Constitution) or fundamental law of the Transvaal Republic declared that there should be no equality in the State or Church between white men and coloured races.

'At a great sacrifice of blood and treasure the Imperial Government acquired the right to determine which of these policies is to be accepted as the fundamental law of British South Africa. The Bill now before Parliament is in fact a declaration, subject to certain temporary provisions, in favour of the policy of no equality between white and coloured men.

'It would be an insult to Your Grace's intelligence that I should do more than invite your attention to the tremendous issue involved. But let me state in a few words what I consider to be my justification in addressing Your Grace on the subject. My father, as an Indian Civil Servant, spent his life in the practice of the principle laid down in the Proclamation of 1858. My brother fought through the Crimean war on the side of Turkish troops, and died in the service of the Queen in the West Indies where the principles of Her Majesty's Proclamation have had the same force as in the East Indies. My son after two campaigns in India fell in action in Somaliland. The European officers who gallantly rescued his body with assistance of native Indian soldiers received for their service special marks of the King's favour. For nearly forty years my own official life in the Colonial Service has been devoted to the education and protection of Indian and African subjects of His Majesty. And I believe the circumstances of my own life are typical of the lives of a group of Englishmen, Scotsmen and Irishmen who have served their King and their country in every quarter of the globe in the spirit of the Queen's Proclamation of 1858 which now seems likely to be rejected in favour of the Grondwet of the Transvaal Republic.'

Lady Violet, who took a similar position, was prepared to use her excellent connections to help Schreiner navigate the shoals of English society. It was she who arranged for Schreiner to gain access to the most powerful media mogul of the day, Lord Northcliffe, the owner of a string of papers and magazines, including *The Times*, *The Observer*, *Daily Mail* and *Daily Mirror*.[93] 'I am venturing to write this note asking you to see him', Lady Violet wrote to Lord Northcliffe from the Ladies Empire Club, 'because he is now on a very important mission, which threatens to be ignored in the general official optimism about South Africa.' She pointed out that Schreiner represented '4 million natives' who were protesting about their treatment in the Act of Union. 'Will you spare him half an hour and will you, if you can see your way, help him to put the case of the dumb and distant natives before a well intentioned public?'

The introduction worked. In less than a week, Dr Abdurahman was writing to Schreiner saying he would collect Jabavu on 3 August and go and see Lord Northcliffe.[94] What transpired between them is unclear, but the meeting is likely to have smoothed the way for the views of the deputation to appear in the British press.

\* \* \*

Towards the end of July the scene was set for the forthcoming debates in Parliament. The white South African politicians were assured of government support, even if the Protectorates of Swaziland, Basutoland and Bechuanaland would not be included in the new Union. The British government, threatened by the rise of German military power and determined to have a united South Africa as part of its Imperial defences, was keen to press ahead with Union. For Schreiner and his deputation the situation became increasingly gloomy. He had done all he could with his allies, inside and outside Parliament. Many of Britain's liberal elite had come out in his support, but it simply did not appear to be enough. Just what could be extracted from Parliament during the debates would be revealed in the next few weeks.

# 7

# London: The parliamentary struggle

It was against this background that the draft constitution was presented to the House of Lords on 27 July.[1] Lord Crewe, as Secretary of State for the Colonies, rose to declare that the Bill before the House 'closes one chapter in the history of South Africa and begins a new one'. Yet at least as important as the Bill itself was the symbolism of the moment, and this was understood by everyone. Lord Crewe had held final meetings with the white leaders on the eve of the debate, to iron out the details of the Royal Instructions to be given to the Governor-General following Union, and, with this out of the way, the debate could begin.[2]

The British newspapers were almost beside themselves in their enthusiasm for the scene that was played out on the crimson carpets of the House of Lords. 'If anyone five years ago had predicted that in the year 1909 General Botha and Dr. Jameson would have been sitting together on the steps of the Throne, while the Colonial Secretary presented to Parliament an Act of Union in the joint name of British and Boer, he would have been thought a mere visionary,' wrote the journalist from the *Westminster Gazette*.[3] 'The British Empire has its critics, but we may at least claim for it that only under its flag could this particular chapter of history have been enacted.'

The *Morning Post* declared: 'The Lords' debate on the second reading of the Bill for constituting the Union of South Africa was not a debate at all in the ordinary acceptation of the term. It was a chorus of congratulation and approval.'[4] And the paper observed that the audience was more important than the speeches. 'On the steps of the Throne among the members of his Majesty's Privy Council was to be seen the man who commanded the Boer forces during the South African War – General Botha. Next to him sat Sir J.H. de Villiers. Chief Justice of the Cape, and close by for a time were Dr. Jameson, ex-Premier of the Cape; Mr. J.X. Merriman, the present Premier; and Mr. F.R. Moor, the Premier of Natal. It is unusual for any but the wives and daughters of Peers to find places in the galleries to right and left of the canopy of the Throne. But the occasion was exceptional, and exceptional measures were taken to meet it. Under arrangements made by the Lord Great Chamberlain, and admirably carried out by Captain Butler, Yeoman Usher of the Black Rod, the Colonial delegates who are not Privy Councillors and the wives or daughters of our distinguished South African visitors, were comfortably seated in these places of vantage.

'Among those who listened to the debate from these galleries were ex-President Steyn and Mrs. Steyn, Mrs. Botha, Mrs. Merriman, Sir Percy and Lady FitzPatrick, Mr. and Mrs. J.W. Sauer, Miss Jordaan, Mr. and Mrs. A. Fischer, General Hertzog, Sir George and Lady Farrar, Mr. A. Browne, Mr. J. Smuts, Mr. and Mrs. T. Watt, Mrs. Plowman, Mr. and Mrs. J. Hofmeyr, Colonel B. Greene, K.C., and Mrs. Greene, Mr. and Mrs. T. Hyslop, Mr. C. Smythe and Miss Smythe, and Mr. and Mrs. H. Hull. Mr. W.P. Schreiner, not being a delegate, was in the ordinary Strangers' Gallery.'

As the *Midland Evening Post* observed, this was a remarkable reconciliation between Boer and Brit, less than a decade after they had been locked in combat. 'The picture is one that will linger long in the minds of those who witnessed it.'[5] Patrick Duncan, who had served in Milner's Kindergarten, and had been legal adviser to the Transvaal delegation to the National Convention, gave a more acerbic assessment in a private letter to Lady Maud Selborne, the wife of the former High Commissioner.[6] 'The 4 Privy Councillors occupied their proper seat on the steps [of the throne]. Facing them, in the gallery over the clock, were Schreiner and his native deputation. Two very black and three brown, sitting cheek by jowl with white men, in a way which must have filled any South African mind with horror.'

In the chamber, beneath Schreiner and his deputation, Lord Crewe began by sketching the 400 years that had led to this moment. He talked of a Union linking the four colonies so that they could take their place alongside Australia, Canada and New Zealand as part of the British

Empire. Lord Crewe then tackled the question of the franchise, which he admitted 'has ... raised a consideration of some difficulty'. He explained that while black men of property could vote in the Cape, this was not the case in the rest of the colonies. 'It was ultimately decided that Parliament was to prescribe the form of the franchise, it being, however, provided that the Cape vote should be saved to the native unless it was decided by a two-thirds majority of both Houses sitting together to abolish the native franchise there. This is said by those who desire to see the interests of the native in every way protected to involve a somewhat serious risk that the Cape franchise itself might be done away with. I think we may assume that as far as the rest of the Union is concerned it will be in future a white franchise.'

This two-thirds requirement was, in Lord Crewe's view, a real safeguard and he believed it would be highly unlikely that the white Parliament would resort to abolishing the black franchise. He suggested that – in the final analysis – the King would step in to save the day, acting to prevent black South Africans from being deprived of their rights. 'It has also to be remembered that this is a matter on which we could not say that the power of disallowance which, of course, belongs to the Crown, would not be exercised. Certainly it is not too much to say that the disfranchisement of a class who had held this power of voting so long would be viewed here with very deep disappointment. Disfranchisement is always an odious thing in itself, and if it were to be applied in this particular manner I am bound to say that it would assume a somewhat specially odious form. Consequently I myself refuse to believe that there is any probability that this particular provision will be carried into effect. Looking at it as a purely abstract question, we could wish that the safeguard might be even stronger, but such as it is I am prepared to consider it strong enough. I may remind your Lordships also that there is a provision for the reservation of all constitutional Bills, and for reservation subject to instructions received from the Crown; and all Bills which desire to alter any provision in the Schedule are automatically reserved.'

Lord Curzon, the former Viceroy of India, underlined the safeguard for the franchise provided by the royal prerogative. 'Your Lordships cannot fail to have been impressed by the serious language used by the noble Earl in this connection,' he said, 'in which he not obscurely indicated that if any such measure were presented at a future date to His Majesty's advisers they would not be oblivious of the fact that they have the power of veto.'

It was left to the Liberal peer Lord Courtney, a former Under Secretary of State for the Colonies and a 'Pro-Boer' during the Anglo-Boer War, to argue that it was quite unacceptable that there was no provision at all for black South Africans to sit as members of Parliament. Lord Courtney pointed out that a limited number of Maori sat in the New Zealand Parliament, and there was no reason why this could not take place in South Africa. 'The native is increasing in numbers and shows a remarkable aptitude for education, insomuch that some of them are occupying honourable positions in the liberal professions; others are engaged in trade, and a larger number every year are going through the practical education which lies in the industrial development of the community. You have some 20,000 native voters in Cape Colony; you have native barristers, native doctors, native editors, native preachers; and it is a most practical question not to stifle the aspirations which we find in the minds of those natives, and which will become stronger and stronger with their progress and development, but to allow the possibility, even though it may not become immediately active, of these natives passing up and going from a position of members of a subject race to a position of equality with the superior race in the government of the country. If you really wish to get a national conscience, if you wish to get a national mind, could you secure better contributions to the magnificent thing you desire than by the co-operation, in however feeble a manner and however slight a degree, of native action with your own in the Government in the future?' But Lord Courtney's was an isolated voice and he received limited support.

The Archbishop of Canterbury took what must rate as one of the most reactionary and racist positions. Black South Africans were, in his view, unready for any part in the democratic process and would remain so for many generations. 'The white man ... is the racial adult: the black man is the racial child. That principle runs through all that is best and most desirable in the legislation we may lay down,' declared Archbishop Davidson. Despite this, even he said it was a pity that the colour bar had been written into the constitution. Like others who spoke, the Archbishop said he was not forcing an amendment to correct it, since this might wreck the Bill, and this would not be in the interests of anyone, 'specially to the native cause'. In the end the Bill was passed by the House of Lords with little trouble to the government; the fight now moved to the MPs in the Commons.

It is clear from the detailed correspondence between Sir Charles Dilke and Schreiner that they were engaged in an intense discussion of the Bill as it went through its committee stage in the House of Commons. There are many letters between the two men as they pored over the details, attempting to extract any concession that might help their cause.[7] But while the Liberals had been the main support in the Lords, it was the Labour Party that became the main assistance in the Commons. This was not unexpected. The Liberals were in office, running the government, while Labour was not. To defy the government whip to support a foreign cause would have been a great deal to ask of any MP. In the end it was Labour that stood by Schreiner, Rubusana, Jabavu, Abdurahman and the rest.

This is not to suggest that Liberal MPs were inactive. A number of radical Liberals were close to Labour at this time and happy to work with them. On 29 July a meeting was held in Committee Room 10 of the House of Commons. This was, as the official invitation put it, to allow MPs 'to hear from Mr. W.P. Schreiner, A. Abdurahman, W.B. Rubusana, and others, Members of the Delegation at present in London, on behalf of the native and coloured inhabitants of South Africa, upon the amendments for which they press in the Draft Act of Union shortly to be presented to Parliament'.[8] The invitation was prepared by Henry J. Wilson, the Liberal MP for Holmfirth in Yorkshire, and supported by six other MPs, including Labour's Ramsay MacDonald.

Wilson took the chair at the meeting, which was attended by about 40 Liberal and Labour MPs.[9] *The Times* reported that the deputation (which included Jabavu) heard them call for the 'elimination of the words requiring all members of the new Assembly to be of European descent, or at least only apply to representatives of the Transvaal and Orange River Colonies'.[10] The deputation also called for the dropping of the clause allowing the 'native' franchise to be removed by a two-thirds majority. After some discussion the assembled MPs agreed to move amendments to this effect during the committee stage of the debate, when the details of the Bill would be discussed. On the face of it the South Africans were making some progress, but Dr Abdurahman knew they faced a huge task. 'Since our arrival here it has been a terribly up-hill fight,' he told his party in a letter home.[11]

At this point the deputation had one – last – opportunity to influence the government. On 6 August they were granted a second interview with

*Alfred Mangena.*

Lord Crewe.[12] Lionel Earle, Lord Crewe's secretary, said that 'Tengo Jabavu and his friend' could come to see the Secretary of State, and that Schreiner could accompany them if they wished. Quite what took place at this meeting is not clear, but there is no indication that they were able to persuade the British government to change its stance at this late stage.

The outlook was grim: all the delegation's efforts had been rebuffed. The impact of these setbacks on Schreiner and his colleagues is not difficult to imagine. They had come thousands of miles, at great expense to themselves and their communities, yet defeat stared them in the face. What did they feel about it? And what did their families back home think of the reports they would have read with great care in the South African press? Sadly, just one letter remains that provides us with evidence of their response. It is from Nellie Abdurahman to her husband, dated 10 August. 'My dearest husband,' she wrote from their home, Albert Lodge, Mount Street, in Cape Town's District Six. 'When you receive this you will be on your way back to "Home Sweet Home" and sunny South Africa. I was so pleased to get your letters today, although the news regarding your Mission to England was not so good as I hoped it would be. However I feel sure that the majority of the Coloured people are satisfied that you have done your utmost for them and time will do the rest.' And she signed herself, 'Your affectionate wife, Nellie.'[13] It was a warm and loving letter, clearly designed to boost her husband's flagging morale at this moment.

By this time the long campaign was almost at an end. Sir Charles Dilke had presented a petition to the House of Commons, signed by Schreiner, Abdurahman, Jabavu and others. *The Times* published a lengthy letter by Tengo Jabavu, in which he specifically raised the issue of the incorporation of Basutoland into the Union. He then went on to deal with the colour bar, accusing the Imperial Parliament of acting like Pontius Pilate and washing its hands of its responsibilities for its black subjects.[14]

Despite their successes in campaigning against the incorporation of the Protectorates, there was little optimism. The ever-observant Betty Molteno had been spending her days flitting between fashionable evenings attended by Botha, Smuts and the white delegates and daytime meetings with the black deputation. Interspersed between these were visits to galleries and listening to the suffragettes – including Christabel Pankhurst and Frederick Pethick-Lawrence, both among the foremost exponents of women's right to vote. On 22 July Betty met a man she only described to Alice as 'a Zulu' while waiting at a bus stop.[15] It is possible that he was either Alfred Mangena or Pixley kaIsaka Seme, both young South African lawyers who had settled in London. The 'Zulu' mistook her for Harriette Colenso, daughter of Bishop John Colenso, a veteran campaigner for the Zulu people. This unidentified figure said he knew Tengo Jabavu's son and that Tengo himself was not living far away. Betty Molteno complained that she had attempted to contact Dr Abdurahman, but that he had failed to reply. The 'Zulu' said this was inexcusable and promised to help the two of them meet.[16]

Seme, who was John Dube's cousin, had spent time in America as a student. At his graduation from Columbia University he had made an award-winning speech entitled 'The Regeneration of Africa' and heard the pioneering African American author, intellectual and campaigner, Booker T. Washington, speak at the Tuskegee Institute in Alabama. In January 1907 Seme came to Oxford University, where he studied law at Jesus College.

Alfred Mangena had represented dock workers in Cape Town before he left for London in July 1902. Mangena enrolled at Lincoln's Inn in London to study law. He also joined the African Society, which promoted relations between the UK and Africa, and became actively involved in campaigning against the imposition of the death penalty during the Bambatha Rebellion in 1906. Mangena took the matter to the Privy Council and appeared at a meeting in the House of Commons in April 1906, chaired by Sir Charles Dilke. The *Daily Mail* reported that a 'Pro-Bambatha Party' had been formed.[17] Standing up for the rebels was, of course, unpopular with the colonial authorities. So it was no surprise that he was accused of having 'incited natives' in Cape Town, but this was followed by a smear. He was accused of having stolen their money – all £150 of it: a huge sum at the time. The allegations were false and Mangena became involved in lengthy libel proceedings after they were published in the official yearbook of Natal. The libel was actually against a newspaper – the *Daily Chronicle* – with a jury deciding in Mangena's favour. However, the official record in the Blue Book remained and Mangena had to petition Parliament to try to have it removed. The clerk of Parliament refused, arguing that it was simply a record of the information presented to the House. It was only after Ramsay MacDonald raised the case in the Commons that John Seely, Under Secretary at the Colonial Office, agreed that a full account should be published, including Mangena's side of the story.

Mangena and Seme were both in London at the time when the draft constitution was making its way through Parliament. They would have followed the discussions avidly. Both had been mandated to represent the Transvaal Native Congress (formed in 1903 as an affiliate of Rubusana's South African Native Congress) to represent its members' views in the debates over the proposed Union.[18] The two men met and held discussions with the South African deputation over the future of their country. Mangena also attended one of the most significant occasions of the visit – a dinner with members of the Labour Party held in the House of Commons on 10 August.[19]

By this time they were sharing lodgings in what Seme described as an 'attic chamber' in Fitzroy Square. Their residence was just a few hundred metres from Gordon Hall on Gordon Square, where Betty Molteno was staying.[20] On 11 August Molteno wrote that she was 'on her way to Queens Road Station [when she] ran almost slap into Dr Abdurahman'. It turned out that he *had* in fact replied to her letter, but it had somehow gone astray. Reconciled, they had a 'good talk and a meeting with Tengo Jabavu is to be arranged'. At this point Molteno wrote: 'He [Jabavu] is most disheartened – Thinks they have not gained anything by coming over.' The following day Molteno again wrote to Alice Greene, telling her that during her meeting with Dr Abdurahman, 'He was very low and seemed to feel no sympathy was being shown them over here – I am sorry for this – for we know very real sympathy does exist – I wish I could help them come into contact with some real sympathizers.'

On Saturday 14 August, Molteno was waiting at Gordon Hall for Dr Abdurahman and Tengo Jabavu, who had said they would call on her at eleven in the morning. Clearly in a good mood and with sun streaming in through her window, she sat down to read the *Review of Reviews* and another liberal weekly, the *Nation*. Both carried articles that were much to her liking. William Stead had written a long article, based on interviews with all shades of South African opinion.[21] Botha, Smuts, Merriman and Schreiner had given their views, as had Betty Molteno herself. But Stead had also talked to Dr Abdurahman, Jabavu, Rubusana and Mapikela. The editor had put it to the white delegates that all they needed to do was get rid of three words – 'of European descent' – and they would receive the backing of most of their critics. Stead had a good rapport with the Afrikaners, since he had backed them during the Anglo-Boer War, but he received a somewhat pained rejection. 'You know that I would be only too glad to accede to any request of yours if I could possibly see my way clear to doing so,' Abraham Fischer, Prime Minister of the Orange River Colony, told him. 'What you ask as to consenting to an alteration in the draft Union Act on a matter which the Convention thought of material importance, and resolved upon after maturest deliberation, is practically impossible. Acceding to your request would at this juncture mean wrecking union; this none of us are prepared to do, including, I hope, yourself.' All the white politicians took a similar stand; wringing their hands while saying they could do no other.

Stead summed up the position of the English-speaking liberals who supported this stand as being particularly odious – 'enforcing upon England the betrayal of her wards is the fly which causes the ointment of the apothecary to stink'. He then went on to quote the black deputation's reaction: '"We only demand justice," said Mr Tengo Jabavu. "And the status quo which was promised us," added Dr Abdurahman. "What becomes of English principles of liberty," said a native from the Orange Free State, "if you are to abandon your guardianship of the native?"' Stead also reported Betty Molteno as saying that what was happening was a betrayal of the liberal principles of previous Cape governors, like Sir George Grey. He concluded the article by quoting General Botha, who had told him that 'natives are not fit to use it [the right to sit in Parliament] and no self-respecting white man would sit beside a coloured man in Parliament'. Stead was outraged: 'I would certainly be better pleased to sit beside Dr Abdurahman or Tengo Jabavu in any Parliament than with certain white men whom I know in South Africa, or even in the British House of Commons.' But in the end he got nowhere. It was – as he recorded – a case of accept the Bill as it stood or leave it. Nothing would be changed.

The *Nation*'s article by Jabavu was of a very different tone.[22] 'Next week the House of Commons will be called upon to sanction disqualification of the natives of Cape Colony based solely on race or colour,' Jabavu wrote. 'Civilised and uncivilised, black and colored [*sic*] (half-castes): partisans of opposing parties in politics; men, women and children – in a word, elements that have never worked together – have been united by a common grievance: the attack on their color, qua color. For be the color line drawn where it may in the new Constitution – at the Union Parliament – or a future disfranchisement – the fact alone that an advantage is being taken of the natives on the ground of color is enough to arouse the deepest feeling in every member of the injured race ... In short, the native communities of South Africa have never been moved by any political act as they have been on this occasion.'

Jabavu went on to deplore what was being proposed, describing it as a 'flagrant breach of faith' and pointing out that many black people had volunteered to come under British rule after being promised in treaties that they would receive even-handed and just treatment. 'They were assured by governors, governors' agents, officials and missionaries of the absolute justice, freedom and liberty, without discrimination of color, they would enjoy under the British Government.' It was a stinging rebuke.

On that sunny Saturday morning, in the week before the Bill was to be debated, Dr Abdurahman and Tengo Jabavu arrived to see Betty Molteno. Her letter to Alice Greene bubbled with excitement.[23] 'Jabavu large and smiling – a sea of human kindness and cheerful light – While Abdurahman looked a beautiful angel almost about to wing its way from dust and turmoil into sunnier skies – Didn't we talk and I read aloud Stead's article – dear Tengo – how good was his large, merry, jovial human laugh at Stead's many sallies – oh he did enjoy and appreciate the article – while Abdurahman was blue as azure – I found myself stopping the reading to beg him to laugh too – saying he could not live much

*The Schreiner delegation was invited to dinner in the Houses of Parliament by leaders of the Labour Party. Those attending included founding members of the ANC.*

longer if he did not laugh more – and he replied "how can I laugh – my wife says I never laugh".'

\* \* \*

One final barrier stood in the way of the Bill: the Labour Party. The party was still in its infancy, with just a handful of MPs. Between them they had to deal with all the domestic and international issues before Parliament. Nonetheless, the party took the South African issue very seriously. Its secretary, Ramsay MacDonald, told Schreiner how difficult he was finding it in raising the issue, given the pressure of time.[24] 'I have not had my clothes off, except for changing, these three days,' he wrote. 'I have not given up hopes, but they are fading.' On 6 August Keir Hardie wrote to Schreiner, inviting him to attend a meeting of Labour members, as well as a few other sympathisers, the following Tuesday at 7:30 p.m.[25] Hardie suggested that two others, 'one coloured and one native', should also speak at the meeting. He asked that Schreiner compile a list of organisations, 'especially the Churches', who supported their cause. Hardie concluded his letter: 'Excuse me for thus intervening, but if a fight is to be made you ought to make the best show possible.'

The meeting was reported by the *Daily Mail*.[26] 'In the deputation were many native gentlemen, "representing" in the words of Mr. Schreiner, "the native and coloured inhabitants of all the self-governing Colonies of South Africa and the territories of Basutoland and Bechuanaland. We are not here", declared Mr. Schreiner, "for the purpose of urging this Parliament to extend to the Transvaal and the Orange River Colony the principles which have obtained for generations in Cape Colony, but to claim that the existing rights and privileges shall be maintained and that the territories under the protection of Great Britain shall not be handed over to the Union Government until the Government has given adequate and reasonable representation to all territories without bar to race or colour."'

It was a last-ditch appeal, with little hope of success. The final act before the debate got under way took place that Tuesday evening in the House of Commons. It was a dinner, presided over by Keir Hardie. The National Library in Cape Town contains in its collections the menu that had been selected for them.[27] The prettily decorated document reveals that a good meal was enjoyed of mutton with green beans, followed by vanilla ice cream and cheese. On the back of the menu are the signatures of all those who attended. These are the signatories, listed in the order in which they signed and with their affiliations and their distinctions given.

Susan Strong (an American opera singer, who had probably been hired for the evening)

Daniel Dwanya (sponsored by Chief Kama from Middledrift in the Eastern Cape)

D.J. Lenders (African Political Organisation)

Matthew Fredericks (African Political Organisation)

Alfred Mangena (already living in London, who joined the deputation)

Agnes P. Hardie (daughter of Keir Hardie)

W.P. Schreiner (former Prime Minister of the Cape and leader of the deputation)

Arthur Henderson (Labour, Barnard Castle, 1903–18)

James Parker, (Labour, Halifax, 1906–18)

Charles Duncan (Labour, Barrow, 1906–18)

Mrs. G.N. Barnes (wife of George Barnes)

George N. Barnes (Labour, Glasgow Blackfriars and Hutchesontown, 1906–18)

George Henry Roberts (Labour, Norwich, 1906–16)

Keir Hardie (Labour, Merthyr Tydfil, 1900–15)

Dr A. Abdurahman (African Political Organisation)

Joseph Gerrans (Mafeking trader representing the Tswana chiefs of the Bechuanaland Protectorate)

Thomas M. Mapikela (South African Native Convention)

Walter Benson Rubusana (South African Native Convention)

John Tengo Jabavu (Cape Native Convention)

Mrs Lillie B. Hardie (wife of Keir Hardie née Lillias Balfour Wilson)

It was a remarkable gathering. Sarah Strong, who entertained the politicians, was the daughter of a New York senator. An opera star specialising in Wagner, she had performed at the Metropolitan Opera in New York before coming to London to sing at Covent Garden.[28] The politicians who listened to her that evening – mostly men from modest backgrounds, who had known their share of poverty – would go on to lead their nations. Of the Labour MPs who sat down with their South African visitors, two subsequently became cabinet ministers and two led the Labour Party. Keir Hardie was Labour's first leader, who did all he could to mobilise international working-class opposition to the First World War. Arthur Henderson also became Labour's leader, and then a

*The American opera star Susan Strong, who entertained the Schreiner delegation at a dinner in Parliament.*

cabinet minister during the 1914–1918 war. He was so horrified by the conflict that he spent most of the rest of his life campaigning against war – for which he was awarded the Nobel Peace Prize. Ramsay MacDonald, who had supported the deputation throughout their campaign but did not attend this meal, became Labour's first Prime Minister in 1924.

The South Africans were just as impressive: including the men who would found the African National Congress in 1912.[29] Alfred Mangena became party treasurer, Thomas Mapikela the ANC's vice-treasurer and Walter Rubusana its vice-president. John Tengo Jabavu was among the foremost journalists of his day, while John Dube (who did not attend the meal but supported the Schreiner deputation) became the ANC's first president.[30] Dr Abdurahman not only led the APO with his colleagues, Lenders and Fredericks, but served on the Cape Town City Council until 1940. These were the cream of the crop of black South Africans, who would go on to build the organisations that shaped their country's future through the twentieth century.

\* \* \*

On Monday, 16 August, the Bill finally came before the House of Commons. Colonel John Seely, as Under Secretary of State for the Colonies, introduced the debate. He reminded the MPs that Britain had been considering a Union for a very long time – it had been proposed for over half a century.[31] He explained that it had been impossible to find a formula that gave a uniform franchise for all four colonies. 'In all the different Colonies which now form the Union, to put it in a phrase, a man who had not got the vote before will not get one under this Bill, and no man who has a vote now will lose it under this Bill.' Thus Coloured, African and Indian men in the Cape would continue to be allowed to vote. But only men who were British subjects and had lived in South Africa for five years and were of European descent would be allowed to sit in either of the Houses of Parliament. This removed the theoretical right black men had had in the Cape since they were granted the vote 55 years earlier, although they could now sit on the proposed provincial councils. But it was a compromise worth having, Seely contended. Without it the Union would not come into being.[32]

'The compromise effected is this, that while every native in Cape Colony retains his right to vote, the chance of being deprived of his vote is specifically made more remote than in the case of other classes of persons. On the other hand, the native is debarred from sitting in the Union Parliament because he was debarred from sitting in two of the Parliaments by our own action here. On that a compromise is arrived at, and I can only assure the House, speaking with all seriousness, that we know that if these words were struck out the Union would be smashed, with results most evil for the natives whom we wish to protect. I am told on all hands by those who have best reason to know that if we here were to break up and smash this great Act of Union for the sake of these words the result on the native races of South Africa in breaking down the rapidly growing sympathy between the two races must be disastrous in the extreme.'

That – in essence – was the government's position, and it refused to budge from it throughout debates over two long days. Seely did, however, have a final consolation for those who took up the 'cause of the native'. He argued that it was highly unlikely that the South African Parliament would attempt to remove the black vote, since it had many more important things to do. But if it did, he had one further piece of information. Any attempt to amend the constitution would require a two-thirds majority of a joint sitting of both Houses of Parliament; but even if this was passed there was one final safeguard: the King would protect this right. The Bill would be considered a reserved Bill and would not receive royal assent.

'It is specially laid down in the Bill that any such attempt as this, if carried, must be automatically reserved – that is to say, if such a law were passed – and I believe it to be impossible – instead of its coming into operation at once, it would have to come over here, weeks later perhaps, to be considered. But after the law has come into operation under this clause it has no force – no action can be taken under it until the Secretary of State has seen his way on behalf of the Government to advise His Majesty to assent to it. South Africa herself has inserted this added safeguard, and I am sure the House will see that in a matter of this kind and of this gravity the safeguard is not illusory. South Africa has inserted those words herself in the Bill; South Africa herself has inserted the safeguard. I am quite confident that all these safeguards would not have been inserted at all unless South Africa meant to play fair by the natives.' The suggestion that the Crown would block any tampering with the franchise was supported by the Prime Minister, Herbert Asquith. Seely laid stress on the fact that any such Bill would be 'bound to be reserved for the assent of the Crown at home'.

Schreiner immediately challenged this statement. In letters to the *Daily Mail* and *The Times*, he said it was based on a misconception.[33] He pointed out, as a lawyer, that both Seely and the Prime Minister were quoting from the wrong section of the Bill and that the provision would not, therefore, be reserved for the King.[34] 'Clause 64 was probably in the minds of the Ministers when they spoke; but a reference to that clause will prove that if the Union Parliament should hereafter pass such a disqualifying measure in accordance with the provisions of Clause 35 no such reservation will be necessary. For such a measure so passed would not, in the words of Clause 64, be a Bill repealing or amending any of the provisions of Chapter IV, under the heading "House of Assembly", and therefore reservation is not provided for. The mistake is as widespread as it is unfortunate. Many think that his Majesty would, under the supposed reservation clause, be in a position to prevent further and future injustice. Colonel Seely and Mr Asquith certainly think so. Yet this is not so.'

On the Wednesday, when the debate resumed, Seely attempted to head off this attack. He said he had asked for the advice of the government's chief legal officer, the Attorney General, and had been reassured. He had also spoken to Schreiner and – in Seely's view – all was well.[35] 'I am glad to be able to announce that I have dealt with the matter, having consulted my hon. friend Mr. Schreiner, and the matter is now merely an academic one. For in order that there may be no possible mistake in the matter it is provided in the Royal Instructions that any such Bill shall be reserved, and therefore the matter becomes purely academic. If anyone takes the view that the Instructions are liable to alteration, I may say that that is not a likely case, because we in our party are not likely to advise His Majesty to alter the Instructions with a view to taking away other people's votes easily. I trust that I have met the points which have been raised.'

In the event the British government was proved wrong and Schreiner's warning was proved correct. When the provisions were finally repealed in 1936, neither the British government nor the King acted to prevent these rights from being abolished; but this lay many years in the future. What was certainly the case was that an impression remained in the minds of many South Africans, and of black South Africans in particular, that the King (or Queen) was their final protection. From these debates it is not difficult to see why they formed this view.

The Labour and Liberal opponents of the Bill put up a strenuous resistance. Sir Charles Dilke argued that it left black South Africans permanently in the hands of the white minority, leaving 'the ultimate fate of 6¼ million people who are to be governed by an absolute and permanent oligarchy of a million people such as has never been established by us before'. He went on to quote Smuts as declaring openly that South Africa should be forever 'a white man's country, whatever ill-informed people in England might say to the contrary'. Sir Charles quoted the case of Dr Abdurahman who was being denied the right to stand for Parliament, despite having chaired the most important committee on the Cape Town Council three times.[36]

Dilke was not the only MP to refer to the Schreiner deputation, which had clearly made its mark. Sir William Byles, the Liberal MP from Salford North in Manchester, quoted extensively from Jabavu's letter to

*The Times*.[37] 'The natives of South Africa have put together their money in order to send over this delegation, and one of them, Mr. J. Tengo Jabavu, the editor of a newspaper at the Cape, is as cultivated a man and as capable a citizen as any white man there is, but his skin is as black as a hat, and that is the only thing against him. He has written an article which I regard as of some importance, as bringing before the country rather emphatically the views of the natives themselves – the opinions they hold with regard to the proposals under our consideration. He says the proposals have occasioned deep and widespread alarm and anxiety among the natives from one end of South Africa to the other.' Byles outlined the assurances given time and again by British representatives to the black population. He then declared that a breach of faith was 'a very serious matter to charge against the British Parliament, and I hope that hon. Members on Thursday, when they come to consider the Amendments to this Bill, will not forget the pledges which have been given by the Imperial Parliament in the past.'

The strongest attack came from Labour. Keir Hardie intervened time and again with the support of Ramsay MacDonald. Both drew on their experience of having travelled through South Africa to make their case. Hardie (a strong suffragette supporter) pointed out that the franchise ensured that, as he put it, 'The Kaffir man and the white woman of European descent are classed together in the Bill as not being fit to be counted.' The Labour leader observed that all the major religious bodies had supported a wider franchise and that, by taking the stand that it did, the Liberal government was in effect slamming the door to democracy in the face of the majority of South Africans. The constitution would leave the absurd situation in which an Indian might sit in the Imperial Parliament in London, yet would be denied the right to sit in the Parliament in Cape Town.[38]

The intellectual case against the racial discrimination written into the constitution was overwhelming. In the end the government's case came down to a single reply: that there was no alternative. On the last day of the debate Seely quoted from a letter he had received from Sir Henry de Villiers, chairman of both the official delegation and the National Convention. Sir Henry had listened to the debates and felt impelled to write to him. This was the key point: 'The Delegation has no power, express or implied, to accept any Amendment of the nature referred to which would destroy a compromise that was arrived at after prolonged discussion.'[39] It was – to put it bluntly – a case of like it or lump it. South African whites had made up their minds on this subject and the British government was unable or unwilling to make them change it.

All that was left was for Asquith – as Prime Minister – to express his regret that such an illiberal maxim had been given the force of law.[40] 'It is not to be understood – it would be a totally false impression if it were suggested – that as regards all the provisions of the Bill there is unanimity of opinion in the House. In particular, as regards some of the clauses which deal with the treatment of natives and the access of native Members to the Legislature, there is, as everybody who has followed these Debates will have seen, not only no difference of opinion in this House, but absolute unanimity of opinion in the way of regret that particular provisions of the Bill have been inserted. I wish, before this Bill leaves the Imperial Parliament, to make it perfectly clear that we here have exercised, and I think wisely and legitimately exercised, not only restraint of expression, but reserve of judgment in regard to matters of this kind, simply because we desire this great experiment of the establishment of complete self-government in South Africa to start on the lines and in accordance with the ideas which our fellow citizens there have deliberately and after long deliberation come to.'

Asquith concluded his address with an appeal to South Africa to amend the constitution to remove the racial restrictions preventing the majority of their countrymen from participating in government. 'I am sure our fellow subjects will not take it in bad part if we respectfully and very earnestly beg them at the same time that they, in the exercise of their undoubted and unfettered freedom, should find it possible sooner or later, and sooner rather than later, to modify the provisions.'

With that the Bill was passed. There had been only one vote on an amendment. Just 55 MPs out of the 670 sitting in Parliament had voted for it: 26 Liberals, 26 Labour and three Irish MPs had stood up to the government. For the Liberals this meant going against the whip, and a loss of favour in the greasy game of politics. For Labour – in opposition – it was a point of principle, but at little cost. Their stand was certainly appreciated by the deputation. Writing in the APO newspaper, Dr Abdurahman declared: 'The only party which is not prepared to sacrifice principle is the Labour Party. It is the one party in whose hands the honour of Old England can be safely trusted.'[41]

In an editorial the day after the final debate, *The Times* congratulated all who had participated.[42] Which other country – it asked – would have seen so many, including 'representatives of the working-class using their position in the legislature, not merely for their advancement of such domestic policies as they may have at heart, but for the assertion of a keen and active interest in the welfare of distant communities of alien race?' The paper argued that if Britain had insisted on the wider franchise it would only have undermined the position of black South Africans in a situation in which London was powerless. If it had attempted to legislate, 'so far from safeguarding the position of the native and coloured population, it could only bring down upon them the inevitable reaction which must result from dictating to a self-governing community proposals which you have power to lay down in black and white, but no power to enforce'. This was a frank admission of realpolitik: Britain could no longer dictate to her dominions – they were beyond her control. London recognised that it was reliant, to a considerable degree, on the support of its former colonies.

The British government did not have long to wait for an answer to its pleas. Less than two weeks after the debate ended, as most of the white delegates were leaving for home, Smuts gave an interview, which was carried by the *Manchester Guardian*.[43] He explained that the size of the official delegation was a reflection of the fear that the British might interfere in their plans, but happily this had not come to pass – 'the people of Great Britain and Ireland have finally decided to trust South Africa and make her work out her own destiny in her own fashion'. This they would now do. At the National Convention they had faced two issues – relations between English and Afrikaners and relations between blacks and whites. 'After weeks of discussion of this latter problem we came to the conclusion that it was impossible to solve both problems at the same time. We solved the one and left the other to the larger and wiser South Africa of the future which could deal with the question much better than we could even hope to do at the Convention.' Clearly there was to be no immediate response to Asquith's call for the removal of the colour bar. Indeed, quite the opposite took place.

Most of the South Africans – official and unofficial, black and white – wasted no further time in London. They left Britain knowing that the constitution had been passed, and the Union of South Africa would come about in 1910. But some did not immediately return home; for them there was still much unfinished business to be concluded.

# 8

# London: Gandhi's campaign

The vote was over and the Bill was now law. South Africa had a founding constitution and the Union would come into force in 1910. But for Gandhi the campaign to win reforms in the Transvaal was nowhere near conclusion. In the next few weeks it would come to a head, with the help of the substantial support base that the Indian community had carefully constructed in London.

* * *

Although, as we have seen, Gandhi did not form part of the Schreiner deputation, he did lend it his support and, when it failed in its objective, his consolation. Just after the final debate on the South Africa Act in the House of Commons, Gandhi wrote to his friend Dr Abdurahman.[1] It was an important intervention at a moment of dark despair. The letter spelt out Gandhi's assessment of the deputation's strategy and, in the gentlest of terms, criticised Abdurahman and his colleagues for their approach to the British. They had relied upon British goodwill, he said, and appealed to a sense of justice and fairness. In Gandhi's view this approach was bound to fail, unless it was underpinned by a vigorous campaign of civil disobedience.

The letter was dated 23 August 1909.[2] 'Dear Dr Abdurrahman [sic]', Gandhi wrote. 'Please accept my sympathy as also congratulations in connection with your mission; my sympathy because you have got nothing substantially; my congratulations because no deputation deserves success as yours did, on account alike of the inherent justice of your cause and the solid work that you put forth. Mr. Schreiner has undoubtedly worked sincerely and like a giant.

'That no amendment would be made in the Draft Bill was a foregone conclusion. One may derive whatever satisfaction is to be had from the fact of almost every member having regretted the insertion of a racial bar in an Imperial Statute-book; neither you nor I can live upon regrets. You are busy, so am I. Were I not busy, I should certainly have come down to you to offer what consolation I could, and yet I know that real consolation has to come from within. I can but recall to you the conversation we had on board. You are disappointed (if you are); you expected something from the Parliament or the British public, but why should you expect anything from them, if you expect nothing from yourself.

'I promised to send you Thoreau's Duty of Civil Disobedience. I have not been able to procure it; I am writing for it to-day and hope to send it before you are off.

'All I can add is a prayer that you may have the strength for it and ability to continue the work in South Africa along internal reform, and, therefore, passive resistance, even though, in the beginning, you may be only a handful.'

The letter ended with a suggestion of a meal together the following day. Its warm and friendly tone reflected Gandhi's care and consideration for Dr Abdurahman's no doubt bruised feelings. After all, he and his colleagues had come so many miles, had expended so much energy and their community's money, yet had so little to show for their efforts. In discussing the issue in his own paper, *Indian Opinion*, Gandhi was more forthright.[3] 'What should the Coloured people do now? The question should not arise. If they have courage in them, let them, with Rama's name on their lips, sound a call for satyagraha [passive resistance or civil disobedience]; otherwise, they are surely as good as dead. To have come over here and made big speeches would avail them but little. The days are past, so it seems, when something could be gained by making speeches.'

Gandhi was right. Had the various black movements that emerged in this period adopted his strategy of civil disobedience, South African history might have been rather different. However, the African leadership and Dr Abdurahman's African Political Organisation did not take this path. Although there were attempts made in the next few years to confront the authorities, this was not the dominant political approach. Instead black movements continued with petitions, deputations and appeals to the authorities for something like four decades. Raymond Suttner suggests that this strategy was an (unsuccessful) attempt to drive a wedge between the Crown and the Union government.[4] André Odendaal argues that we need to avoid patronising the early African elite and appreciate instead the deep-seated constitutionalism that animated their politics.[5] Both may be right and this is not the place to attempt to resolve this complex question. Clearly, the emerging black movements were battling against a confident and resurgent white political class. The risks of confrontation were high and would not necessarily ensure success.

It was really only the formation of the ANC Youth League in March 1944, followed by the election of the National Party government in 1948 and the introduction of apartheid, that finally killed off this approach.[6] The Youth League Manifesto of 1944 accepted that many of the ANC's critics had a point when they attacked the organisation for 'being an unconscious police to check the assertion of the popular will' and standing in the way of 'the avalanche of popular opinion which was tired of appeasing the Authorities while life became more intolerable'.[7] For his part, the young Nelson Mandela saw the ANC as 'obsessed with imperialist forms of organisation' and easily bought off by the government. The arrival of the young radicals – Sisulu, Mandela and Tambo – put an end to a tradition of politics, and set the ANC on a new course.

All that lay many years in the future. The question for Dr Abdurahman, Tengo Jabavu, Walter Rubusana and the rest of the deputation was what to do next. And that would really only become clear once they returned to South Africa.

\* \* \*

For Dr Abdurahman and his colleagues, the long battle for British public opinion was over, but for Gandhi it was still very much in full swing. He had arrived in Southampton on 10 July after a stultifying first-class journey, complaining that he had been fed every two hours and hardly allowed to lift a glass of water to his lips unaided.[8] His aim was to get the British government to force the Transvaal to repeal the Asiatic Act, which had been introduced in 1908. This Act barred Indians from entering the Transvaal and required the voluntary registration of all Indians resident in the colony. The previous year a similar law, known by its critics as

*The sentencing of the Indian 'extremist' Madan Lal Dhingra for the assassination of Sir Curzon Wyllie – a key event in shaping Gandhi's philosophy.*

the 'Black Act', had been passed, requiring Indian men to be registered and fingerprinted. Gandhi led a vigorous protest campaign against both pieces of legislation: he was arrested and went to prison himself.[9] Now he was taking the issue to London. He made the journey with a Muslim trader, Hajee Habib, just as he had brought another Muslim, H.O. Ally, during his previous visit in 1906. It was a well-judged precaution against allegations that he represented only one section of Indian opinion – the Hindus. Gandhi had been given his mandate in June, when a 1,500-strong meeting in the Fordsburg mosque in Johannesburg resolved to send a deputation to appeal to the Imperial government. Ahead of Gandhi and Habib lay lengthy negotiations with the British and with Smuts who, as the Transvaal Colonial Secretary, was in London to finalise the Union constitution.

Important as this work was, it did not prove to be the main focus of Gandhi's time and attention. An event occurred just nine days before he landed in England that so horrified him that it became his central preoccupation. By the time he left on the return journey to South Africa, four months later, the consequences of the startling event had clarified Gandhi's thinking so that he locked himself away in his cabin and wrote furiously, producing a draft of was to be his most influential work – *Hind Swaraj*, or *Indian Home Rule*, as it came to be known in English.

On 1 July 1909 Sir William Curzon Wyllie, a senior officer and civil servant in India, was assassinated while he was on leave in London. He was shot by an Indian student, Madan Lal Dhingra, at the Imperial Institute in Kensington before a large number of British guests and Indian students who had been attending an event organised by the National Indian Association. The assassination caused shock and revulsion in London and in the Indian Raj, but few felt it more keenly than Gandhi. He immediately understood that the murder was a major reversal for his cause. It 'has done India much harm; the deputation's efforts have also received a setback,' he wrote.[10]

To understand why the assassination was so important, one has to see it in its context. In 1909 the Congress Party, which was to lead India to independence in 1947, was in the doldrums. Founded in 1885, it was very much a moderate organisation, dominated by the Indian elite, which attempted to win modest reforms and gain access to the Indian civil service for its sons. By 1906–7 tensions within Congress had led to a split. The 'Moderates' inside the organisation (as they were known) were outflanked by a group labelled 'Extremists', who began making demands for *Swaraj*, or 'self-rule'. It was also a tactical divide, with the Extremists calling for agitation, strikes and boycotts to support their demands. Gandhi's friend and mentor, Gopal Krishna Gokhale, writing in September 1909, lamented the impact of this division on the Congress movement. 'The split, ... followed by the vigour with which the Government came down on the Extremists everywhere, has turned the whole Extremist party into active enemies of the national constitutional movement. And the "Moderates", placed between the officials and the Extremists, have not the necessary public spirit and energy of character to hold together for long.'

It was not long before these divisions found their way to Britain. Congress had gone out of its way to build a presence in London to plead its cause. This took the form of the British Committee, which came into being in the late 1880s. It consisted mainly of former British civil servants who had retired to England after their service in India. As its first chairman remarked, 'In the Indian National Congress, the people of India, hitherto dumb, have found a voice. But the distance to England is great, and the Agency is needed like a telephone, to carry the voice of the people of India to the ears of the people of England.'[11] By the time Gandhi arrived in London in 1909, the British Committee was headed by Lord Ampthill, a former Governor of Madras, who had also served as interim Viceroy of India.

Although the Committee could boast that it had the ear of many senior London politicians, its steady, unspectacular lobbying on behalf of Congress did not endear it to the Extremists. In 1906 a former court official and businessman, Shyamji Krishna Varma, had established an alternative presence in London in the leafy suburban setting of Highgate. India House, under Krishna Varma's direction, became a hotbed of anti-British Indian ferment, in the heart of the British capital.[12] Its weekly *Indian Sociologist* was designed to be a counterweight to the British Committee's staid publication, *India*. While the British might deal ruthlessly with opposition in India itself, the authorities in London were tolerant of almost any publication, no matter how seditious. Periodical publications issued from North London seemed unlikely to shake the foundations of British India. Congress officials were dismissive. As Gokhale commented sarcastically, the Indian revolutionaries had 'put six thousand miles between themselves and the administration they want to overthrow'. It was only in 1906, after a detective was sent to investigate the activities of India House, that Krishna Varma decided (incorrectly) that he was in danger and decamped to Paris.

Krishna Varma's place was taken by other 'Extremists' who were considerably more radical. A Free India Society was formed, led by Vinayak Savarkar. This called for a revolutionary war to drive the foreigner from Indian soil. They looked to the Indian Mutiny of 1857 as a heroic act of resistance, which they christened the First Indian War of Independence. As Savarkar wrote: 'Mother Ganges, who drank that day the blood of Europeans, may drink her fill of it again.'[13] Members of the Society were given physical fitness courses, trained in the use of firearms at gun ranges in London, and lectured on the use of bomb-making.

By 1909 the Indian authorities had begun to be worried by India

House and asked the police to step up their surveillance. As a result, attendance at India House meetings began to fall off. Police reports spoke of a climate of 'distrust' and 'disunity', of a 'marked abatement of activity' and of meetings 'very poorly attended'.[14] In an attempt to halt this decline, Savarkar decided that something dramatic was required. He also had a personal motive: on 9 June 1909 he learnt that his brother had been sentenced to transportation for life for his revolutionary activities in India. Savarkar swore vengeance against the British at a public meeting at India House.[15]

Madan Lal Dhingra had arrived in London three years earlier, to study mechanical engineering at University College. He was soon spending considerable time with the radicals at India House. On 1 July 1909 Dhingra, probably acting on Savarkar's instructions, attended the reception given at the Imperial Institute in Kensington. As Sir William Curzon Wyllie was leaving, he was approached by Dhingra, wearing dark glasses and a blue turban.[16] Sir William had been singled out by the *Indian Sociologist* as an 'old unrepentant foe of India', who had been 'fattened on the misery of the Indian peasant' throughout his career.[17] Dhingra pulled out a revolver and fired twice. Curzon Wyllie fell to the ground. At his trial Dhingra was unrepentant. He accused the British of draining India's wealth and devastating its people by hangings, deportations and starvation, and offered this telling justification for his actions: 'In case this country is occupied by Germans, and an Englishman not bearing to see the Germans walking with the insolence of conquerors in the streets of London, goes and kills one or two Germans, then if that Englishman is to be held as a patriot by the people of this country, then certainly I am a patriot too, working for the emancipation of my motherland.'[18] Dhingra hoped to be sentenced to death, believing that his martyrdom would water the seeds of rebellion. He was hanged at Pentonville prison, aged 25.

For Gandhi the attack was anathema. He was not only philosophically opposed to violence; he believed it was entirely counterproductive. 'No act of treachery can ever profit a nation,' Gandhi argued. 'Even should the British leave in consequence of such murderous acts, who will rule in their place? The only answer is: the murderers. Who will be happy? Is the Englishman bad because he is an Englishman? Is it that everyone with an Indian skin is good ... India can gain nothing from the rule of murderers – no matter whether they are black or white.'[19]

Gandhi did not flinch from taking on his ideological opponents in

India House, whom he met on several occasions. 'I have made a point to see Indians here [in London] of every point of view,' Gandhi told Lord Ampthill. 'I have endeavoured especially to come into contact with the so-called extremists who may be better described as the party of violence. This I have done in order if possible to convince them of the error of their ways … I have practically met no one who believes that India can ever become free without resort to violence.'[20]

It was hardly a debate in which either side gave way. Certainly, if the radicals thought they could convert Gandhi they were mistaken. Gandhi's ideas were deeply rooted both in Indian and Western philosophy and there was no chance that he would abandon his commitment to non-violence. Rather, it was he who set about trying to persuade them. Over many days he also discussed the issues with his patron and friend, the doctor and jeweller Pranjivan Mehta, who was also staying at the Westminster Palace Hotel. Gandhi argued that violent opposition to the British was not just wrong, but destructive of everything Indian independence should stand for. After lengthy debate, Gandhi finally managed to talk Mehta round.[21]

The culmination of this clash of ideas between Gandhi and the 'Extremists' came on 24 October. Gandhi had been asked to share a platform with Savarkar on the occasion of the festival of Dasehra, which commemorates the victory of the god Ram over the devil on the battlefield. It is a festival often associated with war and revolution. Militant Indian students had arranged the meal, and asked Gandhi to preside over the event. He did not hesitate to accept. Indeed, he arrived hours before the dinner, helping to cook and lay the tables.[22] In the debate that followed, it was Savarkar's arguments that were followed with greater attention. But Gandhi's calm, unemotional rhetoric impressed those who heard it. At least three members of the audience became supporters of his movement for Indian independence.[23]

\* \* \*

Important as these debates were for Gandhi's intellectual development, they were not his primary reason for being in London. This was, of course, to fight for the Transvaal Indians who had sent him, and he set about this with a will.

Gandhi had prepared for his clash with Jan Smuts, the Transvaal Colonial Secretary, with some care. Before leaving South Africa he had taken the precaution of dispatching one of his closest friends and allies,

Henry Polak, to India. Polak had met Gandhi in 1904 at Johannesburg's only vegetarian restaurant, the Alexandra Tea Room.[24] Polak, a radical lawyer and journalist, had recently arrived from Britain. He and Gandhi found that they had a shared love for the work of Tolstoy and soon became firm friends. By 1909 Polak was an indispensable member of Gandhi's inner circle of supporters. In June that year, on the train from Johannesburg to Cape Town before setting sail for London, Gandhi instructed Polak to set off for India, to lobby the British administration, publicise the cause of Transvaal Indians, and raise funds.[25]

This was a stroke of genius, and reflected Gandhi's deep understanding of how the British Empire worked, its strengths and weaknesses. Gandhi knew that without exercising maximum pressure on the British authorities, he stood no chance of succeeding, particularly when he was up against as shrewd an opponent as Smuts. Sending a confidant to India to 'stir up the native' there (to use the language of the age) provided Gandhi with an additional lever in his trial of strength with both London and Pretoria.

Landing in Bombay in the first week of August, Polak set about his task with considerable energy, meeting newspaper editors, Indian business leaders and senior members of Congress. On 14 September he spoke at a meeting in Bombay attended by the good and the great of Indian society and addressed by the Congress leader Gokhale. Gandhi and his colleagues were, said Gokhale, 'fighting not for themselves, but for the honour and interests of our motherland'.[26] From Bombay Polak travelled to Surat, Kathor and Ahmedabad in Gujarat before proceeding to Madras and the Tamil interior. He published a pamphlet, *The Indians of South Africa: Helots Within the Empire and How They Are Treated*, which laid out in graphic detail the repression they faced. Polak wrote of the heroism of Gandhi and his supporters, calling for powerful national protest to 'keep the ship of State off the rocks of racialism'. The Transvaal authorities were furious, and denounced the pamphlet.

Polak's campaign was a considerable success and as a result Gandhi gained new converts and supporters across India. Polak was able to write to his friend to assure him that 'with your great modesty you will probably be unable to appreciate the fact that you are regarded as one of India's greatest men today'.[27] Certainly, the British authorities in India took Polak's propaganda very seriously, sending police to spy on his every visit and reporting back on the meetings he attended.

Despite Polak's best efforts, and the pressure his campaign exerted on the British, Gandhi made little headway in London. He had at his disposal two resources that the non-racial deputation led by W.P. Schreiner had not been able to call upon. The first was the substantial and influential Indian community already resident in London. These included the former Conservative MP Sir Mancherjee Bhownagree, whose help he had secured in 1906. The second was the British Committee, led by Lord Ampthill.[28]

The problem for Gandhi was that it was difficult to draw on these two sources of influence simultaneously. While Sir Mancherjee advised Gandhi to pursue a high-profile public campaign against the South Africans, Lord Ampthill took exactly the opposite view. 'It is for you to choose between his advice and mine,' Lord Ampthill wrote.[29] 'Your choice lies between the "diplomatic" and the "political" method. If you choose the former, then you must leave the conduct of your business to me just as the Cabinet leave their diplomacy entirely to Sir Edward Grey [the Foreign Secretary]. Diplomacy is only possible through individual agency and by private action. If, however, you choose the political method, then I will stand aside altogether so as to leave Sir Muncherjee [sic] a free hand. I could not take part in a course of action which seems to me inappropriate and erroneous at the present juncture.'

After meeting Lord Ampthill on 15 July, Gandhi had formed a good opinion of him. 'Transparent honesty, courtesy and genuine humility were written on his face.'[30] Gandhi decided, reluctantly, to entrust Ampthill with the negotiations. Within two weeks Ampthill could report that he had held long talks with the key policy-makers. He had spoken to Lord Crewe as well as meeting Lord Selborne, the South African High Commissioner; Lord Morley, Secretary of State for India; and Jan Smuts. Ampthill had also received the backing of another former Viceroy, Lord Curzon. To have two former Viceroys at one's service – men who were once among the most powerful rulers on earth – was quite extraordinary. They had direct access to the centre of British influence. At the same time, leaving the negotiations in Ampthill's hand took the initiative away from Gandhi himself, a state of affairs he hardly relished.

The British had been pondering for some time what the impact of Union might have on the Indian population of South Africa. In March 1909 a Liberal MP, Harold Cox, put down a question in Parliament asking the Under Secretary for the Colonies, Colonel Seely, 'what position under the proposed new government is intended should be occupied by the 150,000 British-Indians domiciled throughout the several South African Colonies; whether their status is to be uniform; and, if so, is it to be raised to that enjoyed by British-Indians in the Cape Colony or reduced to the present level, with its numerous disabilities, of these British subjects in the Transvaal and Natal'.[31] This was followed by a series of telegrams between London and Pretoria, which also involved the Viceroy, Lord Morley. The essence of these exchanges was that although the British government would like to safeguard the Indians after Union, there would be very little that could really be done and that it would be up to the South Africans to act.[32]

After his discussions, Lord Ampthill came to Gandhi and asked him, if the Transvaal Asiatic Act of 1908 were to be repealed and permission granted for six educated Indians to be admitted to the Transvaal annually, whether the sense of injustice of the Indian community would be assuaged. The proposal that six Indians should be allowed into the Transvaal derived from a suggestion that Gandhi had put to Smuts the previous year as a means of ending the protests.[33] Smuts had rejected it then, believing that once the right of entry was established, there would be further agitation for the number to be increased. Now, in London, Gandhi replied that if the concessions were granted, he would 'certainly be contented'. For him the principle of a racial bar to entry was the main issue, 'involving as it does a national insult'. It was a lawyer's answer, rather than a politician's, and it received a reply from the other lawyer in this debate – Jan Smuts.

Gandhi went to meet Lord Morley and Lord Crewe.[34] Both gave him a sympathetic hearing, but Crewe had bad news. Smuts was prepared to allow six Indians into the Transvaal as an *administrative concession*, but not as a *right*. Smuts was even prepared to repeal the 1907 Act requiring registration. But on the key question of immigration there was no meeting of minds. The Transvaal was not, said Smuts, prepared to allow 'Asiatic immigration' on the 'same footing as the European'. Gandhi was just as determined to resist this administrative concession as Smuts was to reject racial equality. There was an impasse between these two steely legal minds that no amount of quiet diplomacy could budge.

Ampthill advised Gandhi to accept 'for the sake of your community, and the struggle should cease'. But Gandhi was adamant that the principle remained and that he could not agree. It was a decisive moment. This was the last occasion on which Gandhi would entrust the fate of his movement to someone else. While he continued to use intermediaries when they suited him, Gandhi ensured that henceforth it would be he, and he alone, who would take the important decisions.

Gandhi appealed for a further interview with Morley, but this was turned down. He was left facing the conclusion that his quiet, ten-week-long diplomatic campaign had ended in failure. In October 1909 Gandhi wrote to the Colonial Office saying that he would now go public about the negotiations, since a settlement was impossible. He proceeded to speak at a range of public meetings. Lord Ampthill, writing to his ally, Lord Curzon, lamented that a Liberal government had, for the first time in the history of the Empire, allowed a colour bar to be included in the South African constitution and said that he planned to raise the issue in the House of Lords.[35] At the same time, Ampthill said, 'the spirit of the Transvaal Indians has not been broken', and that their cause was now more thoroughly understood in India.

\*\*\*

Having said their goodbyes to the Indian community in Britain, which had tried so hard to support them, Gandhi and Habib boarded the SS *Kildonan Castle* on 13 November 1909.[36] For the next nine days Gandhi remained almost exclusively in his cabin, writing at a furious pace. He completed 275 pages of a manuscript that probably stands as his most important intellectual testament: *Hind Swaraj*. Written in Gujarati, it was a summation of his philosophical cogitations and his political development. Philosophically it drew on Gandhi's reading of both Western and Eastern thinkers, with the preface to the English translation acknowledging his debt to 'Tolstoy, Ruskin, Thoreau, Emerson and other writers, besides the masters of Indian philosophy'.[37] But the politics reflected Gandhi's trajectory since arriving in South Africa. This drew on his development of passive resistance as a technique for confronting the South African and British authorities. It also reflected the deep dissatisfaction and anger that Gandhi felt at the failure of his previous campaigns, both in South Africa and in London. Despite his best efforts, and the heroic support of the Indian community in the Transvaal and Natal, there was little to show for their years of resistance and protest.

Important as these influences were, they were probably surpassed by the immediate circumstances of his visit to London. These were –

as we have seen – dominated by his debates with the radicals aligned with India House, as well as his increasing frustration with the British. His discussion with the 'Extremists', and his long evenings spent with his friend Pranjivan Mehta, helped shape Gandhi's thought.[38] He argued that the path the radical revolutionaries prescribed was 'a suicidal policy' that would not only fail but would transform India into a modernised, Westernised dystopia. The Western form of modernity was complete anathema to Gandhi, who saw it as based on force, and it had – mistakenly – been embraced by misguided Indian radicals. 'The fault is not of men', he explained to Lord Ampthill in October 1909, 'but of the system represented by the present civilization which has produced its blasting effect as well on the people here [England] as on India.'[39] The answer, in Gandhi's view, lay in discarding modern civilisation, which was crushing the human spirit with a 'spirit of selfishness and materialism'.

It was a clever and subtle argument – one that eroded the philosophical base of the India House revolutionaries. In essence it suggested that even if they achieved their goal of driving out the British, they would be left with an India upon whose soul was permanently branded the crippling forces of modernity. The British would have left, but 'little Indian Britishers' would have replaced them. Although the colonisers would have been forced out of India, colonialism would remain. Gandhi put it pithily: 'In effect it means this: that we want English rule without the Englishman. You want the tiger's nature, but not the tiger; that is to say, you would make India English ... This is not the Swaraj [self-rule or independence] that I want.'[40] It was a powerful position and one that presaged the work of later anti-imperialists like Frantz Fanon. In Gandhi's view only 'soul force' and a campaign of selfless non-violence could transform the Indian people into a movement worthy of a new, independent existence, capable of embracing their country's true heritage and philosophy.

The achievement of *Hind Swaraj* lay in encapsulating Gandhi's South African experience, while projecting it forward as a doctrine for the liberation of India itself. It achieved many ends: outlining the weakness of the British position and strengthening Indian self-confidence in their beliefs and their history. At the same time it was more than just a philosophical text. The book was designed as a blueprint for action: one that rejected both violence and supplication. It criticised the terrorism advocated by the 'Extremists' by finding a radical, yet peaceful, alternative to their rhetoric.[41] It positioned Gandhi as a pivotal figure in the South African debates. His rejection of the polite deputations and petitions of his South African colleagues (as evidenced by his letter to Dr Abdurahman) meant that he was not shackled by their limited understanding of how to oppose the local and imperial authorities, without resorting to violence.

This was an extremely difficult balance to maintain: one that only someone of the moral fibre and intellectual stature of its author was likely to sustain. In the months ahead, Gandhi's ability to follow this path would be tested to the limit. He came close to failure before finally emerging triumphant. Yet – as we shall see in the coming chapters – by the time Gandhi left South Africa for the last time in July 1914, he had finally extracted sufficient concessions from Smuts to be able to claim a victory for his people.

# 9

# 'The blow has fallen':
# The reality of Union

The debates and the discussions were over: the South African constitution had been given the seal of approval. For the official delegation the return voyage must have been an occasion for celebration and quiet satisfaction for a job well done. The Union of South Africa – so long desired – would soon be a reality. For the Schreiner deputation the prospects were sombre as they prepared to face the future with little to show for their efforts, although the protection of Swaziland, Basutoland and Bechuanaland was not an insignificant achievement. But there was a glimmer of hope. Before the representatives of the African and Coloured people returned to South Africa, they were able to forge links that would serve them well in the years ahead. And a new understanding was beginning to dawn on sections of the British intelligentsia about the fate of black people in South Africa. When the deputation returned to Cape Town, a very warm welcome awaited them: they were feted as heroes, even though they had made such limited progress. Soon the harsh realities of white rule would become all too evident. How they would react to this onslaught was the most pressing issue confronting them all.

\* \* \*

With the vote in the British Parliament behind them, W.P. Schreiner and his wife took a brief break. Schreiner himself was physically and mentally exhausted by the lengthy campaign. He decided to take his family on holiday to the Netherlands prior to the long journey back to the Cape.

Betty Molteno, keen to find how they were after the debates, visited the Schreiners at Morley's Hotel on Trafalgar Square. There she discovered them busy packing but not too downhearted, despite the defeat.[1] Dr Abdurahman was with them, 'plainly greatly cheered by the debates', Betty Molteno wrote. 'His face wore a quite different expression from what it did when I had that long conversation before Monday's debate.'

John Dube wanted to see the Schreiners off when they left for the Netherlands on 4 September, but arrived too late. He only caught sight of them 'as the train pulled out of Waterloo Station', he wrote in a letter to Schreiner, going on to record his deep gratitude to W.P. for all he had done.[2] 'We appreciate all your efforts in London on behalf of the nations of South Africa. We know that you created quite an impression & we leave the results in the hands of God, although we know that God will not rain down from heaven any good things to us unless we work hard. You have a noble work before you. The greatest people who ever lived on this earth & who are held in lasting memory are those who have championed the cause of the poor & helpless.' These sentiments were echoed time and again by black South Africans in the coming months.

While the Schreiners relaxed in the Netherlands, the rest of the deputation prepared for the voyage home; but their time in Britain was not yet quite over. During the months in London they had met some of their countrymen – African students already living there: Pixley Seme, Alfred Mangena and Richard Msimang. It was an important opportunity to discuss politics in the UK and – more importantly – back home. Sadly we know too little about these conversations, but they would have drawn on the experience they had all gained of Britain as an imperial power, of the unsuccessful attempt to shape London's policy towards their country, and of the need to confront the new Union government. Above all, they considered the urgent need for a national organisation to represent all African opinion. At the time of Dr Rubusana's death, more than a quarter of a century later, Thomas Mapikela recalled that 'the conversations which took place then had reference to the starting of the great African National Congress'.[3]

In the summer of 1909 Seme was living in a house in Fitzroy Square with a number of other South Africans, including Alfred Mangena.[4] Seme was in touch with a number of sympathetic white South Africans. These included Georgiana Solomon, widow of the liberal Cape politician Saul Solomon, and Alice Werner, a lecturer in African languages at King's

College, London. Betty Molteno was part of this circle: she lived in Gordon Square, within a few hundred metres of the lodgings of the South Africans, and seems to have met Seme on one occasion in the street, where they held an animated conversation.[5] These connections were important since they formed the foundations for the supportive relationships that were available to the African members of the Schreiner deputation. The white South Africans resident in Britain – articulate, well connected and with funds – were sympathetic to the black cause and could generally be relied upon to open doors that would otherwise have been closed to their compatriots. At the same time this was a social network, not an organised force. This meant that they relied on personal introductions, which had to be maintained over time. For some Africans and Coloureds coming to London, this worked and worked well.

One major source of support has not been touched on so far. Before returning to South Africa some members of the deputation made contact with an evangelical Christian movement, the Brotherhood. This movement – once a mighty force – was holding its annual conference in Cardiff, and unspecified members of the deputation travelled to the Welsh capital to attend it. Today the Brotherhood is almost forgotten, but in the early 1900s this Christian movement was huge: by 1912 it claimed more than 200,000 members.[6] It had senior politicians among its membership. As David Killingray has pointed out, it was supported by leading nonconformist clergy and lay people, as well as prominent figures in the Labour and Liberal parties. The Labour leader Keir Hardie was an active member. Founded in 1875 as the 'Pleasant Sunday Afternoon', its motto was 'One is your Master, even Christ, and all ye are Brethren'. By 1909 it had a national federation and supporters across the British Empire, as well as in the United States, France and Belgium. Its symbol was two hands clasped in friendship. Black people were welcomed into membership and given the opportunity to address the movement's meetings.

In September 1909 members of the Schreiner deputation took a trip to Cardiff to attend the Brotherhood conference.[7] They received a warm welcome and made a considerable impact. 'It was the privilege of the writer to meet in conference a dozen men of colour from South Africa, who had come to this "Christian land" to plead the cause of their race with our statesmen,' recorded an unnamed author in the Brotherhood journal.[8] 'As these lines are read they are on their way back to South Africa with heavy hearts, and with a feeling that there must be something wrong with our conception of Christianity, when we deny to those fitted to exercise them, the most elementary rights of citizenship. Amongst those referred to were medical men, lawyers, literary men, and those who had won their degrees at British Universities, but who, because they had been created with black instead of white skins, are to be debarred from exercising either the right to vote or to represent in legislative assembly those of the same race and colour as themselves.' The writer concluded with a prediction: 'This is sowing to the wind, and will produce the usual whirlwind harvest. It is a mistake of a very grave character to thus stamp the coloured races as inferior beings. It is against God's order.'

Their backing must have been heartening and over the next few years Africans turned to the Brotherhood for support and inspiration. When Alfred Mangena returned to South Africa in 1910, he would establish the 'African Brotherhood and Commercial Co-operation Society' with the aim of giving economic and political support to Africans.[9] Its headquarters was in Pretoria and it aimed to have branches countrywide. A short-lived newspaper, *African Native Advocate*, with Alan Soga as editor, may have been the result of its work. In time senior African leaders, including Sol Plaatje and Walter Rubusana, would build on these initial links with the Brotherhood.[10] When Plaatje led a five-man delegation to London in 1914 to protest about the Natives Land Act, he was warmly received at the Brotherhood headquarters. A photograph of the delegation was published in the Brotherhood's journal, along with an article by Sol Plaatje entitled 'An Appeal to the British Brotherhood: Shall Injustice Be Sanctioned under the British Flag?'[11] On his return to South Africa three years later, Plaatje set about establishing Brotherhood branches across South Africa – spending more time on this activity than on the emerging ANC, of which he was a senior member.[12]

While the majority of the deputation (including the Schreiners after their Dutch vacation) soon set sail for Cape Town, some remained in Britain. They were Joseph Gerrans, Tengo Jabavu and John Dube. Dube had been a semidetached member of the group because of his work as an educationist. His activities on its behalf were curtailed by his central concern: his school at Ohlange in Natal. This is not to suggest that he had been inactive. At the time of the National Convention Dube had been a leading opponent of the terms on which Union was proposed. He had attempted to form a 'Vigilance Committee' to unite Africans from across all four colonies to lobby the Convention.[13] When this failed, he

*John Dube, first president of the ANC, and his wife, Nokutela.*

participated in a national gathering of Africans in May 1909, which was also attended by Dr Abdurahman. But there were clear limits to how far he could go. The sugar magnate Marshall Campbell, chair of Ohlange's board of trustees, had warned him sternly against being involved in politics. Dube must have found this deeply frustrating, but he felt he had little option but to accept these constraints. He announced that he would take a fundraising trip to Britain in 1909 to raise external backing for Ohlange's work. He was also forced to give explicit assurances to the government in Natal that he would only work on educational issues while he was abroad. As Dube explain to Rubusana in a telegram, he would not be able to participate openly in the work of the deputation. 'Cannot go as Deputation. My educational work debars me from taking part in politics.'[14]

Despite this, Dube managed to do what he could to support his fellow South Africans. He participated in the breakfast organised by the Aborigines' Protection Society on 27 July, but could not be part of the deputation that met the Colonial Secretary, Lord Crewe. When the rest of the deputation left for home in September, John Dube and his wife, Nokutela, remained in London, raising money for the school. He spoke at churches and in halls in London, Sheffield and Nottingham. Then, on 12 February 1910, they left to continue their fundraising in the United States.

Tengo Jabavu, the editor of *Imvo*, also stayed on in Britain a little longer. He had the good fortune to meet Helen Clark, a leading Quaker and suffragette who lived in the remote Somerset village of Street, south of Bristol. It was here that the Clark family, major shoe manufacturers, had established a model village to house their workforce. Helen Clark had a strong interest in South Africa, being a friend of Emily Hobhouse and a supporter of the Boer cause during the Anglo-Boer War. She knew many of the Afrikaner leaders personally, and when they arrived in London in 1909 she went out of her way to meet them.[15] Her friendship was reciprocated: from her diary we know that the delegates, including Steyn, Merriman, Botha and Smuts, sent her a bottle of wine. On 22 July she travelled by train to London to meet them, dining at the Hyde Park Hotel with Jan Smuts, who was a particular friend. From then on, hardly a week went by without some mention of a meeting with Smuts and other South African leaders in London or Oxford, or at her home in Somerset.

On 21 October, on another visit to London, Helen Clark came across another South African. She wrote in her diary: 'New Reform Club [where Liberal politicians met] to hear Tengo Jabavu to my great interest.' Two days later she described Jabavu as 'our black friend'. He had come to see them in Street, staying with the family for three days.[16] 'We have greatly enjoyed his visit & had much talk about S. Africa,' she recorded. 'It is very touching to see his appreciation of his helpers amongst white men – and his gratefulness for anything done for him or his people. It has been altogether good for us to see him.'[17]

It is evident that the Clarks had become firm friends with the Jabavus – both John Tengo and his son, Davidson Don Tengo (better known as D.D.T.), who was studying in London. The visitor's book contains evidence of Davidson visiting Street as late as 5 August 1914, while his father continued to correspond with Helen Clark until 1918, just three years before his death.[18] Throughout the correspondence there are repeated references to the support and affection John Tengo received from the Clark family and from the wider Quaker community. Money was raised for his work as a journalist and to support his paper, *Imvo Zabantsundu*.

Christians like the Clarks made an indelible and lasting impression on the Jabavus. Davidson joined the Hampstead Brotherhood orchestra, part of the wider Brotherhood movement, becoming their principal violinist.[19] His father, on yet another visit to Britain in 1911, wrote to Helen saying, 'It may interest you to hear that owing to the influence of the lives and examples of Quakers in this country I have after long and careful consideration decided on joining the Society of Friends. I desire to live their life in the Gospel; and although I may be the first and only Native Quaker I trust I may not be the last – with your help & prayers. I think how on the educational side an influence can be brought to bear on my countrymen that may so operate that I may not be the only Friend out there, and that indeed I may be the nucleus of a Quaker Mission.'[20]

The support of British organisations was clearly appreciated by black South Africans. Christian groups as well as the Labour Party and radical Liberals had rallied to their cause. Despite this, the Schreiner-led deputation had failed to convince the Liberal government to give black South Africans the rights they had been promised. Overall the appeal to the British public had not been a success, despite the concession on the Protectorates. Nonetheless, their time in England was not wasted. A small but influential group of British men and women had come over to their side. Many who had been the backbone of the 'Pro-Boer' movement during the Anglo-Boer conflict had revised their ideas about the Afrikaners. While Smuts managed to maintain his personal links with some of his Pro-Boer friends (and with women in particular), a more sceptical attitude towards South African whites was emerging among the British left and a section of the intelligentsia. Ramsay MacDonald and Keir Hardie had no illusions about the new rulers in Pretoria; and others were beginning to agree.

\*\*\*

For all the assistance the deputation received in London, the situation that faced them on their return was grim and getting grimmer. Louis Botha provided an inkling of what was to come in an interview with a German paper, reproduced by the *Cape Times*.[21] 'On the native question in South Africa', Botha told the Berlin *Lokal-Anzeiger*, 'the first decade was necessary for the consolidation of the Union. The whites ... have laid the foundations of, and must continue the erection of, that edifice to make it habitable. Afterwards they would negotiate to see how much room was left for the natives.'

It was a chilling statement, presaging what was to follow. Yet it did not dampen the enthusiasm of the welcome the deputation received from their own communities. They sailed into Cape Town harbour on 21 September 1909 on board the RMS *Saxon*.[22] There to greet them at the docks was a welcoming committee from the APO. After breakfast, speeches were made on the promenade deck of the ship. The APO general secretary, N.R. Veldsman, speaking on behalf of his party and the 82 branches they represented, gave the formal address.[23] 'We desire to express to you all, more especially to you, Mr Schreiner, our heartfelt appreciation of your noble efforts, on behalf of the coloured races of South Africa. We are fully aware of the magnitude of the task you had undertaken ere you left these shores. We watched with the keenest interest the reports of your doings in Great Britain ... Though your mission has in some quarters been pronounced a failure, we feel that it has been a glorious success. The failure is but temporary. Truth and Justice must ere long prevail, and such success seems miraculous in face of the forces arrayed against you.

'You succeeded in convincing all British statesmen, if their words are to be believed, that the clauses affecting our political status were blots on the South African Act of Union. That admission was made by every Lord and Commoner who took part in the debate on the Bill.'

Veldsman's words set the tone for many of the contributions by Coloured and African communities in the coming weeks and months: thanks to the deputation for what they had achieved and the hope that more would be delivered when Union came about. Replying, Schreiner made the same point. The racial discrimination was a 'blot' on the new constitution, but the deputation had, he said, received support at the highest level in British society. 'We have done what we could, and we have received from the Prime Minister the assurance that he expected that the Union Parliament would take steps in the direction that we desired, and we [are] determined to stand on that.'[24] But, he said, appeals to Britain were a thing of the past. Now, declared the former Cape Prime Minister, it was 'in South Africa [that] our future work must be done'.

Dr Abdurahman – somewhat reluctantly – also made a short address, again thanking Schreiner for all he had done and calling on his supporters 'with level heads and cool temperaments' to continue their fight.[25] Rubusana, who followed, mentioned that he had received a communication from his own community in the Eastern Cape, saying: 'they will give a welcome peculiar to the natives.' The dockside ceremony was followed by a grand reception in the Banqueting Hall of the City Hall, complete with a 'capital musical programme' arranged by the Ladies Committee. The arrival of the Schreiners was greeted with an ovation. When Dr Abdurahman, Lenders and Fredericks entered, the orchestra was, fortuitously, playing 'The Gladiators Return'.[26]

Others were more cautious. The Rev. Ramsden Balmforth, who had done so much to persuade Schreiner to lead the deputation, was unable to attend the celebrations. He wrote admitting that the trip to London had not achieved its purpose, even if all sides in the House of Commons had implicitly condemned 'so unanimously' the racism now enshrined in the South African constitution.[27] 'Our course is now clear,' he said. 'It is, never to rest until every civilised human being in the country, whatever his race, creed, or colour may be, is granted that freedom of opportunity which is the inalienable right of every man and woman wherever freedom is something more than a name.'

It was a ringing declaration, probably written more in hope than in anticipation of rapid fulfilment. Perhaps the most well-judged summary of the situation came in Jabavu's *Imvo*.[28] 'The blow has fallen, and the British Government and the House of Commons have passed the Union Constitution Act without the amendments we had hoped for ... The Native and Coloured people must now realise that an entirely new chapter in South African history is opening, in which they have to depend on ourselves and their South African European friends for the securing and maintenance of their civil and political rights. They must become united politically and, refusing to cling to any of the present political parties, must work for the creation of a new political party in the State which will unite the religious and moral forces – European and Native – of South Africa upon lines of righteous legislation, justice and fair play, irrespective of race or colour.'

\* \* \*

All too soon the reality of the new Union became evident. White politicians set about establishing a uniform system of administration across the country. This included bringing conformity to the 'native policies' of what had, previously, been four individual colonies. When the Transvaal's Louis Botha beat the more liberal Cape politician John X. Merriman to become the first Prime Minister, there was disappointment among many Africans and Coloureds. Despite this, Rubusana sent a message of congratulations to Botha, saying that it was 'the earnest prayer and wish of the natives of this country that you and your government may be wisely guided in the discharge of your onerous duties of State – by Him from which all true wisdom proceeds'.[29] The initial omens were positive. Among the first acts after Union on 31 May 1910 was the release of the imprisoned Zulu king, Dinuzulu, who had been jailed following the Bambatha Rebellion of 1906.

Yet even before the Union had officially been inaugurated, a different, less conciliatory tone was asserting itself. It was soon clear that racial supremacy was the order of the day. 'Another dose of Botha and Smuts,' ran the headline of the APO newspaper in its first edition of 1910.[30] 'Ever since the institution of representative government in the Transvaal, Generals Botha and Smuts ... have given ample proof that they ... are absolutely unfit to have control of civilised coloured people. Since their return from England they are, if anything, worse than ever. They have made all sorts of restrictive regulations and continue to imprison men who are in many respects their superior. Now they have issued regulations that coloured people and natives will be allowed to travel over the C.S.A. [Central South African] Railways on journeys between Transvaal stations in third class compartments only. Well-dressed and good looking coloured persons may travel in a first or second-class compartment marked "reserved" but only when it is practicable to reserve a compartment.'

Segregation was not confined to the former Boer Republics. Coloured people were soon being refused access to Cape Town's latest craze – the roller-skating rink or 'Rinkeries'.[31] The Women's League of the APO registered their 'emphatic protest' against the regulations. But it was in the Transvaal and Orange Free State that the worst measures were introduced. The Pretoria Town Council was only prevented by the courts from introducing a regulation preventing Coloured people from walking on any pavement.[32] Then Pretoria attempted to force Coloured people to carry passes. Dr W. Godfrey, a Coloured attorney, protested that he would 'sooner allow himself to be shot than carry a pass'.[33]

There was clearly little to celebrate. When, in February 1910, the Cape Town City Council met to discuss plans to spend £4,600 on the festivities to mark the Union, Dr Abdurahman used the opportunity to register his displeasure and refused to vote for the expenditure. 'No coloured man can feel happy: no coloured man, I hope, will sing "God save the King" on that day. I know I won't.'[34] How could any black man find anything to celebrate – he argued – when the right to stand for Parliament had been denied them? 'No coloured man will see the Prince of Wales coming through the streets and feel happy, for he will know it is the consummation of robbing him of something he has had for fifty years.'

Worse was to follow. Botha's South African Party won the first Union election in September 1910, beating the pro-British Unionists by 121 seats to 39. There was a feeling among many Afrikaners that they had finally won back 'their' country. But they were still apprehensive. Afrikaners, along with most English-speaking whites, still perceived the black population as a threat: a mood summed up in this verse:

> The caffre first comes; the white man he comes later
> The white man seizes the land; the black man seizes later ...
> The white man he lives now, the caffre he lives later
> The white man he laughs now, the caffre he laughs later.[35]

One day the tables might be turned. There was – in the view of whites – no time to lose in adopting more restrictive legislation. J.B.M. Hertzog, another Boer War general, called for 'Native policy' to be based on the laws of the former Afrikaner Republics.[36] A string of measures was enacted extending racial segregation. The government introduced the Mines and Works Act of 1911, prohibiting strikes by contract labourers and reserving certain categories of work for whites only.[37] The so-called 'friends of the natives', like Merriman, appeared powerless to oppose the Bills. When Sol Plaatje appealed to the former Cape Prime Minister to prevent the dismissal of African waiters from the South African Railways, Merriman could only reply: 'What can I do? I can only talk and that does not seem to help your people at all.'[38] The Defence Act of the following year created an armed force in which only whites would serve. These were a foretaste of what was to follow. It was clear to black South Africans that they would have to resist a rising tide of racist legislation. Unity was essential.

\* \* \*

One of the options that lay before the Schreiner deputation was to build on the relationships they had forged in London. These men – African, Coloured and white – had worked together successfully. They had a common agenda and fought hard for shared goals. Why not build a political movement, without regard to race, that might become a powerful bastion against the racist policies that were becoming so evident? Some, certainly, understood the need for unity. As we saw earlier, Jabavu had explicitly called for 'the creation of a new political party ... which will unite the religious and moral forces – European and Native – of South Africa upon lines of righteous legislation, irrespective of race or colour'.[39] The question was the form it might take.

Rubusana, who on his return toured South Africa tirelessly, reporting back to his African constituency, made a point of attending the April 1910 conference of the Coloured APO held in Port Elizabeth.[40] The gathering was – said Dr Abdurahman in his presidential address – 'one of the most important that has ever met'. Although it was, he said, his role to deal with the 'rights and duties of the coloured people of South Africa, as distinguished from the native races', the two were now in much the same position. 'We have a deep interest in the native races of South Africa, and the Union Act of South Africa puts us all into one fold.'

The meeting suspended its business to hear from Rubusana, who 'conveyed to the Conference the greetings of the South African Native Convention, and expressed his conviction that there should be more co-operation between the native and coloured people of the country'. A unanimous vote of thanks for the speech was passed and Dr Abdurahman followed, 'endorsing the view that the coloured and native people should amalgamate in political matters, and fight together for the welfare of all coloured people'.[41]

This point was underlined in the following edition of the party's newspaper.[42] Reporting on the APO conference, it said that the racial bar in the constitution had 'done more for the coloured people than could have been achieved by any other means. It had produced a feeling of solidarity that will work wonders. The coloured races have been fused into one whole body, whose disintegration will defy the efforts of all ages and all the white races of this planet. The interests of all non-whites are identical. That lesson has been relentlessly driven home in the hearts and minds; and it will not be long ere the coloured races learn the increased power they have acquired by their fusion into one undivided and indivisible people.'

These declarations were all very well, but no one took the next step of forming a non-racial party. Dr Abdurahman was entirely sincere in his quest for unity. In recent years he had worked hard for the rights of Africans as well as Coloureds. He had attended the Queenstown conference of 1907 that brought both groups together and rejected the draft South African Act as an attack on both races. He had participated in the 1909 deputation to Britain, personally giving a contribution of

£100 to Jabavu to meet his expenses in London.[43] But Dr Abdurahman also faced pressures from inside the Coloured community to move in the opposite direction. There were voices calling for the APO to take a stronger stand on exclusively Coloured issues. Dr Abdurahman was attacked by James Curry from the right. Curry, founder of the short-lived South African Coloured Union, denounced the doctor's radicalism. Two other Cape activists, John Tobin and F.Z.S. Peregrino, requested the Minister of Railways to bring in segregated railway carriages for Coloured people, because of the abuse they were suffering from white passengers. The APO, which opposed all forms of segregation, denounced them as 'traitors to the cause'.[44]

The Coloured people were not the only ones suffering from divisions. In late 1910 Rubusana decided he would stand for the Cape Provincial Council.[45] No African had offered himself for election to a legislature before. Theo Schreiner wrote to his brother W.P., asking whether it would be legal and the latter confirmed that it would. When it was announced that Rubusana would take the plunge, the news caused consternation among the white community. The Transkeian *Territorial News* denounced it as a 'political bombshell'. Rubusana faced two white opponents, who attempted to do a deal to reduce his chances of winning, but only succeeded in falling out between themselves.

For a while it seemed that there might be three black candidates: Dr Abdurahaman and Jabavu both considered putting themselves forward, but in the event neither did. Rubusana went out of his way to encourage Jabavu to try to win a seat. He went to see Jabavu, appealing to him to stand, and organised a petition from African voters assuring Jabavu of their support. But divisions and mistrust between the men were too deep-seated: Jabavu refused. In his newspaper, *Imvo*, he criticised Rubusana and suggested to voters that they should judge his candidature on its merits and not back him just because he was an African. 'Let voters consider his qualifications and qualities apart from colour.'[46] Despite this lack of support Rubusana won the election, beating his nearest white rival by 25 votes. He became the only African ever to hold a seat in a Provincial Council. Although Jabavu continued to be lukewarm about the achievement, the *APO* and other African papers were jubilant.

Dr Abdurahman and Rubusana were not alone in considering non-racial unity. In September 1910 L.W. Ritch, secretary of the British India Committee, and one of Gandhi's white supporters, gave an interview to the Reuters news agency. Ritch was about to travel to South Africa to meet Gandhi and Polak, 'to discuss the prospects of the British Indians in the Transvaal and throughout the Union in the light of the Government policy indicated by the utterances of Generals Botha and Smuts'.[47] He told the *Reuters* journalist that there were some 150,000 Indians living in the Union but that they faced different policies depending on which of the former colonies they resided in. Ritch hoped that the more liberal policies of the Cape would prevail, but that was by no means certain. 'If the policy adopted towards British Indians domiciled in South Africa should unhappily prove to be one framed upon the Transvaal model, the Asiatics and "coloured" peoples of the Cape and Natal will almost certainly combine with the British Indians and Chinese, who during the last four years have successfully resisted the Transvaal Government over the registration laws and form a solid phalanx against which the Union Government will almost certainly beat itself in vain.'

In the event this 'solid phalanx' did not materialise. It is perhaps less than surprising that this unity across the races could not be achieved. Coloured politics had its fair share of divisions. African political movements, prior to the formation of the ANC, were at least as fractured. There were also the problems of geography. The country was vast and communication was frequently difficult. Finally, there was the reality of the emerging white political agenda, which considered different racial groups as separate entities and treated them differentially. Nor was this a perspective driven by the whites alone: it is worth noting that Ritch (reflecting the views of Gandhi himself) continued to refer to Indians as 'British Indians domiciled in South Africa'. For both men, Indians in South Africa were only temporary residents, in a category rather different from the whites, Coloureds and Africans, who had lived in the country for longer. The centrifugal forces were simply too powerful to be overcome by the warm words and good intentions of individual leaders. An all-encompassing non-racial unity would lie years in the future.

All the same, links were made and views exchanged. In 1911 the young lawyer Pixley Seme went to see Gandhi at Phoenix farm in Johannesburg. Gandhi told Seme about his 'passive resistance movement and how he had settled women and children on the farm. [Seme] remarked on how satisfactorily it had all worked out.'[48]

\* \* \*

Around the time of Union there was an influx of fresh blood into the leadership of the African people, many of them recently returned from studies abroad. Pixley Seme was among this group of young, ambitious South Africans.[49] He had been sponsored by the American Board Mission to be educated at Columbia University, before going on to Oxford. Seme passed his law exams and was called to the bar at London's Middle Temple. Three other returnees had also received legal training. There was Alfred Mangena, who had challenged the Natal government's crushing of the Bambatha Rebellion in 1906.[50] Richard Msimang, another lawyer, also came home in 1910. He had been educated at Dube's Institute at Ohlange before spending ten years at Queen's College at Taunton in Somerset. It was from there that Msimang had written to Schreiner in August 1909 wishing the deputation 'every success' and asking Schreiner to 'associate my name with those of your supporters'.[51] The fourth was George Montsioa from Pietersburg, who had, like Mangena, been called to the bar at Lincoln's Inn. Montsioa, Msimang and Seme established law practices in Johannesburg. The final member of this group was S.M. Molema, who had been studying medicine in Edinburgh. He wrote that the South Africa to which he was returning would be dominated by 'adversity or, to be plain, repression'.

This group of brilliant and well-educated men set about establishing themselves back home. They were determined to build on the discussions they had held in London to establish a single organisation to confront the emerging menace represented by white racism. It was Seme who took the lead. His office was just across the way from Gandhi's in the centre of Johannesburg. Seme's younger brother, Selby, a clerk in the firm, would consult Gandhi when Pixley Seme was absent.[52] Pixley had the assertiveness and resolve that some of the more old-school African leaders lacked. He wasted no time in showing that he was not easily cowed. Soon after his return to South Africa, Seme boarded a train, having booked himself a first-class ticket. 'Like all solicitors I of course travel first class,' he later explained.[53] When a group of whites took violent exception to his presence, he drew a loaded revolver and prevented them from ejecting him. A court found Seme guilty of having used a firearm in a threatening manner, but the incident appears to have done little to dent his confidence.

On 17 June 1911 Seme held a meeting of the South African Native Convention in his office. The aim was to reach out to other organisations. By July the press reported: 'Preliminary arrangements have been completed ... for the union of the various native associations throughout South Africa and a congress of the new organisation will be held next month.'[54] In the event the meeting took longer to organise and further preparatory discussions were held during which some key actors were absent. Walter Rubusana and John Tengo Jabavu and his son Davidson – as well as Alfred Mangena and W.P. Schreiner – were away in London once more. This time they were attending the Universal Races Congress.[55] Held in July, it was designed to encourage understanding and unity among blacks and whites worldwide. Close to a thousand people attended, including the leading African American, W.E.B. Du Bois.

The temporary removal from the scene of the two rivals for African leadership – Jabavu and Rubusana – may have been fortuitous. In October 1911 Seme sent a circular to the key players – African leaders, newspapers and community groups – outlining the need for unity and calling for a South African Native Congress to bring this about. The aim would be to get 'all the dark races of this subcontinent to come together, once or twice a year'.[56] Seme issued this ringing challenge: 'The demons of racialism, the aberrations of the Xhosa-Fingo feud, the animosity that exists between Zulus and the Tongaas, between Basothos and every native, must be buried and forgotten; it has shed among us sufficient blood. We are one people. These divisions, these jealousies are the cause of all our woes and our backwardness and ignorance today.'[57]

African unity had the wind in its sails and in November 1911 a caucus was held to lay the groundwork. Sol Plaatje made a closing speech at the gathering 'exhorting the members to be united'.[58] It was finally agreed that an inaugural meeting of the new organisation would be held in Bloemfontein in January 1912. On 8 January over 60 delegates representing all four provinces of South Africa, as well as the Protectorates, came together for four days. Traditional leaders rubbed shoulders with educated, Westernised delegates. Seme pointed out that they had come together with difficulty, overcoming the divisions brought by 'different tongues and tribes'. He then made what became a famous declaration for African unity: 'Chiefs of royal blood and gentlemen of our race, we have gathered here to consider and discuss a theme which my colleagues and I have decided to place before you. We have discovered that in the land of their birth, Africans are treated as hewers of wood and drawers of water. The white people of this country have formed what is known as the Union of South Africa – a union in which we have no voice in the making of laws and no part in its administration. We have called you therefore to this Conference so that we can together devise ways and means of forming our national union for the purpose of creating national unity and defending our rights and privileges.'[59] The motion, supported by a powerful speech from Rubusana, was passed unanimously. The delegates stood and cheered. The South African Native National Congress, or as it was later renamed, the African National Congress, had been born.

Clearly, they had much to celebrate. They had overcome real difficulties and divisions to initiate what would in time become among the most important organisations on the African continent.[60] They also made another wise decision. Appointing either Rubusana or Jabavu as their new party's leader could have reignited old feuds. Instead they chose John Dube. The 41-year-old Zulu from Natal had sufficient stature to lead the movement, even though he was not present at the founding conference.

The new party adopted a series of objectives, ranging from the 'promotion of unity and mutual co-operation between the Government and the Abantu Races of South Africa' to the 'promotion of the educational, social, economical and political elevation of the native people'. All of this was done while encouraging 'a spirit of loyalty to the British crown, and all lawfully constituted authorities'.[61] Sol Plaatje had been among the moving forces behind the new congress and was elected its first secretary-general. But as Plaatje's biographer accurately observed, 'By no stretch of the imagination could Congress's aims be described as radical.'[62]

# 10

# Gandhi: Defeat and victory

After his return to South Africa from London in 1909, Gandhi spent the next five years confronting the new Union government in a campaign that would be the climax of his two decades in the country. Yet he began his final confrontation almost bereft of support. Many of the most militant members of the Indian community had abandoned the cause, exhausted by years of conflict. Despite this, Gandhi was to end the campaign in triumph, leaving South Africa to be hailed as the Mahatma ('great soul') in his native India.

This chapter is not a blow-by-blow account of how this took place. There are many excellent accounts of Gandhi's campaign.[1] Instead, drawing on archival sources that have hitherto received little attention, I try to give an outline of what happened, provide an alternative perspective and draw some wider conclusions. Why was it that Gandhi was able to emerge successful, when so many other campaigners failed? And how did he reignite the support that he had established in the previous decades to gain leverage over the South African government? Central to all this was the contest between two men: Gandhi and Smuts. Theirs was a relationship marked by periods of intense conflict followed by attempts at reconciliation. Both were men of the highest intelligence and ability. Both represented the interests of their communities and both were determined to emerge victorious.

\*\*\*

Gandhi had been locked in a fight for the rights of Indians in South Africa, and in the Transvaal in particular, for many years. Yet by the time of Union, support for resistance was waning among Gandhi's followers, as the businessmen and professionals who were the backbone of his campaign gradually tired of the apparently endless strife.

At the same time the South African government was anxious to calm the situation prior to the coronation of George V. This event was to be followed by an Imperial Conference where delegates from India were certain to bring up the treatment of Indians in South Africa. The moment seemed opportune for another attempt at reconciliation, so, taking advantage of the circumstances, Gandhi wrote to Smuts, once more seeking a resolution of the issue. This time Smuts was more receptive, promising new legislation in 1912 that would abolish restrictions on the immigration of Indians to the Transvaal. By April 1911 it seemed that a deal had been concluded.

In October and November of the following year the Indian Congress leader G.K. Gokhale visited South Africa at Gandhi's invitation. He was received with considerable respect by the authorities and at the end of his visit he held a meeting with Prime Minister Louis Botha. Africans, like John Dube, could only look on in envy at the attention the Indian leader received. 'We Natives of South Africa have not been given the opportunity of taking any part in the affairs of our fatherland, and consequently cannot boast such leaders,' Dube wrote.[2] Gandhi was excluded from these discussions and exactly what was agreed between Gokhale and Botha has been a matter of dispute ever since. Gokhale announced that a consensus had been reached: the so-called 'Black Act' would be repealed together with another piece of hated legislation: the £3 tax on indentured Indian labourers who wanted to remain in South Africa as free citizens at the end of their contracts.[3]

But the government denied that any such agreement had been concluded. Gandhi and the wider South African Indian community believed the assurances had indeed been given.[4] Gokhale's welcome from the Botha government had been respectful, raising hopes among ordinary Indians that their lot might improve. Their optimism was then reinforced by Gokhale's announcement. When this proved to be a mirage the frustration and anger of the community were palpable.[5] The foundations for Gandhi's final campaign had been laid.

By early 1913 Gandhi was complaining to Gokhale that his deal was not being honoured. Worse was to come, and from an unlikely quarter. In June 1913 a Cape Town court issued a judgment which brought into question traditional Indian marriages. Justice Malcolm Searle ruled that marriages performed according to the rites of a religion that permitted polygamy were not legally valid. Writing of this ruling from an Indian prison cell a decade later, Gandhi described the judgment as 'an event ... which none had expected'. It was, he said, a 'terrible judgment', which 'nullified in South Africa at a stroke of the pen all marriages celebrated according to the Hindu, Mussulman and Zoroastrian rites. The many married Indian women in South Africa in terms of this judgment ceased to rank as the wives of their husbands and were degraded to the rank of concubines, while their progeny were deprived of their right to inherit the parents' property.'[6]

There was no way that Gandhi could ignore such an attack on Indian family life. He went through the motions of pleading with the authorities to rescind the judgment, but he was blocked at every turn. Supported by his wife, Kasturba, he wrote to Gokhale saying that *satyagraha* might have to be recommenced and warning: 'this time the struggle, if it comes, will involve more suffering than before.'[7] At the same time the South African government was determined to press ahead with further anti-Indian legislation. A new Bill was introduced in Parliament in April 1913, including even more rigorous immigration regulations and maintaining the £3 tax. W.P. Schreiner, by this time a Union Senator nominated to look after African interests, pointed out that the Bill flouted the assurances given to Gokhale, but his words had little impact. As one MP put it, apart from a 'few cranks', white South Africa was unanimously against the 'importation of Asiatics'.[8]

By the middle of 1913 it was clear that the government had no intention of backing down. In May the Bill had passed through the South African Parliament and in June it received the royal assent. Knowing that he had to act, Gandhi did what he had done with such success during his deputation to London in 1909: he deployed Henry Polak. His trusty lieutenant began bombarding the government of India and the Colonial Office with letters, asking them to intervene.[9] Henry's sister Maud, who was living in London, briefed Gandhi's old supporter Lord Ampthill, providing him with a detailed 78-page analysis of the conditions of Indians in South Africa. Speaking in the House of Lords, Ampthill asked his fellow peers just what they would do if Gandhi launched a new campaign: 'how are you going to meet the untold scandal which will be created if there shall be a renewal of passive resistance?' They were little moved.

Gokhale, in London at the time, also waded in. He declared that unless the deal he believed he had brokered between Gandhi and the South African government was adhered to, 'there is sure to be renewal of a bitter struggle'. In June Gandhi wrote to Gokhale warning that 'the Bill is so bad that passive resistance is a necessity ... So far as I can judge at present 100 men and 13 women will start the struggle.' Although Gandhi continued to make appeals to the South African authorities, even leaving his telephone number for Smuts to phone him, it was clear that the stage was set for a major confrontation. For Gandhi success was vital. There were already those in the Indian community who were deeply critical of his leadership, describing him as a 'failure'.[10] He had one final card to play before the struggle commenced: he dispatched Henry Polak to London to make a last-ditch appeal to the Imperial government. There Polak, together with Gokhale, met the South African Interior Minister, Abraham Fischer, who happened to be in London as well. But Fischer refused to compromise, saying that 'further legislation was out of the question', although he was willing to see that the law was not harshly implemented.

It is important to consider just how difficult Gandhi's position really was. His previous campaigns had fizzled out without success, and he had lost much support from the shopkeepers and traders who had been the bedrock of his movement. Deep divisions had emerged within the Indian community and soon there was open revolt.

A Parsi merchant was quoted in the *Transvaal Leader* as saying: 'We can't do anything. I might as well run my head against the brick wall. Trade is not good, and we suffer much in the past.'[11] By October 1913 the differences had become so acute that Gandhi could no longer control the Natal Indian Congress. After a series of confrontations, he walked out of a Congress meeting, to found a new, rival body, the Natal Indian Association.[12]

As Maureen Swan has suggested, Gandhi's final push in 1913 was launched from a position of considerable weakness.[13] 'The movement in the Transvaal was in a state of collapse, the deputation to London a failure ... He wanted a successful end to *satyagraha* (passive resistance) in the Transvaal not only for its own sake, but also as the necessary prerequisite for returning to India, taking *satyagraha* with him, making it the basis for Indian nationalist politics.'[14] Much was therefore at stake.

The authorities, aware of Gandhi's diminishing support, were remarkably cool about the challenge. 'Gandhi was suffering from one of his periodic attacks of mental derangement, and was, for the time being, attracted by the role of prophet and martyr,' said Smuts, then Minister of the Interior, concluding that he 'doubted whether there was much real enthusiasm or financial support' behind the campaign, which he 'rather expected would soon collapse'.[15] The British were also not particularly concerned. The Governor-General of South Africa, Viscount Herbert Gladstone, remarked calmly to Lord Crewe, then Secretary of State for India: 'I do not think that any further concessions will be obtainable this session.'[16] The only warning sounded by anyone in authority prior to the confrontation came from India. The Viceroy, Lord Charles Hardinge, telegraphed the India Office in London: 'We have been under the impression that the bill was drafted in general agreement with Mr Gandhi's views, but the very strong opposition to its terms of which evidence is reaching us seems to indicate that this is not the case, and in the circumstances we feel constrained to withdraw acceptance of the bill as revised and passed.'[17] His views, although important, carried insufficient weight in London or Pretoria to bring about a change in policy. There was no offer of a last-minute compromise.

\* \* \*

Faced with such obduracy, and with his credibility with his own community at stake, Gandhi launched his campaign. On 13 September 1913 he wrote a detailed account of the negotiations and why they had failed in *Indian Opinion*.[18] His editorial concluded with these words: 'The fight this time must be for altering the spirit of the Government and of the European population of South Africa. And the result can only be obtained by prolonged and bitter suffering that must melt the heart of the Government and of the predominant partner. May the community have the strength and the faith to go through the fire!' With this call to arms the campaign was launched.

On 15 September 1913 Gandhi sent 16 protesters, including his wife, Kasturba, from his farm at Phoenix near Durban to march across the Natal border into Transvaal without permission.[19] Simultaneously, a group of Transvaal women crossed into Natal, to visit the coal-mining areas around Newcastle.[20] The hardships they faced were immense: one of the women lost the baby she was carrying. Once in the Newcastle area the women went from mine to mine, speaking to workers and their families.[21] The 'mere presence of these women was like a lighted match-stick to dry fuel', wrote Gandhi. 'Women who had never before slept except on soft beds and had seldom so much as opened their mouths, now delivered public speeches among the indentured labourers. The latter were aroused and … by the time I reached there, Indians in two mines had already stopped work.' The women moved on to mobilise the Indian railwaymen. Yet despite their apparent success, there was little indication that their protest would change government thinking. Would the campaign end as ignominiously as the authorities had expected?

Gandhi wrote to the government on 28 September, informing the Minister of the Interior that he intended to take *satyagraha* to a new group: he would organise a strike of the indentured labourers.[22] 'I know what responsibilities lie on my shoulders in advising such a momentous step, but feel that it is not possible for me to refrain advising such a step,' Gandhi informed the Minister. He would now ask 'those who are now serving their indenture and who will be liable to pay the £3 tax upon the completion of their indenture, to strike work until the tax is withdrawn'.[23]

This was a complete reversal of Gandhi's tactics, for he had previously relied very little on support from workers.[24] Maureen Swan notes that it was only during Gokhale's 1912 visit to South Africa that Gandhi really came into contact with indentured labourers, when attending a mass rally on the giant Mount Edgecombe sugar estate.[25] Certainly, the miners represented a substantial pool of potential supporters. The Natal coal mines were among the largest employers of indentured and free Indian labour.[26] Together with the indentured labourers on the sugar plantations, they offered exactly what any astute political organiser would want: a large group of workers living in close proximity to one another, who were employed in industries vital to the local economy. These were impoverished men yet they had real clout, and – in the £3 tax – a real grievance. By 15 October, having received no reply from the government, Gandhi issued a press release declaring that the use of indentured labour would be part of his campaign.[27] The following day the strikes began on the coalfields of northern Natal.

On 16 October Hermann Kallenbach, Gandhi's friend and financial backer, and two of his closest supporters, Thambi Naidu and Mrs Bhawani Dayal, went to a coal mine south of the town of Newcastle. The Ballengeich mine employed a thousand Indians. Kallenbach and his colleagues were confronted by the managers, who were determined to prevent them from reaching the miners.[28] 'There was a small stream on the way. On the one side of the bank of the stream stood the white mine manager with his bayonet along with his black hirelings who were armed with heavy sticks. There were some white employees of the mine owner with them. The whites each carried a whip in one hand and a double barrel gun in the other … They shouted at the *satyagrahi* leaders and told them to beware and not to cross the stream. If they stepped on their soil on the other side of the stream they would not go back alive, they threatened. Kallenbach shouted back, "Brothers, We are not afraid of losing our lives, but we are not keen to cross the stream at this time of the night. We will go now and come back in the morning when we will be glad to accept your challenge." The three men came back to Newcastle and went to sleep. When they woke up in the morning … There were a crowd of miners from Ballenguich [*sic*] all around their place.'

On 21 October Gandhi left Phoenix for Newcastle, in another attempt to mobilise the miners.[29] These combined efforts were a huge success. A day later Gandhi wrote to Kallenbach triumphantly: 'The strike is the real thing. It is now making itself felt.'[30] He asked Kallenbach to publicise the opposition and to prepare a camp on his farm outside Johannesburg to receive the protesters, in the event that they were not arrested en route. Public meetings were held and the strike began spreading across northern Natal. Gandhi urged the indentured miners to support his call for action. By the last week in October 1913 some 3,000 coal miners had gone out on strike and had been joined by railway employees. A decision was taken by 1,500 workers to walk from Dannhauser in Natal to the Transvaal border, to provoke arrest.[31] On 23 October Gandhi announced that he would lead miners out of their compound.[32] What had begun as a protest was becoming a mass movement.

The authorities responded by resorting to increasingly draconian measures. Mine compounds were declared outstations of Dundee and Newcastle jails; European staff were appointed as temporary prison warders. Miners were whipped and fired upon, in an attempt to force them underground.[33] The repression failed to halt the protests. By 23 October about 1,700 miners were on strikes at ten mines. The

*Indian protesters move through Volksrust, November 1913.*

*Dundee and District Courier* reported that miners and railway workers had joined the industrial action. 'There is no disorder,' the paper wrote, but it called for government action.[34] 'The situation is an awkward one and calls for some very definite treatment on the part of the authorities.' The mine managers had come to much the same opinion. They met and called on the government to immediately mobilise a 'full and efficient force of regular police or troops to protect life and property'. They were particularly worried that the Indians would try to bring African workers out on strike as well.[35]

Although the managers were willing to contemplate force, the owners were initially more wary. The Natal Coal Owners' Society invited Gandhi to its meeting on 25 October, at which he made it plain that it was the Union government's failure to honour its promises to abolish the £3 tax that was at the root of the problem.[36] This was the promise apparently made to Gokhale a year before; and when the coal owners contacted the Indian Congress leader, he assured them that it had been given to him. Smuts – also contacted by the owners – gave the opposite view: 'Government never gave such promise as Gandhi alleges either to Gokhale or anybody else.' The owners sided with the authorities. In October their organisation expressed its concern at the government's 'inaction and failure to enforce the Law'. On 13 November a meeting of the Natal Coal Owners' Society passed a resolution stating that in its

*Indian protesters reach the Transvaal border, November 1913.*

opinion 'it is not desirable to repeal the £3 and that the Government be so advised'.[37]

Despite the brave talk, white opinion was rattled. The *Natal Mercury* called for the £3 tax to be abolished. Thousands more Indians joined the protests, and on 28 October 2,037 men and 127 women set forth from Newcastle to march towards the Transvaal border. They had just a pound and a half of bread and an ounce of sugar each as a daily ration.[38] Gandhi's newly formed Natal Indian Association provided considerable material support for the marchers. Its leaders paid heavily for this, and eight of its officials were charged with inciting violence.[39]

By 6 November the march had reached Volksrust on the border with the Transvaal. Whites in the town threatened to 'shoot the Indians like rabbits'. When Gandhi tried to contact Smuts by phone to warn him of possible trouble, Smuts refused to take his call.[40] Despite the harassment, the crossing of the border went ahead at 8:30 p.m. Gandhi was arrested and released on bail.[41] Within days he, together with Kallenbach and Henry Polak, was arrested and finally jailed, awaiting trial. On 11 November Gandhi was sentenced to 'nine months' rigorous imprisonment'. [42] But this did nothing to quell the unrest, which had by now spread into southern Natal.

As the weeks went by, support for the protest continued to spread. At the end of November strikes had closed the Mount Edgecombe sugar estate; the towns of Durban and Pietermaritzburg were disrupted and industries in coastal Natal were affected.[43] Some of Gandhi's supporters, ignoring his calls for non-violence, began taking matters into their own hands.[44] Sticks and knives were hidden in the sugar plantations. Policemen were ambushed and white farmers besieged and taken hostage. The Durban chief magistrate wrote on 17 November that the strike was 'practically universal'.[45] Detachments of British troops were rushed to Natal from the Eastern Cape and Pretoria. The Coal Owners' Society called for a 'strong display of force' and the 'immediate arrest of leaders'. Smuts assured them by telegram that troops under General Lukin were being deployed to the 'perturbed area' and that additional police would be brought from the Transvaal.[46] By the end of November more than 1,000 people were in jail, yet still the protesters held firm.[47] More than 20,000 Indians were on strike, paralysing key sectors of the economy.[48]

\* \* \*

The public in India followed every twist and turn of the dispute. News reports of the events unfolding in South Africa were published daily across India in the more than 1,300 newspapers and journals that flourished in this period.[49] Pressure on the Indian government increased. On 27 October the Viceroy, Lord Hardinge, took the extraordinary step of publicly criticising the South African and British governments' handling of the crisis.[50] 'It is not easy to find means whereby India can make its indignation felt by those holding the reins of Government in South Africa,' he said at a gathering in Madras. 'Recently your compatriots in South Africa have taken matters into their own hands by organising what is called passive resistance to laws which they consider invidious and unjust – an opinion which we who watch their struggles from afar cannot but share. They have violated, as they intended to violate those laws, with full knowledge of the penalties involved, and ready with all courage and patience to endure those penalties. In all this they have the sympathy of India – deep and burning – and not only of India, but of all those who like myself, without being Indians themselves, – have feelings of sympathy for the people of this country.'

The speech was hugely popular in India, but there must have been a sharp intake of breath when it was read in London and Pretoria. What Hardinge had to say caused a real stir. It broke a powerful British tradition, which held that colonies and dominions did not interfere in one another's affairs. The Secretary of State for India, Lord Crewe, wrote a lengthy and carefully worked letter to Hardinge, marked 'Private'. In it he conceded that the situation had made matters difficult for the Viceroy, who had to deal with the fallout from the blanket newspaper reports of the brutality being meted out in South Africa.[51] 'The South Africa business is very disturbing', Lord Crewe said, 'and one cannot be surprised that opinion with you is greatly agitated ... We heard that some hundreds of Indians have been flogged, one version is that they have been tied up to the triangles in compounds converted into gaols and given six dozen with the cat, while the other is that a crowd of coolies were forced back to the plantations by men armed with sjamboks, when they were beginning a march across country.'

Crewe said that he had done what he could to discuss the situation with the South African authorities: 'uphill and down-dale with all the more important of them, from Botha downwards and I believe that they wish to be just and humane; but South African public opinion is really not to be trusted in relations to Indians any more than it is to the African Natives.' Crewe then delivered what amounted to a thorough ticking off to the Viceroy. 'As you know, we have never wished to check the semi-independent utterances on proposals of your Government on this subject, because it would clearly be unfair to expect you to hold a balance between Indian interest and claims and those of a self-governing Dominion, as His Majesty's Government are obliged to do. But I find that your direct communication, as Viceroy, with Gladstone [the South African Governor-General] is considered to be technically incorrect, and as I am telegraphing you today, your Madras speech has somewhat fluttered the dove-cotes.'

The British government was clearly worried that the Empire might be damaged if its senior representatives fell out with each other and began intervening directly in one another's affairs. Elevated in standing though the Viceroy no doubt was, the idea that he might tell another government how to behave was a violation of entrenched protocol. That he had intervened in the affairs of a self-governing dominion made the issue doubly difficult. If the Viceroy had wished to express his concerns, he should have gone through London. The India Office would have contacted the Colonial Office, which would then have taken up the matter (circumspectly and in private) with the Botha government. No wonder Hardinge's Madras speech had 'fluttered the dove-cotes', as Crewe put it so gently.

Hardinge tried to mend fences by attempting to convey to the India Office the pressures he was confronting.[52] 'I do not think people in England quite realise the depth of feeling existing in this country on the subject of the differential treatment meted out to Indians in the British colonies, and especially in South Africa,' he complained to Crewe. 'There is a feeling of bitter resentment and, as an Indian said to me a few days ago, England will have to choose one day between the retention of India and the retention of her colonies, as India will not put up indefinitely with the treatment that she is receiving, and will in the end not tolerate a position in the Empire inferior to that of the colonies.' This was no exaggeration. Telegrams poured into the Indian government from across the country.[53] There were protests and petitions across the subcontinent. Botha and Smuts were burnt in effigy in the holy city of Benares. A five-act play was written and performed in which a Gandhi character presented an extended soliloquy on the evils of life in South Africa.

What had begun as a local difficulty in one dominion continued to grow in its impact. Then, in December 1913, an incident occurred which must have been deeply embarrassing to the British government: King George intervened by writing directly to Hardinge. Crewe wrote to the Viceroy expressing his frustration and humiliation that the King was being drawn into the crisis.[54] 'The King tells me he has written to you about the South Africa business. He quite appreciates the necessity of your speaking in response to popular emotion, and I was able to make this clearer to him; but he was rather alarmed by one or two of your expressions, and begged me to impress on you the need to keep on good terms with the self-governing Dominions.'

For the King to feel the need to become involved in an Imperial dispute was a devastating blow for all concerned. Hardinge replied with a contrite letter to Crewe, in which he accepted his mistake and promised that he had 'no intention, under present circumstances, of saying a word more on the subject of the Indians in South Africa, unless some unforeseen situation should arise which is hardly likely'. The South African High Commissioner, Prime Minister Botha and Smuts all called for the Viceroy to be recalled; and though the British government considered removing him, his stand had received such support from the Indian public that this sanction was simply impossible to impose.[55]

The clamour for action by the Imperial authorities to sort out the South African situation continued to grow. On 18 November a meeting of the

Natal Indian Association demanded London's intervention.[56] Gladstone telegraphed the Colonial Office in London, summarising the situation. His tone had an air of desperation.[57] 'Indian mass meeting, over 5,000 present, strongly condemn Government of South Africa attitude, arrest and imprisonment of Gandhi, Kallenbach, Polak, and others for striking demonstration of feeling against £3 tax. Strikers imprisoned. Mines proclaimed temporary gaols. Brutally assaulted, flogged, some shot at, wounded. One died to-day result flogging. Strikers confined to estates under police guard. Thousands continue to come out. Situation getting more serious every hour. Increasingly difficult feeding people and keeping order. Active, prompt, intervention by Imperial, Indian Governments necessary lest greater hardships ensue, even more lives lost.'

On 11 December, under acute pressure from both home and abroad, Smuts finally took the step that broke the impasse. He announced a commission of inquiry into the causes of the strike.[58] A week later Gandhi, Polak and Kallenbach were released unconditionally. But Gandhi – as a good lawyer – was suspicious of Smuts's intentions: after all, establishing a commission is frequently used by governments as a means of burying an issue. Gandhi declared that he was not happy with the membership of the commission. He wrote to Gokhale in India, saying that it was a 'packed body intended to hoodwink the public in England and India'. Gohkale was not very sympathetic with Gandhi's refusal to participate in the commission's work. 'Gandhi had no business to take a vow and tie himself up,' he complained.[59] Although the commission provided a line of communication between the two main parties, the outcome of their deliberations was still far from certain. The *satyagraha* campaign had not yet been officially called off.

\* \* \*

At this critical juncture Gandhi received help from a most unexpected quarter. On 27 December Emily Hobhouse wrote to Jan Smuts on Gandhi's behalf.[60] Of all the people who could have intervened, few were held in greater regard by the former Boer War leader. Hobhouse was revered by Afrikaners for her intervention to end the suffering in the concentration camps.[61] The friendship between her and Smuts went back many years. It was the product of the network of remarkably progressive South African women who had supported the Boer cause. They included Betty Molteno, Alice Greene, Olive Schreiner and Emily Hobhouse herself. In 1902, with the war over, Molteno travelled to Europe with the defeated Boer Generals. There, at the dockside in Southampton, was her friend Hobhouse waiting for her. As a result of this dockside meeting Hobhouse came to know the Generals.[62] She later entertained Botha, De Wet and De la Rey individually at her London flat and also accompanied them to a briefing with the British Liberal peer Lord Courtney in late October.[63] It was in 1903 that Hobhouse first met Jan Smuts and was immediately struck by him. 'Smuts is a charming man, clear-headed and clever.'[64] It was an admiration that was clearly reciprocated. After Hobhouse's death in 1926, Smuts declared of her: 'at that darkest hour, when our race seemed almost doomed to extinction, she appeared as an angel, a heaven-sent messenger.'[65]

Given her status in the eyes of the Afrikaners, Emily Hobhouse was in an ideal position to address the continuing strife between the government and the Indian community. And it just so happened that her friend and ally Betty Molteno was perfectly placed to bring the issue to her attention, since she was with the Indians in Natal and could provide first-hand accounts of the strike.

Molteno, as we saw, had spent time with the Schreiner deputation in 1909, supporting their campaign to halt the inclusion of racial discrimination in the Union constitution. Having come to know and befriend John Dube at this time, she decided to build a cottage near his school at Ohlange, outside Durban, with the hope of using it as a base from which she and her partner, Alice Greene, could get to know the African people and involve themselves in educational matters and economic development. As for Gandhi, Molteno met him for the first time during the same London visit. In September 1909 Gandhi recorded in *Indian Opinion* that she was someone who had 'much sympathy [for our cause]' and had offered her help.[66] Molteno wrote to Gandhi from her home in Geneva, asking him to lay out his thoughts on how she could help South Africa become a truly united country.

In early 1912 Molteno and Greene returned to South Africa from their home in Europe, going to Natal to visit Dube's school and see the progress being made on their cottage. As it was not yet ready to be lived in, they went to stay in Cape Town until it was completed. The two women followed Gandhi's unfolding campaign in Natal avidly. Molteno was deeply moved by the reports she read of the plight of the Indian women. As the daughter of a Prime Minister of the Cape, she had access to the highest circles. On 17 November she visited Prime Minister Louis Botha at his residence in Cape Town. There she tried to persuade him that the Indian women were being jailed not because they were criminals, but because they were protesting about the government's refusal to recognise their marriages. Molteno said she was going to Natal and promised to report back to Botha on what she found there.

Because Alice Greene did not accompany Molteno to Natal, the two corresponded almost daily, and sometimes more frequently than that. It is this record that allows us to piece together what Molteno observed from her base at Ohlange, from where she could walk to Gandhi's settlement at nearby Phoenix. On 24 and 25 November this is just what she did. There she met Gandhi's supporter Albert West, who was editing *Indian Opinion* and maintaining the settlement in Gandhi's absence. He told her of the floggings and brutal treatment being inflicted on the Indians. When she arrived the following day she found 300 Indians seeking refuge in Phoenix. At the same time she witnessed West being arrested and bundled into a police car. Twenty mounted police arrived and ordered Gandhi's relative Maganlal to instruct the Indians to return to work. As the refugees streamed out of the settlement carrying their children and few possessions, Molteno wrote 'that the white men looked ashamed of their job. I stood near the leader of the band, when poor, white-faced terribly excited Mrs West went to speak to him. Men always feel the distress of the wife and this tall fine Captain looked but ill-satisfied with himself.'

One policeman remained to ensure that no more Indians came to Phoenix overnight. Another policeman was to arrive in the morning. Molteno slept at the settlement and on the next day she set off to discover the fate of Albert West at Verulam on behalf of a distraught Mrs West. Later that day Molteno, Mrs West and Miss West met Albert at Phoenix station after his case was remanded for a week, and they walked back together 'in triumph', relishing the 'joy of the settlement' on their return. At this stage of her growing involvement with Phoenix, Molteno was still keen to keep the information of her whereabouts from her Cape friends. An unsigned message for Greene, written on *Indian Opinion* notepaper, reads, 'Don't tell anyone I am having any connection to Phoenix – Keep that strictly for yourself.' Molteno was soon so caught up in events around her, though, that hiding her close ties with Phoenix became impossible.

On 27 November Molteno learnt from West that 'several poor Indians had returned and complained that they had been beaten and very roughly handled'. Among the new arrivals was an injured labourer named Soorzai, who had with him his common-law wife and baby. Molteno sat with West as he recorded their stories of abuse, witnessing the evident strain he was under when he broke down himself as the young wife began to cry. Soorzai tried to lodge a complaint before the magistrates, but was arrested, charged with desertion and imprisoned. On 10 December he died of his injuries. Molteno was closely involved in Soorzai's case and was one of the few people to see his body in hospital before he was taken to the crematorium at Umgeni for burial. She was therefore in the thick of the strike – information about which she relayed daily in her letters to Alice Greene. These were personal and private communications, but soon they would help shape Gandhi's campaign.

In late 1913 Emily Hobhouse sailed to South Africa from Britain with the intention of taking her place at the unveiling of the Women's Monument in Bloemfontein on 16 December to commemorate the Boer women and children who had died in the war.[67] After spending some weeks in Cape Town, she left for Bloemfontein on 24 November. Even though she tried to ignore her deteriorating health, she found herself stranded in Beaufort West, five hundred kilometres from Cape Town, a few days later, under doctor's orders to proceed no further. She had a heart condition which had become dangerously unstable. Not wanting to be a burden on her hosts, Hobhouse had written jestingly to Smuts from Beaufort West on 2 December: 'My dear Oom Jannie, Which is the greater plague – the Indians or me?'[68]

Hobhouse returned to Cape Town on 6 December in a desperately weakened state, unable to walk or even speak above a whisper. In the end Betty Molteno's partner, Alice Greene, was left with the main burden of caring for Hobhouse. This continued until the end of January 1914, when Hobhouse's strength had returned and she was moved to the Prime Minister's official residence in Cape Town, Groote Schuur, as the guest of General and Mrs Botha.

During her time with Greene, Hobhouse became acquainted with the full magnitude of the events taking place in Natal. Greene read her Molteno's letters, which provided a graphic insight into the brutality being inflicted on the strikers. For a woman like Hobhouse, this was a call to arms. In a letter to Molteno, Greene recorded the beginning of Hobhouse's engagement with Gandhi on 27 December: 'Directly I told her I had sent off a telegram to Gandhi, and that you had suggested her sending one too, she instantly took pencil and paper and wrote down a long telegram, which I sent off from Kenilworth. It cost 5/7 so you can judge of the length. She sent it to Maritzburg to catch him at the mass meeting this afternoon. It was to the effect that her personal sympathy was intense, but that she would venture to advise patience. It would not do to alienate sympathy and even endanger the very cause itself. Could he not wait until the meeting of Parliament before having recourse to further resistance? Even yet English women had not achieved full freedom. She used much gentler language than this, but that was the gist of it. She told him also that everything was being followed with much sympathy and feeling. I don't know how you will feel about such a message, but I did not see that it could do harm.'[69]

Indeed, Hobhouse's telegram helped ease the stand-off between Smuts and Gandhi. But she was not the only person calling for a respite. Gandhi was contemplating a march on Pretoria and had discussed it in daily telegrams with Gokhale between 11 and 28 December.[70] Gokhale had told Gandhi that boycotting the commission was a grave mistake, which would alienate friends and sympathisers, and argued against the march. By endorsing a delay in the resumption of hostilities Hobhouse helped defuse a tense situation. As E.S. Reddy has written, 'On December 27th, Gandhiji received a telegram from Miss Hobhouse, whom he and the Boers admired so greatly, appealing to him as a "humble woman" to postpone the march for fifteen days. Gandhiji consulted his colleagues and agreed because of his esteem for her.'[71]

It would appear that this was part of an implicit bargain, and to keep her side Hobhouse wrote Smuts a long letter on 29 December. She urged him in the strongest terms to give the Indians cause to hope for a speedy resolution. 'My dear Oom Jannie, Probably an invalid like myself who has hardly come back from the brink of the grave, ought in your opinion to lie quiescent and not mix in public affairs. But somehow I was not born that way ... I should not presume (since you are a Minister) to write to you, had it not been that Gandhi has *asked* me to do so and that gives a sort of right to do what might otherwise be deemed interference, were we not such old friends. Besides we have all been busy exerting each our little influence to prevent or at least postpone the threatened New Year march on Pretoria and that, you see, is conceded, for oh! how many *little* things done by *little* people go to make up the turning points in history. It is not just what you big people do in your powerful offices ... You see 15 January is the date proposed for another march. Before then some way should be found giving private assurance to the leaders that satisfaction is coming to them. Their grievance is really moral not material and so, having all the power of the spiritual behind him, he [Gandhi] and you are like Mrs Pankhurst and [Home Secretary Reginald] McKenna and never never never will governmental physical force prevail against a great moral and spiritual upheaval. Wasted time and wasted energy dear Oom Jannie.'[72] Hobhouse went on to offer her services as a go-between in the impending negotiations with Gandhi, on the basis that she was a sympathetic but independent observer of the struggle for Indian rights.

Molteno left Natal and travelled to Cape Town over Christmas 1913, before returning to be with Gandhi. There is little doubt that her five-day visit brought new life and interest to the ailing Hobhouse. With her recent experiences, Molteno would have been a breath of fresh air to a woman stranded in a foreign country, literally without a voice, and under doctor's orders to see no one other than Greene and her servant. Greene watched her charge's mounting enthusiasm and corresponding collapse over the two days following Molteno's suggestion that Hobhouse write to Gandhi. '[Emily Hobhouse is] in a state of utter and complete exhaustion, but I could not be surprised when I saw all she had done this morning ... The fact is she is not strong enough to be working for Gandhi. She throws into everything such a heart and such a brain that it would leave a normally strong person pretty exhausted. There was a letter to you (fastened up) and a letter to G which I read. Telegrams also, sent and received, all of which she gave me to read. As you are at head-quarters I need not go into detail. G is demanding two more members to the Commission, one to represent the Indian Community and the other, if they so please, the planters and coal-owners' interests, and this he wants to make sine qua non. E sympathizes with the demand, but does not want him to be too stiff about it. "Take what you can get" is practically her advice, but she also thinks pressure and persuasion should be employed to induce the Government to give up their stiffness and try and meet the Indians half way.'[73]

Molteno in turn acknowledged the impact that Hobhouse's first telegram had had in Durban. 'V. soon we were up on our way to Parsee Rustomgee's where I was to see Mr Gandhi – who had received your telegram ... Whilst I was engaged with Polak dear Gandhi was suddenly beside me – so small – so gentle – looking well – as though possessed of a deep inward peace – We clasped hands as we have done twice before and that seemed to mean more than words ... My welcome was as warm as could possibly be and your telegram had well prepared the way for me – There was also excitement about Miss Hobhouse's telegram and a long reply telegram to her was read to me.'[74]

Some days later Molteno encouraged Hobhouse to write again: 'E. Hobhouse's telegram and sympathy has been and is very greatly appreciated here – Please tell her so – that I am so very glad that she sent it and hope she will send another should she at anytime feel she has good grounds for doing so.'[75]

\* \* \*

While Hobhouse was intervening on Gandhi's behalf, his cause was further bolstered by arrivals from India. A senior Indian civil servant, Sir Benjamin Robertson, had been asked to join the commission of inquiry. It was a development warmly welcomed by the Viceroy. Writing to Lord Crewe on Christmas Day 1913, Lord Hardinge said there was nobody in India 'who knows all the history and details of the question better than he does, and I have a very high opinion of his sound common sense and power of handling men without rubbing them up the wrong way. In a similar question in Assam he entirely disarmed the hostility of the planters who resemble in some ways the South Africans.'[76] Robertson was carefully briefed by Gokhale. The Congress leader showed him copies of *Indian Opinion* from mid-1913 to indicate that Gandhi had done all he could to try to avoid a confrontation with the authorities. Robertson had to play a neutral role as a commission member, but his arrival signalled an important departure from the confrontation that had been the hallmark of the Smuts–Gandhi relationship since 1907. Since the Botha government had sanctioned Robertson's role, it meant that they accepted outside intervention in and scrutiny of South African internal affairs. It was an important development and one that was likely to strengthen Gandhi's hand.

Two others arrived from India to assist Gandhi. The English clergymen C.F. Andrews and W.W. Pearson had been teachers at St Stephen's College in Delhi. Andrews had previously written to Gokhale offering to help in any way in furthering the Indian cause, and – with Gandhi in jail – Gokhale called on Andrews and Pearson to travel to South Africa

*Jan Christiaan Smuts.*

and try to mediate between the two sides.[77] Gandhi met them in Durban with a welcoming committee that included Betty Molteno. Andrews immediately became immersed in Gandhi's campaign. He provides an eyewitness account of the importance of Hobhouse's intervention: 'The day after my arrival in Durban a long letter came for Mr Gandhi from Miss Hobhouse. It was one of the first letters I saw among his large correspondence, and it greatly touched me. There was no blame or recrimination for Mr Gandhi's unbending attitude which had stirred General Smuts' resentment but an intelligent understanding of it and an appreciation of the Indian position. There can be no doubt that during the days that followed the influence of Miss Hobhouse with the Boer leaders did much to pave the way to a reconciliation.'[78]

As E.S. Reddy concludes: 'Gandhiji was surprised to see a great change in the attitude of General Smuts and that was undoubtedly due to Miss Hobhouse.'[79] Andrews ascribed this change to Hobhouse's influence on 'Oom Jannie' and was clear that both sides of the negotiations received numerous encouraging letters from Hobhouse in the first weeks of 1914. Andrews, very much a conciliator, saw an opportunity to resolve the dispute. He managed to persuade Gandhi to write to Smuts once more on

6 January, asking for a face-to-face meeting. Relations had deteriorated so badly that Smuts was quite surprised to receive the letter.

Smuts had other pressing problems on his plate at the time.[80] There had been growing white labour unrest over the past year – first on the mines and now on the railways. Smuts believed he was facing an incipient uprising led by foreign-born revolutionaries and he acted decisively, declaring martial law. He deployed commandos under Boer War Generals to surround the headquarters of the trade union federation in the Johannesburg suburb of Fordsburg.[81] Artillery was trained on the building and the strikers were given an ultimatum to surrender. Hundreds were arrested and nine syndicalists were deported from the country under armed guard.[82]

The deportation caused an outcry, both in South Africa and Britain. In March 1914 a trade union demonstration in London, seven miles long, comprising half a million workers, protested against their treatment.[83] The deportation allowed Lord Crewe a moment's private amusement with Viceroy Hardinge.[84] 'The rather startling action of the South African Government in placing the labour men on shipboard is going to arouse a sort of storm here, and Loulou [Lewis] Harcourt [Secretary of State for the Colonies] will have a lively time in the House of Commons. With you, on the contrary, the news ought to have a soothing effect; it can be argued that Gandhi and Polak have never been sent off to sea under the Jolly Roger; and that to be a white man is a positive disadvantage, unless one is prepared to sit still and make money. Quite seriously, I am disposed to ascribe the sweet reasonableness of the Union Ministers, at least to a certain extent, to the emergence of these bigger troubles; when a formidable gang of poachers is devastating your coverts, you cannot waste time over a labourer who is suspected of having snared a rabbit.' If Crewe was right, the South African government's decision not to deport Gandhi and some of his supporters, and Smuts's willingness to give some ground by establishing the commission of inquiry, may have been at least in part because he needed to concentrate on a larger enemy – the 'gang of poachers'.

Despite the pressures on Smuts, he granted Gandhi an appointment. On 8 January Gandhi travelled up to Pretoria. Always careful not to take advantage of an opponent's weakness, Gandhi assured the government that his *satyagraha* protests would be suspended until the railway strike was settled. The authorities were taken aback, but his stand won him friends in unexpected places. One of Smuts's secretaries candidly informed Gandhi: 'I do not like your people, and do not care to assist them at all. But what can I do? You help us in our days of need. How can we lay hands upon you? I often wish you took to violence like the English strikers, and then we would know at once how to dispose of you. But you will not injure even the enemy. You desire victory by self-suffering alone and never transgress your self-imposed limit of courtesy and chivalry. And this is what reduces us to sheer helplessness.'[85]

The appointment was postponed several times, as Smuts dealt with the strikes. It was only on 16 January that Smuts and Gandhi finally met. It would take a series of protracted negotiations, in which Andrews and Robertson participated, before a compromise agreement was hammered out. It was a long and complex process. The mediators went out of their way to try to resolve what had become as much a rupture between two men of steely resolve, as a division between the communities they represented. It was not easy going, and Gandhi received much criticism for his stubborn refusal to compromise.

Viceroy Hardinge, utterly frustrated by what he saw as Gandhi's intransigence, threatened to deal directly with the Botha government.[86] 'That the Indians have behaved themselves during the strikes in South Africa is indeed very satisfactory', he wrote to London, 'and I hope that it may be counted to them for righteousness. Robertson's influence should soon show itself, and if the Indian leaders prove recalcitrant the only course open, in my opinion, is to treat with the Union Government over the heads of the community. I am not sure that in many ways this will not be preferable, as Gandhi & Co. are likely to open their mouths too wide.'

\* \* \*

In the end Gandhi got a good deal of what he, and the Indian community, had been looking for.[87] The £3 tax on former indentured labourers would finally be scrapped. The marriage law would be amended to allow for traditional Indian marriages, except where they were polygamous, and these would neither be banned nor legalised. Immigration restrictions on Indians with a record of prior residence in South Africa would be eased.

Andrews wrote to Gokhale suggesting that Gandhi's time in South Africa was at an end.[88] It was time for Gandhi to return to India. 'His work in S. Africa is done – and nobly done: and this time it was very near to a collapse. Everyone here says he is "played out". Polak, Kallenbach,

Ritch, etc. – All say the same. He must go, both for his own sake and for the community's. Yes! For the community's: for if he stays on he will dwarf everyone else and there will be no leaders here for at least another generation ... He is one of the best men in the world! ... He has made the noblest fight that has been made for years, and I cannot bear to think that it should all end in some great and huge mistake made in haste ... but persisted in because of a mind distracted or outworn.'

With the Indians being gradually released from jail in batches, Gandhi accepted the advice of friends and began to make preparations to depart. The seemingly interminable conflict was moving to a conclusion, with an apparent victory for Gandhi.[89] In reality he had been forced to abandon several of his demands. Indians were still banned from entering the Orange Free State and restrictions against Indian immigration remained. Smuts described the result as constituting 'a complete and final settlement of the controversy', while Gandhi considered it the 'Magna Carta' of Indians, providing them with room to resolve their outstanding grievances.[90] Gandhi's critics were not as kind. One declared: 'The Indian community has materially gained nothing ... The whole of this so-called settlement presents the ugly look of a farce.'[91]

In March 1914 the commission reported, endorsing the Gandhi–Smuts compromise, and this was embodied in legislation. Gandhi spent June in Cape Town, lobbying ministers. Botha and Smuts steered the Bill through Parliament, carefully neutralising opposition. Gandhi had many farewells to make and was hailed by Indian communities around the country. Old friends, like W.P. Schreiner and Dr Abdurahman – as well as his close supporters in the Indian and white communities – paid him their respects. Finally, on 18 July Gandhi – in fulfilment of his long-held wish – left South Africa, to almost universal acclaim. Even Smuts, with whom he had so long been in conflict, was later to remark that 'It was my fate to be the antagonist of a man for whom I had the highest respect'.[92]

What had led to Gandhi's 'victory', limited though it was? It is not really possible to ascertain for certain why Smuts and the Union government decided to settle. Clearly, there was an accumulation of pressure from a variety of sources. The Imperial government had used its influence. There was the threat to the economy from the strikes by the indentured labourers and white railway workers. South African whites were distinctly nervous that there might be further trouble from the Zulu. And finally there was the quiet intervention of Emily Hobhouse, armed with the eyewitness accounts with which Betty Molteno had provided her.

Gandhi was also a supreme tactician and publicist. He had mobilised his supporters in Britain and across the Indian subcontinent. And his stream of letters, articles and statements meant that the whole English-speaking world was kept abreast of every twist and turn of the struggle, seen from Gandhi's point of view. His mixture of determination and sweet reasonableness was an extraordinary achievement. Gandhi knew when to compromise, and was always ready to settle for less than he had asked for, yet dress it up as a victory.

Smuts certainly found Gandhi the most difficult of opponents. As an early biographer of the General put it: 'Smuts understood force. He could deal with it. He had dealt with it. But passive resistance baffled him. It was so perplexingly resilient. He threatened Gandhi. But Gandhi remained calm and unruffled. He sent some Indians to prison. Gandhi led them into prison himself. Smuts then decided to compromise.'[93] Smuts himself, writing to Sir Benjamin Robertson, the Viceroy's representative, no doubt expressed the relief of many in the white community when he said: 'the saint has left our shores – I sincerely hope for ever.'[94]

Ten days after Gandhi's boat sailed, Austria declared war on Serbia following the assassination of Archduke Franz Ferdinand. For South Africans the battlefields of South West Africa and East Africa lay ahead, and then the trenches of Flanders. The world was about to be convulsed by a global conflict that would transform the certainties of the past.

# 11

# Aftermath: The road to war

While Gandhi was fighting Smuts for the rights of the Indian community, Africans were confronting new threats on two fronts. The first related to their employment on the mines. Vast quantities of cheap labour were needed by the mine owners. This was necessary because although the mines had plenty of gold ore it was buried deep in the earth and could only be mined by large numbers of labourers. So a two-pronged strategy was devised.[1] The Native Labour Regulation Act of 1911 was enacted to prevent African workers from deserting the mines. They could be traced to their homes and forced to return to work or be jailed. The second piece of legislation was the Natives Land Act of 1913, which outlawed sharecropping or African farming on 'white' land. It also prevented Africans purchasing land outside the reserves. Initially this left just 7.7 per cent of the country available for African farmers. In 1936 the reserves were finally increased to encompass 13.5 per cent of South Africa.[2]

J.B.M. Hertzog, the first Union Minister of Native Affairs, was the driving force behind the Land Act. A segregationist who looked to the southern United States for inspiration, Hertzog believed that the policy was vital for white South Africa. He thought it was not possible to deny black people the franchise in the long run and – just as importantly – he argued that it was vital that whites should continue to farm their own land. Ancient Rome and Greece had fallen, he argued, because they relied on freed slaves and did not do the work themselves. Whites would suffer the same fate if they left agriculture to African labourers and tenant farmers.[3] The aim of the legislation was to deprive Africans of the right to farm white land. Instead of being sharecroppers or tenants, they would be forced into paid employment. Farmers would have an ample source of cheap labour and any excess would be available for the mines. In backing the concept of 'Native reserves', the government was building on proposals drawn up by the South African Native Affairs Commission of 1903–5.

W.P. Schreiner, by this time a Union Senator, opposed the Bill, delivering two speeches against it.[4] He explained his opposition in terms of the message it sent to the black population: 'To the bulk of the people we are saying: "I lay it down as hard and fast law, ... there is no home for you except in a tiny portion of the country which is the only country open to you."' Schreiner's was an isolated voice and he made no headway; the Bill soon became law. When criticised by English-speakers some years later for establishing 'Native Reserves', Louis Botha pointed out angrily that 'the principles ... were originally passed by British citizens. I refer to the commission of 1903–1905 ... I say that the whole principle of territorial segregation came out of the head of [these] people.'[5] There was a good deal of truth in Botha's assertion. At the same time it was his government's decision to implement the proposals. The laws went a long way towards establishing a policy of segregation. Cheap wages, rigorously controlled labour and 'Native reserves' were the cornerstones of the new South Africa – policies that would, after 1948, culminate in apartheid.

The importance of the Land Act was immediately recognised by Sol Plaatje, the ANC's secretary-general. His summary of the impact the law had on African communities has echoed down the years: 'Awakening on Friday morning, June 20, 1913, the South African Native found himself not actually a slave, but a pariah in the land of his birth.'[6] Plaatje toured the country to assess the damage the legislation was inflicting. In the Free State he soon came across families driven from the farms they had worked, travelling on the roads in the hope of finding new homes. There were suggestions that some form of strike action should be used to fight the law, but this received little support in the ANC and was voted down.[7] In July 1913 the ANC president, John Dube, held discussions with his party about the best way forward. Plaatje had already written to Lord Gladstone, the Governor-General, asking him to withhold assent to the Bill. Gladstone had refused; he would not even meet the ANC to hear their views. Dube contacted the Anti-Slavery Society in London to seek

*Sol Plaatje, first secretary-general of the ANC, went round South Africa campaigning against the 1913 Land Act.*

their support. The Society was not encouraging, taking the view that the Land Act would protect Africans from further encroachment by whites on lands still in the hands of Africans.[8] The ANC decided, after much deliberation, to make further representations to the South African authorities. If these failed, they would take their case to London.[9]

Everyone, including W.P. Schreiner, counselled against sending another deputation to Britain. Dube himself was sceptical about its value, but what other options did he and his party have?[10] In the end Prime Minister Botha did meet them. He gave the ANC a hearing, but nothing more. 'If I went to Parliament with a Bill to amend the law,' he told the deputation, 'they will think I am mad.'[11]

There was nothing for it but to scrape together enough funds, hold a farewell public meeting in Cape Town and set off for Britain once more. The delegation's only real encouragement had come from a newly formed South African Society. Supported by W.P. Schreiner, Alice Greene and Betty Molteno, its aim was to 'promote the welfare of the native and Coloured Races'.[12]

John Dube led the deputation to London. Their aim, as Dube explained to Botha, would be to 'bring the facts of their grievances to the English public with a view to bringing influence to bear on the British government, and then lodging their protest through His Majesty's Ministers with the King, and asking the King to exercise his powers by disallowing the Act'.[13] They sailed on 16 May 1914. The group consisted of veterans of the 1909 deputation: Dube, Mapikela and Rubusana, together with Sol Plaatje and Saul Msane, another of the ANC's founding members.

In London the Anti-Slavery Society impressed on the deputation that they should say nothing in public, for fear of damaging the hearing they might receive from Lord Harcourt, then Secretary of State for the Colonies.[14] Reluctantly the ANC agreed. When the meeting with Harcourt finally took place at the end of June, it was clear he had no intention of intervening: South Africa was a self-governing country and Prime Minister Botha was held in high esteem, he informed them.

Sol Plaatje described their reception. 'Mr Harcourt made no notes and asked no questions at the interview accorded to our deputation. He listened to how desperately we resisted the passing of the law; how the Government ignored our representations, and those of all the churches and missionary bodies on our behalf; how we twice applied to Lord Gladstone for opportunities to inform him of the ruin which is wrought by the law among our people; how Lord Gladstone wrote in each instance saying it was "not within his constitutional functions," to see us. To all this Mr Harcourt replied with another "assurance of General Botha" that "we have not exhausted all remedies before coming to England".'[15] That was really the end of the matter, as far as the British were concerned: this was an internal South African affair.

Harcourt's response must have been deeply dispiriting, but the South Africans were not without support. The Anti-Slavery Society had given assistance of a kind: they helped Dube publish a pamphlet, outlining the achievements of his school, the Ohlange Institute.[16] Dube and his colleagues were warmly received by the Brotherhood, the Christian movement which the 1909 deputation had met in Cardiff. Jane Cobden, Sophie Colenso, both well-known 'friends of the Native', and the Liberal MP Sir Alfred Spicer organised receptions for them.[17] There were public meetings to speak at and newspapers to be interviewed by, but nothing was going to change the policies of the British government. Europe was on the brink of war and a deputation from a troublesome dominion was the last thing on the Imperial mind.

By mid-July Dube had returned to South Africa, leaving the rest of the deputation behind him, penniless. Rubusana and the others were perplexed by his sudden departure, as he had given them no explanation. It seems that Dube had been persuaded by the Anti-Slavery Society that his presence was required in southern Africa to deal with the land issue in Southern Rhodesia – a venture which finally led nowhere.[18] The rest of the deputation had to make their way home as best they could. Only Plaatje remained in Britain. In May 1916 he finally succeeded in publishing his major work, *Native Life in South Africa before and since the European War and the Boer Rebellion*. Exposing the iniquities Africans faced in the country, it was well received. The *Birmingham Post* commented that it made a serious case and described the issues it raised as 'disquieting'. 'Here at any rate is a book which makes the native agitation intelligible and may conceivably have an influence on future events in South Africa – and at home, for by no legal fiction can Imperial power dissociate itself from responsibility for Native affairs.'[19]

\*\*\*

Any hopes that black South Africans might have entertained that the British government would step up to its 'responsibilities for Native affairs' were misplaced. On 4 August 1914 Britain declared war with Germany and all attention was focused on the conflict. For the Botha government the decision to support Britain appeared to be a foregone conclusion. After all, Louis Botha and Jan Smuts had participated in Imperial Defence Conferences even before Union in 1910. The South African authorities were closely tied with those of the Empire. Churchill wrote that in 1913 Botha had returned from a visit to Germany warning that the situation was ominous. 'I can feel that there is danger in the air,' the General had warned Churchill. 'And what is more, when the day comes I am going to be ready too. When they attack you, I am going to attack German South-West Africa and clear them out once and for all.'[20]

When war was declared, the first response London received from Pretoria seemed promising. On 4 August the South African government offered to take over the duties of guarding their country, relieving the British garrison of the responsibility, so that they could be transferred elsewhere. On 7 August the Colonial Secretary, Lord Harcourt, accepted Botha's offer and enquired whether South African forces would seize ports in the neighbouring German colony of South West Africa.[21]

The South African cabinet met the same day to consider the request. Acceding to London's wishes was not going to be easy. There was opposition from many Afrikaners, who questioned why they should take up arms on behalf of their old enemy, especially since Germans had backed the Boer cause. Even within his own cabinet Botha encountered resistance. It took the Prime Minister three days of persuasion to achieve a unanimous vote in cabinet in favour of going to war – and even then only by promising that the army would be composed solely of volunteers. Outside government the opposition was led by Hertzog. He had refused to accept Botha's policy of reconciliation between English- and Afrikaans-speaking whites and had been excluded from the government. Then, in January 1914, he broke with Botha to form the National Party. While Hertzog accepted, as the government did, that as a dominion South Africa was effectively at war once Britain was involved, he considered this a technicality. Hertzog argued that it was the right of each dominion to decide whether it should actively participate in the conflict or not.[22] Many agreed with him, as Smuts accepted in private when he described what he called 'the people's genuine dislike of the German South-West African expedition'.[23]

When a rebellion broke out among Afrikaners opposed to the war, the government had its hands full trying to put it down. It was not until early 1915 that Botha could finally take up command of the South West Africa campaign and lead his troops into the territory. It took six months of hard fighting to force a German surrender, but in July 1915 this was achieved. With internal troubles behind him and South West Africa under his control, Botha could concentrate on playing a full part in the wider war.

Smuts was dispatched to lead the attack on German forces in Tanganyika (present-day Tanzania). White South African troops were also sent to join the war in Europe, dying in their thousands. More than 2,300 white soldiers were killed in the battle of Delville Wood alone. Disaster struck when more than 600 African volunteers, sent to dig trenches in France, were drowned after the SS *Mendi* was accidentally rammed off the Isle of Wight in February 1917. Oral history records that the poet and close ally of Tengo Jabavu, the Rev. Isaac Wauchope, comforted the men with these words: 'Be quiet and calm my countrymen, for what is taking place now is what you came here to do. We are all going to die, and that is what we came for. Brothers, we are drilling the

*Louis Botha sweeping the Germans out of South West Africa.*

death drill. I, a Zulu, say here and now that you are all my brothers …
Xhosas, Swazis, Pondos, Basotho and all others, let us die like warriors.
We are the sons of Africa. Raise your war cries, my brothers, for though
they made us leave our assegais back in the kraals, our voices are left
with our bodies.'[24] On hearing of the tragedy, Prime Minister Botha led
Parliament in standing to pay tribute to their courage and sacrifice.

\*\*\*

For South Africa's African and Coloured communities, the First World
War offered the same opportunity as the Boer War: a chance to show
their loyalty to their country and the British Crown.[25] On hearing of the
outbreak of conflict, the ANC halted its agitation against the 1913 Land
Act.[26] Sol Plaatje declared that Africans were keen to join up and 'proceed
to the front'. In October 1914 Walter Rubusana offered to raise a force
of 5,000 men. The Secretary of Defence's reply to Rubusana was brusque
to the point of rudeness.[27] 'The Government does not desire to avail itself
of the services in a combat capacity, of citizens not of European descent
in the present hostilities. Apart from other considerations the present
war is one which has its origins among white people of Europe, and the

Government is anxious to avoid the employment of coloured citizens in a warfare against whites.' Even though they were forbidden to carry arms, large numbers of Africans did participate, mostly as labourers. Some 74,000 Africans served in South West Africa, East Africa and France.[28]

The Coloured people were just as enthusiastic as the Africans. The APO of Dr Abdurahman was keen to help with the enlistment: 'By offering to bear our share of the responsibilities', said Abdurahman, Coloured men would prove themselves 'not less worthy than any other sons of the British Empire'.[29] Their offer was not rebuffed. While Africans were forbidden to carry weapons, Coloureds were not. In September 1915, the government decided to raise an infantry battalion, known as the Cape Corps. They were to see action in East Africa, Turkey, Egypt and Palestine.

The political parties representing Coloured and African people were not under any illusion that their show of patriotism would sweep away the racism and segregationist policies at home. In August 1914 the *APO* newspaper reminded its readers that 'whatever British liberty means in abstract, few of us can honestly say that we love it much in practice'.[30] But participating in the war did bring its rewards. As D.D.T. Jabavu concluded in 1920, 'the Native Labour Contingent ... has imported into this country a new sense of racial unity and amity quite unknown heretofore among our Bantu races. Common hardships in a common camp have brought them into close relation.'[31] Africans also noted their favourable treatment by French civilians and compared it with the racist behaviour of some of their own officers. 'The result is that there is amongst the diversified Bantu tribes of this land', Jabavu wrote, 'a tendency towards mutual respect and love founded upon the unhealthy basis of an anti-white sentiment.'

# 12

# Conclusion

By the time the First World War broke out, the political movements that would dominate South African political life during the twentieth century were mostly in place.[1] The Africans had the ANC, the Coloured people the APO, and Indians had their Congresses. Only the Communist Party of South Africa had yet to be formed. The Afrikaners were in firm control of the country, with a confident leader in Louis Botha. There were soon rifts within Afrikanerdom when Hertzog broke away to form the National Party, but Afrikaner control of the country's future would last for most of the rest of the century.

From the previous chapters six trends emerge.

Firstly, Britain had lost influence over the country that it had conquered at such cost during the Anglo-Boer War, just twelve years earlier. While outwardly supremely confident and powerful, London was less dominant than it appeared. There was the nagging worry that unless it tied its dominions firmly to itself, they might drift away and form alliances of their own, or even join the United States. White politicians in South Africa, Australia and Canada were prepared to co-operate with each other if they believed London was attempting to interfere in their domestic issues. They also looked favourably on the segregationist policies of the American South. Senior civil servants in London were worried. Charles Lucas in the Colonial Office described race as 'a question second to none in difficulty and importance' for the Empire: 'There is also to my mind a constant and serious danger that, if we do not take the initiative the

United States may stand out on and through this question as the leaders of the English-speaking peoples in the Pacific as against the coloured races. This is not my own view alone.'[2]

This was a real conundrum for the British: how to keep their dominions contented without the 'coloured races' revolting against Imperial rule. At the height of the crisis that resulted from the Gandhi–Smuts showdown in 1913, similar sentiments were expressed. The Indian Viceroy, Lord Hardinge, explained to the India Office the intense pressures Indians were exerting on him because their countrymen were being so foully treated in South Africa.[3] The resentment was bitter, and, as we have seen, Hardinge quoted an Indian as warning him that the day would come when the British would have to choose between her white dominions and India. A sense of fragmentation and possible Imperial decay was beginning to be evident.

These concerns arose at a time when the growth of the German navy and the superiority of the German army meant that Britain needed its dominions and colonies as never before. London knew that if there was to be a European war, it would require the Empire to provide it with men and materiel. In the circumstances there was little chance that the British government would have acceded to the pleas of Schreiner and his deputation in 1909. Even if racism had played no role in Britain's thinking, self-interest would have dictated that they fall in with the demands of the white South Africans, who had participated in Imperial Defence Conferences even before the country was a Union. The decision to support the white establishment brought its rewards: Louis Botha took the country into the First World War despite the opposition of many Afrikaners. The British could withdraw their South African garrison and leave the conquest of German South West Africa to Botha's forces. South African troops, black and white, went on to play an important role in East Africa, as well as on the Western Front and in Palestine.

At the same time the British liberals and the emerging left had been forced to reassess their understanding of southern Africa. Men like Labour's Keir Hardie had been solid 'Pro-Boers' during the Anglo-Boer War and he himself was a member of the 'War against War' committee.[4] For Hardie this was a question of principle; he supported the Boers, arguing that they were serving humanity in the struggle against capitalist imperialism.[5] 'This war is a capitalist war,' Hardie wrote. 'The British merchant hopes to secure markets for his goods, the investor an outlet for his capital, the speculator more fools out of which to make money, and the mining companies cheaper labour and increased dividends.'

It was only after the Boer War was over that Hardie and Ramsay MacDonald had an opportunity to travel to South Africa and see the situation for themselves. MacDonald did so quietly, but was convinced that many whites were racists and could not be trusted to treat their fellow citizens with anything like respect. London, he argued, should not trust the 'man on the spot'. Hardie was much more outspoken in Johannesburg and Pretoria, and as a result he was almost beaten up. These experiences convinced them – and, through them, the wider British left – that racism was deeply ingrained in South Africa. By the time the Schreiner deputation arrived in London in 1909, the Labour Party and radicals within the Liberal Party were there to welcome them. As Hardie put it, to leave Africans unrepresented in the new dispensation was like writing above the portals of the British Empire 'abandon hope all ye who enter here'.[6]

Nor was it just politicians who had their political perceptions altered. A number of influential British women, like Helen Clark, had been close to the Boer leaders. By the time the Jabavus – father and son – returned home, she had heard a rather different account of the country. This transformation would, in time, see a gradual but permanent shift in public opinion in favour of black, rather than white, South Africans. It was not fast in coming, but by the 1960s suggestions that whites were 'kith and kin' were unravelling as the Anti-Apartheid Movement got into its stride.

At the same time Smuts managed to maintain strong relations with a network of liberal-minded women, inside South Africa and abroad. These included some of the most progressive feminists of their age, like Emily Hobhouse, Olive Schreiner and Helen Clark.[7] These were women who were not inclined to entertain, let alone accept, the racist views and behaviour of anyone, let alone a senior politician. At times they were unflinching in their criticism. Yet they tolerated Smuts's opinions and continued a friendship with him that endured down the years. 'The passions which drew these women to Smuts', as an historian has commented, 'are well nigh impossible to unravel.'[8]

Secondly, the Afrikaners were clearly in the ascendancy. They had recovered remarkably swiftly from the terrible suffering that had been inflicted on them during the Boer War. The prisoners of war had been brought home and the farms rebuilt. Even the mines had been brought back to life – largely thanks to Chinese indentured labour. Of course, many Afrikaners remained impoverished by the conflict and the cattle diseases that swept the country, providing the bedrock of the 'poor white' problem that was to haunt the country in the coming years. But as a people they were back on their feet. They had the confidence to establish the organisations that were to form the building blocks of Afrikaner power. These ranged from Sanlam (founded in 1918 to provide insurance) to the Broederbond (established in 1920 to provide clandestine political leadership). Botha and Smuts were keen to reach a compromise with their English-speaking white compatriots. They established a process of reconciliation that was – largely – successful. Certainly, the British had been won over by Botha's magnanimity. One only needs to think of the rapturous reception with which the press greeted his taking his seat on the steps of the throne in the House of Lords to see that this was so.

There was another strand to Afrikaner politics, which was represented by J.B.M. Hertzog. It was one that remained deeply distrustful of British intentions. Hertzog was determined to ensure South Africa's complete sovereignty, an issue discussed at a series of Imperial Conferences. One, held in 1917 while the First World War still raged, passed what was known as Resolution IX dealing with the existing and future government of Empire. Smuts had had a considerable role in its drafting.[9] The resolution called for 'the readjustment of the constitutional relations of the component parts of the Empire' as soon as possible after the war. It went on to suggest that what was required was new relations between the different parts of the Empire which, 'while thoroughly preserving all existing powers of self-government and complete control of domestic affairs, should be based upon a full recognition of the Dominions as autonomous nations of an Imperial Commonwealth'.

In 1924 Hertzog won the South African election and became Prime Minister. He attended the 1926 London Imperial Conference and demanded complete autonomy for the country. By the time Hertzog sailed for home he could claim victory.[10] 'No declaration could be devised', Hertzog said on his return to Cape Town, 'by which the country's liberty in a most unlimited manner could be so clearly demonstrated as was done in the document as it stood. No one need bother in future about South Africa breaking away from the Empire. As a result of the Imperial Conference, the old Empire no longer exists. The old Empire was a domination of States under which South Africa and other Dominions had to, and did, submit for years. All that remains is a free alliance of

*Prime Minister Louis Botha (standing, right) at the Imperial Defence Conference in London, 1911.*

England and the six Dominions, co-operating as friends and, so to speak, forming their own League of Nations.'

At home Hertzog's aim was to deprive black South Africans of the vote. On becoming Prime Minister he wasted little time in making his views known. He introduced a 'civilised labour policy', reserving jobs in a number of areas for whites. In 1925 he attended (for the first and only occasion) the annual conference held by the white Native Affairs Commission with African chiefs and other prominent black figures. Hertzog spelt out why he was seeking to strip them of the Cape franchise: 'It is clear that the arrangement which was come to in 1909 was only a compromise. Now we must accept it as a fact that the European portion of our population is against the enfranchisement of the Natives on the same basis as themselves. The European feels, quite rightly, that the right to vote is the fruit of centuries of civilized government and that he is the result and heir of a civilization in which the Native does not share.'[11] As we shall see, Hertzog's ambition, although not immediately realised, was finally attained.

Thirdly, by 1914 major African and Coloured organisations – the

ANC and APO – had come into being and begun to establish themselves. In itself this was a real achievement. At the same time they failed to build on the non-racial unity and solidarity that had been established in London in 1909. Members of both parties had worked closely together during the Schreiner deputation over many weeks. They had travelled to and from London and had plenty of opportunity to discuss their country's politics on board ship and then co-operate during the campaign. Yet this bond was not translated into a permanent political organisation. There was certainly mutual support, but the parties did not manage to combine their activities or their organisations to resist the rising tide of racism.

This was not because African and Coloured political leaders did not understand the need for unity. Dr Abdurahman, giving his presidential address to the APO conference in April 1910, said, 'We have a deep interest in the native races of South Africa, and the Union Act of South Africa puts us all into one fold.'[12] His words had been well received. Walter Rubusana was a guest at the conference and was warmly welcomed. He supported what Dr Abdurahman had said. Rubusana was reported as having 'expressed his conviction that there should be more co-operation between the native and coloured people of the country. He instanced the native labour question as one which could be solved very soon by such united action.' As the APO's own newspaper put it, 'The interests of all non-whites are identical. That lesson has been relentlessly driven home in the hearts and minds; and it will not be long ere the coloured races learn the increased power they have acquired by their fusion into one undivided and indivisible people.'[13]

Despite these positive declarations, little concrete action was taken. The establishment of the ANC in 1912 did not result in the development of a wider unity of all those opposed to racial domination, irrespective of their colour. That would take much longer. Co-operation did gradually increase and was given added urgency as the threat to remove the franchise increased. The All-African Convention was formed in the 1930s to 'co-ordinate the activities and struggles of all African organizations in their fight against oppression and as a mouthpiece for the African people'.[14] Dr Abdurahman and the APO participated. But relations between Africans, Coloureds and Indians would only really be cemented during the Defiance Campaign of the 1950s. It took until 1969 for the ANC to finally open its ranks to all South Africans, irrespective of race, at a conference held in exile in Morogoro, in Tanzania. As the party itself now explains, it was at this conference that 'the non-racial character of the ANC was further consolidated by the opening up of the ANC membership to non-Africans'.[15]

This is not to suggest that an iron wall was erected between the ANC and other movements. The new party did attempt to build relations with other like-minded organisations. In March 1912 Sol Plaatje went to Cape Town to organise meetings with government ministers. He took the opportunity to visit Dr Abdurahman and discuss the possibility of co-operation between the two parties.[16] Plaatje arranged a meeting of the executive of the ANC and the APO at the APO's offices in Loop Street. The two organisations agreed that 'there should be closer co-operation between the Coloured and Native races of South Africa'. They would 'keep in touch with each other', discuss issues of mutual interest and 'where necessary take united action'.[17] Nothing more permanent was suggested. Perhaps resistance from within the Coloured community would have prevented this development. The APO had its competitors for the community's support and Dr Abdurahman would have been aware of this.

The emergence of the ANC was also applauded by Gandhi, who had hitherto shown only limited interest in African politics. He used his paper, *Indian Opinion*, to welcome the founding of the party.[18] 'Our friend and neighbour, the Rev. John L. Dube, the Principal of the Ohlange Native Industrial School,' he wrote, 'has received the high honour of being elected the first president of the newly inaugurated Inter-State Native Congress. Mr Dube has issued a manifesto so good that we regret we cannot find sufficient space for it.' The foundation for friendly relations between the ANC and the two most important Coloured and Indian movements had been established – but nothing more formal than that. Each movement ploughed its own furrow, fighting for the rights of its own community.[19]

Perhaps the parties were still in their infancy and needed time to consolidate their positions before looking for broader alliances. Each represented sections of society that had, in reality, rather different interests and agendas. The discrimination they faced was a uniting factor, but none was then to know the lengths to which it would be taken in the future. Nonetheless, the founding of the ANC was a vitally important development. It had brought Africans together as never before, even though ethnic identities remained strong and the national organisation remained weak.[20] The APO welcomed the founding of the organisation, saying that it would allow greater Coloured–African co-operation in political matters.[21] *Indian Opinion*'s headline captured the moment, in the language of the day. It was, as Gandhi put it, 'The Awakening of the Natives'.[22] Gandhi was right: the creation of the ANC marked the founding of the party that would play the decisive role in the attack on racism and the ending of apartheid.

This brings us to the fourth trend that is evident from this period: the moderation and deference of the black leadership. Despite the growing threat from the newly installed Union government, the organisations representing the African and Coloured populations remained essentially conservative. The APO and ANC were movements built by and speaking for the elite of their communities. Although their rhetoric might sometimes be powerful and even radical, there were few attempts to confront the authorities. This led to key opportunities for protest being lost. If a more vigorous, confident and united strategy had been adopted, the assault on their rights might have been more successfully resisted. This is, of course, speculation. As has been observed, these early organisations shared a 'reliance on deputations and appeals to morality and Cape and British liberal ideals'.[23]

This was really no longer a way forward. After 1909 they were not dealing with the British colonial administration, which was open to liberal pressures from London; they were confronting far more implacable local white politicians. Petitions and deputations were no longer effective. Yet the suggestion that civil disobedience would be more fruitful had gone unheeded. Gandhi made the point to Dr Abdurahman in his letter of 23 August 1909, but the advice appears to have been largely forgotten or ignored. As Gandhi had warned at the time, if the opposition continued on this path their movements would be 'as good as dead'. As he put it, 'The days are past, so it seems, when something could be gained by making speeches.'[24] Gandhi himself was about to put an alternative to the test: the belief that the path of non-violent protest would prove a more effective lever to prise rights from the government.

Having said this, it is important to point to an observation made by Dube about Gandhi's non-violent resistance strategy. During the 1913–14 campaign Dube was in an excellent position to gauge the effectiveness of Gandhi's modus operandi. Dube lived very close to Gandhi's Phoenix settlement and visited his campaign headquarters in Durban. Dube's paper, *Ilanga*, reported the strikes, ending a commentary with a Zulu expression meaning 'Go for it, Gandhi!'[25]

Dube told a visitor from India, 'After being an eye witness to the struggle, instead of taking the Indian workers as uncivilised and treating them disdainfully, I have acquired a sense of respect for all Indians.'[26] At the same time Dube laid out precisely why he thought Gandhi's methods could not be used in the ANC campaigns.[27] Indians, he believed, 'could display extraordinary endurance. If our Natives come in their place, nobody can control their violent nature. For their safety they would certainly retaliate. The white men of this place require only this much. If any brother of mine kills a white man after being excited, it would precipitate a great disaster upon us. Thousands of brothers of mine would be put to death in no time and we would be totally ruined. We do not possess so much prowess also to wage a *satyagraha* struggle. Only the strength of the Indians can endure it.' With the evidence of the vicious retaliation by whites following the Bambatha Rebellion, who could disagree with this assessment?

While these parties were taking shape, the first stirrings of another movement were beginning to be evident: black trade unionism. As we have seen, Alfred Mangena had been active among dock workers before leaving for England in 1901.[28] And the Cape Town dockers continued to make their presence felt: in 1919 they formed the backbone of the Industrial and Commercial Workers' Union, organised by Clements Kadalie.[29] Nor were they alone. The shortage of white labour during the First World War led to rising demand for Coloured labour in the Cape.[30] Dr Abdurahman encouraged Coloured workers to establish their own, separate unions, with the APO even forming its own Federation of Labour.[31] Other artisanal unions took the opposite policy, encouraging Coloured and white workers to join the same organisations. In 1917 white members of the International Socialist League joined with the Transvaal Native Congress (the least conservative of the ANC provincial organisations) and attempted to form an industrial union.[32] These were small beginnings, but from them would come – in time – powerful, militant movements. Theirs was not a tradition of deputations and petitions; strikes and protests were in their bloodstream. This trend was reinforced by the Transvaal Native Congress, which attempted forms of resistance against the pass laws just after the First World War.[33] White vigilantes and the police broke up these protests, but they were an indication that a small section of African society was prepared to break with the dominant liberal paradigm of their leaders.[34]

Fifthly, it is clear that Gandhi succeeded (at least in some of his aims) because he really understood how power operated. He knew just how the Empire worked and which elements might be mobilised to serve his cause. The legal skills he had acquired in Britain and honed in South Africa allowed him to confront the authorities in general, and Smuts in particular, on equal terms. He understood how the official mind worked and was able to play on the sentiments and values of the British upper class. While black lawyers like Mangena, Richard Msimang and Pixley Seme all had a legal background like Gandhi, none had yet the experience Gandhi had accumulated since the 1890s. Gandhi also appreciated the importance of India to the British and the need to mobilise support across the world. His decision to send one of his key white associates, Henry Polak, to spread his message in India and mobilise the support of the Indian population in 1909 and 1913, was vitally important. Polak was important in raising pressure on the British in general and on the Indian Viceroy in particular. This was, of course, a lever on London that was not available to African and Coloured leaders.

His relationship with Polak underlines another of Gandhi's strengths: his ability to work across the colour bar. Polak was among a string of whites who were his passionate supporters and advocates. Gandhi also had close relations with Coloured families in the Cape, including the Abdurahmans and the Gools, with whom he stayed.[35] This warmth was reciprocated. Dr Abdurahman's APO established an Indian Passive Resistance Fund to back Gandhi's campaigns.[36] Gandhi's relations with Africans were more difficult and more complex, as has already been mentioned. His language until late in his time in South Africa could be racist and his attitude dismissive. It should, however, be noted that Africans – and the ANC leadership in particular – were not always complimentary about the Indians in their midst. John Dube, for example, frequently criticised Indians for encroaching on his people's land. As late as 1912 he told a large gathering of Zulu chiefs that 'people like coolies have come to our land and lorded it over us, as though we, who belong to the country, are mere nonentities'.[37] As suggested earlier, this attitude mellowed, especially following Gandhi's campaign of 1913–14, when the two leaders became considerably closer to each other.[38]

Gandhi also had an extraordinary ability to use the media – from his own paper, *Indian Opinion*, to his interviews, letters and articles for other publications. His output was truly astonishing. Few have ever matched his energy and intellectual agility. It gave him a global prominence and recognition. Finally, there was the importance of the British India Committee, established by the Congress Party in 1889. It may have been a plodding, bureaucratic body, but it offered a permanent presence in London. Together with influential British Asians, including the MPs Dadabhai Naoroji and Mancherjee Bhownagree, they provided Gandhi with a solid base of support from which to work. By contrast, every African and Coloured deputation that arrived in Britain in the late nineteenth and early twentieth century had to begin building a support base anew. There had been at least four missions to England by 1894.[39] Others followed in 1906, 1909 and 1914. Yet all failed to establish a permanent presence in Britain. They had to rely instead on personal contacts with 'friends of the natives' like the Colenso family. These factors, taken together, provide the background to Gandhi's success.

Sixth was the black leadership's persistent belief that the British Crown would come to their rescue. This faith underpinned many of their decisions. A large number of black South Africans were strong supporters of Empire, at least until the First World War. Today this may seem anachronistic, yet these leaders of African and Coloured opinion were among the ablest of their generation. So what explains their attitude? It is true that their loyalty was cultivated by the Imperial power through schooling, sport and royal tours. As the ANC president, John Dube, put it in 1907, 'loyalty to the Throne' was 'one of the fundamental principles of education'.[40] In 1912 he called on the ANC to adopt a policy of 'deep and dutiful respect for the rulers God has placed over us'.

At the same time this was more than just the result of pomp and circumstance paraded before gullible subjects. The warmth many felt for the British was probably the result of a combination of factors. They valued the education they received from the missionaries. The lesson this education had taught them – that a polite, well-drafted request or petition could change official policy – was a powerful one. In some circumstances it could produce results. It failed when the issues they raised clashed with interests that were central to British concerns: such as improving relations with white South Africans in general, and Afrikaners in particular. Only on the question of the Protectorates did London hold out against the South African white politicians – and even then this was as much the result of concerns about the possibility of Basotho military resistance as a sense of duty to their black subjects.

When confronted with the looming threat posed by the First World War, the British authorities felt they had little option but to ignore appeals from South Africa's black population, no matter how well delivered or persuasive they were. Yet the lessons that leaders like Dube had received were so deeply inculcated that it was quite impossible for many in the African and Coloured leadership of that generation to abandon them. It would be years before it became self-evident that this approach was a dead end. Others – outside the ANC – understood this earlier, with the Industrial and Commercial Workers' Union becoming a vigorous force in the mid-1920s, before it went into decline.

An important moment was reached in 1936. The Cape's non-racial vote had been under attack from the Hertzog government for years. Now the franchise was finally being removed from the African people. A promise of royal protection had been delivered with clarity on 16 August 1909 in the British Parliament by no lesser figure than the Prime Minister, Asquith, at the end of the Union debate.[41] As he had assured the public, any attempt to remove African rights would be 'bound to be reserved for the assent of the Crown at home'.

Whites might have forgotten this undertaking, but Africans had not. When the issue of removing the Cape 'native suffrage' was first being debated, D.D.T. Jabavu and Walter Rubusana went before a South African parliamentary committee.[42] They described the 'memorable speeches' made by Asquith. It was in this context, they argued, that 'King Edward VII took the extraordinary step of preserving the right of the Cape Native franchise against future dispossession in his "Letters of Instruction" to all future Governors-General'. They looked to Britain and the King for protection, but none was forthcoming. Their protests were ignored. In reality the royal prerogative was only ever going to be exercised on the advice of the South African (and not the British) government.[43] On 6 April 1936 Hertzog finally persuaded his Parliament to abolish the Cape franchise – to the loud cheers of the white MPs.[44] For the first time since 1853, Africans across South Africa could no longer vote. After a battle of ten years Hertzog had finally managed to abolish the rights Africans had held, at least in the Cape, since that time and offered instead a limited number of 'Native Representatives' – white politicians entrusted to represent Africans – throughout the Union. In the end the assurances that Asquith had given had proved to be worthless.

It was a tragic end to this sorry process. Race had not always been the motivating factor in deciding these issues: all parties – from the British authorities to the various South African ethnic groups – defended their interests tenaciously. It is evident that the denial of the vote to Africans, and later Coloured and Indian South Africans, was to deform the country's politics and then its society. Racism was the great curse that hung over its people. It was a fate that Olive Schreiner had foreseen all those years earlier when she wrote: 'South Africa must be a free man's country. The idea that a man born in this country, possibly endowed with many gifts and highly cultured, should in this, his native land, be refused any form of civic or political right on the ground that he is descended from a race with a civilisation, it may be, much older than our own, is one which must be abhorrent to every liberalised mind. I believe that an attempt to base our national life on distinctions of race and colour, as such, will, after the lapse of many years, prove fatal to us.'[45]

# Appendix
## Franchise timeline

| | Event | Outcome |
|---|---|---|
| 1836 | Cape municipal boards created | Men of property and income given the vote, irrespective of race |
| 1853 | Cape Parliament established with a non-racial franchise | Men of property and income acquired the vote, irrespective of race |
| 1854 | Orange Free State established by the Bloemfontein Convention | White men can vote |
| 1856 | Charter of Natal | Men of property and income can vote, irrespective of race |
| 1858 | Transvaal constitution | White men can vote |
| 1865 | Natal Law no. 11 | African men can only vote if registered by the Lt Governor following a petition; as a result, almost all Africans excluded from franchise |
| 1887 | Parliamentary Voters Registration Act passed by Cape Parliament | Vote extended to the newly incorporated territories of the Transkei, but land held under communal or tribal title was not to be counted as part of the property franchise qualification |
| 1892 | Franchise and Ballot Act passed in the Cape | This raised the property and income requirement for the vote, and also introduced an educational qualification; affected many African and Coloured voters |
| 1894 | Franchise Amendment Bill passed in Natal | The franchise for Asians limited to those who were registered prior to 1893 |
| 1909 | South African National Convention | White politicians decided that only white men would vote in the new Union, except in the Cape where the existing franchise was maintained |
| 1910 | Union of South Africa established | Race entrenched in the South African constitution: only white men could stand for Parliament |

| | | |
|---|---|---|
| 1920 | Native Affairs Act | Local advisory councils established for Africans |
| 1926 | General Hertzog introduced four 'Native Bills' | Provided for abolition of Cape African franchise and for representation by seven white MPs; bill halted |
| 1929 | Parliamentary Select Committee proposed new Native Representation Bill | Provided for two white senators and a further two after 10 years; Cape Africans to retain franchise but on separate roll; bill failed to obtain two-thirds majority |
| 1930 | White women granted unqualified franchise | African vote devalued, as no African women were given the vote |
| 1935 | Parliamentary Select Committee recommended abolition of African representation in House of Assembly, but retaining four white senators | All African Convention met to oppose the bill |
| 1936 | Representation of Natives Act passed by two-thirds majority | Cape Africans lost the vote; instead, they were to be represented by three white MPs ('native representatives') and four white senators; an advisory Native Representative Council formed |
| 1946 | Native Representative Council adjourned in protest | |
| 1951 | Native Representative Council abolished | |
| 1956 | Separate Representation of Voters Act | Coloured voters removed from common roll and allowed to elect one white senator and four white MPs |
| 1959 | Promotion of Bantu Self-Government Act passed and Representation of Natives Act repealed | African representation in parliament entirely abolished |
| 1968 | Coloured Persons' Representative Council Act | Coloured representation in Parliament abolished; a Coloured Persons' Representative Council established |
| 1970 | Bantu Homeland Citizenship Act | Africans given right to vote in nominally independent 'homelands' |
| 1983 | Tricameral Parliament established | Coloureds and Indians given separate chambers in white-dominated Parliament |
| 1994 | End of apartheid, new constitution | All adult South Africans given the vote in an unqualified franchise |

*Source*: C.M. Tatz, *Shadow and Substance in South Africa: A Study of Land and Franchise Policies Affecting Africans, 1910–1960*, University of Natal Press, Pietermaritzburg, 1962; Tom Lodge, Denis Kadima and David Pottie (eds.), *Compendium of Elections in Southern Africa*, Election Institute of Southern Africa, Auckland Park, 2002.

# Notes

**Chapter 1**

1 This description is from the *Cape Times*, 24 June 1909.

2 www.unioncastlestaffregister.co.uk/SHIP_KENILWORTH_CASTLE_%282%29_01.html.

3 *Cape Times*, 16 June 1909.

4 The 1910 Union constitution gave Parliament considerable leeway in determining who was granted the vote, subject to the proviso that in the Cape it should not be removed from any man on the grounds of race without a two-thirds vote of a joint sitting of both Houses of Parliament.

5 *Cape Times*, 1 July 1909.

6 Not all of the black delegates departed on this voyage. John Dube, for reasons that will be clear later, was not on the *Kenilworth Castle*. He left Cape Town for London on 7 July 1909. Heather Hughes, *First President: A Life of John L. Dube, Founding President of the ANC*, Jacana Media, Auckland Park, 2011, p. 151.

7 *Cape Times*, 1 July 1909.

8 E. Walker, *W.P. Schreiner: A South African*, Central News Agency, Johannesburg, 1937, p. 12.

9 Ibid., p. 148.

10 André Odendaal, *The Founders: The Origins of the ANC and the Struggle for Democracy in South Africa*, Jacana, Auckland Park, 2012, p. 408.

11 Walker, *W.P. Schreiner*, p. 165. W.P. Schreiner had already sailed for London, leaving on 16 June with his wife.

12 Schreiner and Gandhi were members of London's Inner Temple, while Smuts was at the Middle Temple. Walker, *W.P. Schreiner*, p. 12; J.C. Smuts, *Jan Christian Smuts*, Cassell, London, 1952, p. 23; Ramachandra Guha, *Gandhi before India*, Allen Lane, London, 2013, p. 46.

13 *Cape Times*, 16 June 1909.

14 Karel Schoeman, *Only an Anguish to Live Here: Olive Schreiner and the Anglo-Boer War, 1899–1902*, Human and Rousseau, Cape Town, 1992, p. 6.

15 *Cardiff Times and South Wales Weekly*, 20 September 1909.

16 Olive Schreiner to Abdullah Abdurahman, 9 April 1909, UCT Manuscripts and

212

Archives, BC16 Box 4 File 2/1909/21.

17 *The Collected Works of Mahatma Gandhi*, Indian Government, New Delhi, 1999, vol. 9, p. 287.

18 Olive Schreiner, *Closer Union: A Letter on the South African Union and the Principles of Government*, 22 December 1908, http://webapp1.dlib.indiana.edu/vwwp/view?docId=VAB7036&doc.view=print.

19 Ibid., p. 18.

20 Olive Schreiner to W.P. Schreiner, 9 April 1909, UCT Manuscripts and Archives, BC16 Box 4 File 2/1909/20.

21 In 1912 the organisation was called the South African Native National Congress, becoming the African National Congress in 1923.

22 Mohandas Gandhi, *Satyagraha in South Africa*, in *Collected Works*, vol. 34, 1928, ch. 5, p. 30.

23 W.E.B. Du Bois, *The Souls of Black Folk*, A.C. McClurg, Chicago, 1903.

24 See, for example, Jack and Ray Simons, *Class and Colour in South Africa, 1850–1950*, IDAF, London, 1983 [1969].

25 I am indebted to Richard Rathbone for this insight.

## Chapter 2

1 This was the era of male suffrage and the right was not extended to women, but this was almost universally the case and South Africa was no exception.

2 The Natal Parliament passed a law in 1896 by which men should not be entitled to register as voters 'who (not being of European origin) are Natives or descendants in the male line of Natives of countries, which have hitherto possessed the electoral franchise, unless they first obtain an order from the Governor in Council exempting from the operation of the Act'. *Report of Commission of Inquiry Regarding Cape Coloured Population of the Union*, U.G.54–1937, Government Printer, Pretoria, 1937, p. 217, par. 1066.

3 Ibid., p. 213, par. 1034.

4 Stanley Trapido, 'The friends of the natives: merchants, peasants and the political and ideological structure of liberalism in the Cape, 1854–1910', in Shula Marks and Anthony Atmore (eds.), *Economy and Society in Pre-industrial South Africa*, Longman, London, 1980, p. 262.

5 André Odendaal, *The Founders: The Origins of the ANC and the Struggle for Democracy in South Africa*, Jacana, Auckland Park, 2012, p. 33.

6 Ibid., p. 34.

7 Brian Willan, *Sol Plaatje: South African Nationalist, 1876–1932*, University of California Press, Berkeley, 1984, p. 21.

8 Heather Hughes, *First President: A Life of John L. Dube, Founding President of the ANC*, Jacana Media, Auckland Park, 2011, pp. 30–40.

9 Odendaal, *The Founders*, p. 29.

10 Ibid., p. 35.

11 Ibid., pp. 56–57.

12 Ibid., p. 58.

13 Ibid., p. 74.

14 Ibid., p. 103.

15 Ibid., p. 104.

16 Ibid., p. 38.

17 Ibid., p. 39.

18 Ibid., p. 98.

19 Ibid., p. 99.

20 Ibid., p. 96.

21 Ibid., p. 100.
22 Ibid., pp. 43–44. The poem was published in *Isigidimi* in June 1882. Hoho was a reference to the mountain refuge from which Chief Sandile resisted the British, before being killed in 1878.
23 Ibid., p. 114.
24 Ibid., p. 119.
25 Ibid., p. 122.
26 Ibid., pp. 124–125.
27 Ibid., p. 126.
28 Bernard Magubane, *The Making of a Racist State: British Imperialism and the Union of South Africa, 1875–1910*, Africa World Press, Trenton, 1996, p. 108.
29 G.W. Eybers, *Selected Constitutional Documents Illustrating South African History, 1795–1910,* George Routledge and Sons, London, 1918, pp. 73–74.
30 Odendaal, *The Founders*, p. 130.
31 Ibid., p. 195.
32 Ibid., p. 200.
33 T.R.H. Davenport, *South Africa, a Modern History*, University of Toronto Press, Toronto, 1987, p. 65. More recently, this interpretation has been questioned, with suggestions that the Mfengu (far from being refugees from the Zulu wars) were nearly all Xhosa who were captured by British and colonial forces in the 1835 frontier war, and carted off to the colony as a labour force. See J. Cobbing, 'The Mfecane as alibi: thoughts on Dithakong and Mbolompo', *Journal of African History*, 29 (1988), pp. 513–514; A.C. Webster, 'Ayliff, Whiteside, and the Fingo "emancipation" of 1835: a reappraisal', BA Honours essay, Rhodes University, 1988, quoted in Richard Bouch, 'The Mfengu revisited: the 19th century experience of one Mfengu community through the eyes of historians and contemporaries', Institute of Commonwealth Studies, University of London, 1990.
34 www.sahistory.org.za/people/dr-walter-benson-rubusana.
35 Odendaal, *The Founders*, p. 141.
36 Ibid., p. 145.
37 Ibid., p. 459.
38 Robert I. Rotberg, *The Founder: Cecil Rhodes and the Pursuit of Power*, Oxford University Press, Oxford, 1988, p. 603.
39 Gavin Lewis, *Between the Wire and the Wall: A History of South African 'Coloured' Politics*, David Philip, Cape Town, 1987, p. 11.
40 Again, this is not universally true. Men like Dr Abdurahman were 'Malays', most of whom were Muslim.
41 Richard van der Ross, 'A political and social history of the Cape Coloured people, 1880–1970', PhD thesis, University of Cape Town, 1973, p. 11.
42 Lewis, *Between the Wire and the Wall*, p. 10.
43 The Progressive Party was beaten by the Afrikaner Bond. It must have come as a bitter personal blow for Rhodes that his old friend W.P. Schreiner was the Bond's choice of Prime Minister, even though he was not a Bondsman himself.
44 Van der Ross, 'A political and social history', p. 13.
45 *Cape Argus*, 1898, quoted in ibid., p. 44.
46 Rotberg, *The Founder*, p. 611.
47 Chinese were also classified as 'Asian' but they were small in number.
48 Ramachandra Guha, *Gandhi before India*, Penguin Books, London, 2013, p. 66.
49 Ibid., p. 66.
50 Ibid., p. 72.
51 Ibid., p. 77.
52 Davenport, *South Africa*, p. 117.

53 Tom Lodge, Denis Kadima and David Pottie (eds.), *Compendium of Elections in Southern Africa*, Election Institute of Southern Africa, Auckland Park, 2002, p. 292.
54 E.H. Brookes, *The History of Native Policy in South Africa from 1830 to the Present Day*, J.L. van Schaik, Pretoria, 1927, quoted in C.M. Tatz, *Shadow and Substance in South Africa: A Study of Land and Franchise Policies Affecting Africans, 1910–1960*, University of Natal Press, Pietermaritzburg, 1962, p. 4.
55 Tatz, *Shadow and Substance*, p. 4.
56 Guha, *Gandhi before India*, p. 126.
57 Ibid., pp. 126–127.
58 Gandhi continued to demand that Indians should be treated as equal members of the Empire throughout his period in South Africa. In November 1909, for example, he attacked Smuts for failing to introduce a non-racial law in the Transvaal. This – he argued – 'cuts at the very root' of the principle of 'elementary equality' of all British subjects. Ibid., p. 356.
59 Ibid., p. 132.
60 Ibid., p. 133.
61 Ibid., p. 133.

**Chapter 3**

1 Thomas Pakenham, *The Boer War*, Random House, New York, 1979, p. xv.
2 See J.S. Marais, *The Fall of Kruger's Republic*, Oxford University Press, Oxford, 1961, pp. 1–3 for a discussion of this issue.
3 Hermann Giliomee and Bernard Mbenga, *New History of South Africa*, Tafelberg, Cape Town, 2007, p. 211. In 1897 the British decided to increase the garrison in South Africa to 8,000 men and 24 field guns. G.H.L. Le May, *British Supremacy in South Africa, 1899–1907*, Clarendon Press, Oxford, 1965, p. 6.
4 Dennis Judd and Keith Surridge, *The Boer War*, John Murray, London, 2002, pp. 91–92.
5 Arthur Davey, *The British Pro-Boers, 1877–1902*, Tafelberg, Cape Town, 1978, p. 61.
6 Judd and Surridge, *The Boer War*, p. 60.
7 Hermann Giliomee, *The Afrikaners: Biography of a People*, Hurst, London, 2003, p. 252.
8 Judd and Surridge, *The Boer War*, p. 191.
9 Ibid., p. 193.
10 Giliomee, *The Afrikaners*, p. 255.
11 Ibid., p. 256.
12 G.B. Pyrah, *Imperial Policy and South Africa, 1902–1910*, Oxford University Press, London, 1955, p. 53.
13 Giliomee, *The Afrikaners*, pp. 260–262.
14 Pyrah, *Imperial Policy*, p. 91; Judd and Surridge, *The Boer War*, p. 203; Cecil Headlam, *The Milner Papers: South Africa 1897–1899*, Cassell, London, 1933, vol. 2, p. 212.
15 Pyrah, *Imperial Policy*, p. 90.
16 Judd and Surridge, *The Boer War*, p. 204.
17 Marilyn Lake and Henry Reynolds, *Drawing the Global Colour Line: White Men's Countries and the Question of Racial Equality*, Cambridge University Press, Cambridge, 2008, p. 212.
18 Le May, *British Supremacy*, p. 77.
19 André Wessels (ed.), *Lord Kitchener and the War in South Africa, 1899–1902*, Sutton Publishing for the Army Records Society, Stroud, 2006, p. 197.
20 Judd and Surridge, *The Boer War*, p. 149.

21 W.K. Hancock, *Smuts, the Sanguine Years: 1870–1919*, Cambridge University Press, Cambridge, 1962, p. 159.

22 Hancock, *Smuts*, Ibid., p. 159.

23 Judd and Surridge, *The Boer War*, p. 291.

24 Ibid., p. 161.

25 Judd and Surridge, *The Boer War*, p. 296.

26 Pakenham, *The Boer War*, p. 564.

27 Ibid., pp. 564–565.

28 Ibid., p. 565.

29 Geoffrey Searle, '"National efficiency" and the "lessons" of the war', in David Omissi and Andrew S. Thompson (eds.), *The Impact of the South African War*, Palgrave, Basingstoke, 2002, p. 204.

30 Calculated using http://safalra.com/other/historical-uk-inflation-price-conversion/.

31 Searle, 'National efficiency', p. 205.

32 Pyrah, *Imperial Policy*, pp. 41ff.

33 Ibid., p. 78.

34 Pakenham, *The Boer War*, p. 572. Others give different figures. Elizabeth van Heyningen quotes the official figures from the monument to the women in the camps at 26,251 women and children and 1,676 men, but others have given even higher figures. Elizabeth van Heyningen, *The Concentration Camps of the Anglo-Boer War: A Social History*, Jacana Media, Auckland Park, 2013, p. 18.

35 Giliomee, *The Afrikaners*, p. 180. See also Odendaal, *The Founders*, pp. 21–22.

36 Odendaal, *The Founders*, p. 261.

37 House of Commons Debates, 19 October 1899, vol. 77, cols. 254–371, http://hansard.millbanksystems.com/commons/1899/oct/19/third-days-debate#S4V0077P0_18991019_HOC_178.

38 Odendaal, *The Founders*, p. 260.

39 Milner to Asquith, 18 November 1897, Milner Papers, Bodleian Library, Oxford, NRA12685.

40 Pakenham quotes this phrase without giving any context. See *The Boer War*, pp. 119–120.

41 Odendaal, *The Founders*, p. 263.

42 Pakenham, *The Boer War*, p. 402.

43 Odendaal, *The Founders*, p. 264.

44 Sol T. Plaatje, *Mafeking Diary: A Black Man's View of a White Man's War*, ed. John Comaroff with Brian Willan and Andrew Reed, Meridor Books, Cambridge, 1973, pp. 19–20.

45 Bill Nasson, *Abraham Esau's War: A Black South African War in the Cape, 1899–1902*, Cambridge University Press, Cambridge, 1991, p. 5.

46 Ibid., p. 18.

47 Ibid., p. 18.

48 Ibid., p. 22.

49 Ibid., p. 47.

50 Odendaal, *The Founders*, p. 265.

51 Paul S. Landau, 'Transformation in consciousness', in Carolyn Hamilton, Bernard K. Mbenga and Robert Ross, *The Cambridge History of South Africa, vol. 1, From Early Times to 1885*, Cambridge University Press, Cambridge, 2010, p. 417.

52 Nasson, *Abraham Esau's War*, p. 93.

53 Ibid., p. 94.

54 Ibid., p. 97.

55 Ibid., p. 99.

56 Ibid., p. 98.

57 Pakenham, *The Boer War*, p. 572.

58 Van Heyningen, *The Concentration Camps*, p. 150.

59 Ibid., p. 154.

60 Quoted in Marika Sherwood, *Origins of Pan-Africanism: Henry Sylvester Williams, Africa, and the African Diaspora*, Routledge, Abingdon, 2011, p. 136.

61 Judd and Surridge, *The Boer War*, p. 234.

62 Pakenham, *The Boer War*, p. 573.

63 David E. Torrance, *The Strange Death of the Liberal Empire: Lord Selborne in South Africa*, Liverpool University Press, Liverpool, 1996, p. 102.

64 Martin Meredith, *Diamonds, Gold and War: The Making of South Africa*, Simon and Schuster, London, 2007, p. 494.

65 Ibid., pp. 494–495.

66 Nasson, *Abraham Esau's War*, pp. 170–171.

67 Ibid., p. 181.

68 Rudyard Kipling, 'The Lesson'.

**Chapter 4**

1 Quoted in Ronald Hyam, *Elgin and Churchill at the Colonial Office: The Watershed of the Empire-Commonwealth*, Macmillan, London, 1968, p. 3.

2 Ramachandra Guha, *Gandhi before India*, Penguin Books, London, 2013, p. 310.

3 Hermann Giliomee, *The Afrikaners: Biography of a People*, Hurst, London, 2003, p. 265. In the 1950s and 1960s the bitter memory of the humiliation of having their language regarded as second rate was frequently referred to by Afrikaners speaking to English-speaking whites.

4 L.M. Thompson, *The Unification of South Africa, 1902–1910*, Oxford University Press, London, 1960, p. 16.

5 Ibid., p. 16.

6 'If I had known as well now the extravagance on the part of almost all the whites – not only the Boers – against any concession to any coloured man, however civilized, I should never have agreed to so absolute an exclusion, not only of the raw native, but of the whole coloured population, from any rights of citizenship, even in municipal affairs.' Marilyn Lake and Henry Reynolds, *Drawing the Global Colour Line: White Men's Countries and the Question of Racial Equality*, Cambridge University Press, Cambridge, 2008, p. 215.

7 Thompson, *The Unification of South Africa*, p. 14.

8 Melanie Yap and Dianne Leong Man, *Colour, Confusion and Concessions: The History of the Chinese in South Africa*, Hong Kong University Press, Hong Kong, 1996, p. 106.

9 Rachel Bright, *Chinese Labour in South Africa, 1902–1910*, Palgrave Macmillan, Basingstoke, 2013, p. 162. The decision provoked a considerable backlash in South Africa and across the Empire. White South Africans considered the ending of Chinese labour might result in increased unemployment for them, while in some parts of New Zealand and Australia there was anger that London had interfered in a white colony.

10 Lake and Reynolds, *Drawing the Global Colour Line*, p. 220.

11 Charles Lucas, *The Self-Governing Dominions and Coloured Immigration*, British National Archives, Kew, CO 886/1, July 1908, p. 47.

12 Ibid., p. 53.

13 Lake and Reynolds, *Drawing the Global Colour Line*, p. 167.

14 Charles Pearson, *National Life and Character: A Forecast*, Macmillan, London, 1894.

15 Ibid., pp. 89–90.

16 Marilyn Lake, 'The white man under siege: new histories of race in the nineteenth

century and the advent of White Australia', *History Workshop Journal*, 58 (2004), p. 44.

17 Lucas, *The Self-Governing Dominions*, p. 54.

18 Ibid., p. 52.

19 Ibid., p. 54.

20 Lake and Reynolds, *Drawing the Global Colour Line*, p. 203.

21 W.K. Hancock, *Smuts, the Sanguine Years: 1870–1919*, Cambridge University Press, Cambridge, 1962, pp. 213–214.

22 'The mandarins of the colonial office, and many politicians too, held colonial and non-European societies in contempt. Smuts, Gandhi, Deakin, Mullah Muhammad of Somaliland: the significance of each of them in the history of their own peoples was underestimated. They were regarded in Whitehall merely as "cunning", "half-mad", "boring" and "mad" respectively.' Hyam, *Elgin and Churchill*, pp. 3–4.

23 Hancock, *Smuts*, p. 215.

24 Ibid., p. 217.

25 Thompson, *The Unification of South Africa*, p. 32.

26 Ibid., p. 35.

27 Phyllis Lewsen (ed.), *Selections from the Correspondence of John X. Merriman, 1905–1924*, Van Riebeeck Society, Cape Town, 1969, pp. 16–17. Emphasis in the original.

28 Ibid., pp. 17–18.

29 Gavin Lewis, *Between the Wire and the Wall*, David Philip, Claremont, 1987, p. 46.

30 Lewsen, *Selections*, p. 18.

31 Universal male suffrage was only introduced in Britain in 1918; women gained the vote in 1928.

32 Thompson, *The Unification of South Africa*, p. 121.

33 *Cape Times*, 9 January 1901, quoted in Lewis, *Between the Wire and the Wall*, p. 31.

34 Giliomee, *The Afrikaners*, p. 264.

35 André Odendaal, *The Founders: The Origins of the ANC and the Struggle for Democracy in South Africa*, Jacana, Auckland Park, 2012, p. 270.

36 Ibid., p. 269.

37 Ibid., p. 274.

38 Ibid., p. 289.

39 Hansard, House of Commons Debates, 11 July 1906. The Keir Hardie archive, London School of Economics, ILP/4/1900/ 66A, contains several letters from the Colenso family to Hardie.

40 Hyam, *Elgin and Churchill*, pp. 239–261.

41 Ibid., p. 251.

42 Lake and Reynolds, *Drawing the Global Colour Line*, p. 221.

43 Ibid., p. 222.

44 Shula Marks, *Reluctant Rebellion: The 1906–1908 Disturbances in Natal*, Clarendon Press, Oxford, 1970, p. 191.

45 Radical Liberals had been pushing for African rights since 1906.

46 Hansard, 13 May 1908, http://hansard.millbanksystems.com/commons/1908/may/13/native-affairs-south-africa.

47 Ibid. First a Conservative MP, he was later a Liberal MP and was given the post of Under Secretary for the Colonies, which he held in 1908–1911.

48 Odendaal, *The Founders*, p. 349.

49 E. Walker, *W.P. Schreiner, a South African*, Central News Agency, Johannesburg, 1937, pp. 139ff.

50 Thompson, *The Unification of South Africa*, p. 110. Note that the 'Coloureds' included Indians and Chinese.

51 Ibid., p. 111.
52 Secret Dispatch from Selborne to Crewe, 24 October 1908, British National Archives, Kew, PRO CO879/106/8.
53 Ibid.
54 Odendaal, *The Founders*, p. 363.
55 Secret Dispatch from Selborne to Crewe, 24 October 1908, PRO CO879/106/8.
56 Odendaal, *The Founders*, p. 351.
57 Ibid., p. 352.
58 Lewis, *Between the Wire and the Wall*, pp. 20–21.
59 Ibid., p. 27.
60 Ibid., p. 27.
61 Ibid., p. 36.
62 Ibid., p. 36.
63 Ibid., p. 38.
64 Ibid., p. 38.
65 A. Abdurahman to Hardie, 30 July 1906, enclosing 'Coloured people franchise in South Africa', Keith Hardie Papers, LSE Archive, ILP4/1906: 284. Hardie did not raise the franchise during a debate in the House of Commons in 1906, but he spoke to ask why women were not given the vote rather than the black population. Instead, he asked whether land would be reserved for Africans. Hansard, 17 December 1906.
66 Lewis, *Between the Wire and the Wall*, p. 39.
67 Ibid., p. 50.
68 Ibid., p. 51.
69 Ibid., p. 52.
70 See, for example, Guha, *Gandhi before India*; Maureen Swan, *Gandhi: The South African Experience*, Ravan Press, Johannesburg, 1985; Robert Huttenback, *Gandhi in South Africa: British Imperialism and the Indian Question, 1860–1914*, Cornell University Press, Ithaca, 1971.
71 Guha, *Gandhi before India*, p. 204.
72 Arthur Herman, *Gandhi and Churchill: The Epic Rivalry That Destroyed an Empire and Forged Our Age*, Arrow Books, London, 2009, p. 150.
73 Guha, *Gandhi before India*, p. 223.
74 Ibid., pp. 228ff.
75 Paul F. Power, 'Gandhi in South Africa', *Journal of Modern African Studies*, 7, 3 (October 1969), p. 448.
76 *Indian Opinion*, 13 February 1909.
77 The experience of the indentured is complex and there is no single narrative that covers all their experiences. See Ashwin Desai and Goolam Vahed, *Inside Indian Indenture: A South African Story, 1860–1914*, HSRC Press, Cape Town, 2010, pp. 2–3, 423–435.
78 Shula Marks and Stanley Trapido (eds.), *The Politics of Race, Class and Nationalism in Twentieth Century South Africa*, Routledge, Oxford, 2014, p. 33.
79 Lewis, *Between the Wire and the Wall*, p. 52.
80 Christopher Saunders, 'F.Z.S. Peregrino and the South African Spectator', *Quarterly Bulletin of the South African Library*, 32 (1977/78), p. 87.
81 Gavin Lewis (*Between the Wire and the Wall*, p. 49) briefly mentions that he reported Tobin, Abdurahman and others to the authorities as 'reckless radicals' and wrote to the Secretary of Native Affairs about the activities of the APO in campaigning against the Draft Act of Union.
82 Ibid., pp. 49–50.
83 Ibid., p. 53.
84 *Cape Times*, 22 June 1909.

85 *APO*, 3 July 1909.
86 *Cape Times*, 16 September 1909.
87 *The Times*, 8 July 1909.
88 *The Times*, 12 July 1909.

Chapter 5

1  *The Times*, 5 July 1909.
2  *The Observer*, 27 November 1932.
3  Henry James, *Essays in London and Elsewhere*, Harper and Brothers, New York, 1893, p. 4.
4  Selborne to Crewe, 24 March 1909, British National Archives, PRO CO417/479.
5  *Kelly's Post Office Commercial Directory*, 1909.
6  André Odendaal, *The Founders: The Origins of the ANC and the Struggle for Democracy in South Africa*, Jacana Media, Auckland Park, 2012, p. 425. John Dube (not officially a member of the deputation) stayed at 23 Woburn Place, Russell Square, WC. Schreiner to Dilke, undated, Dilke Papers, British Library, Add MSS 43941 (199).
7  Ramachandra Guha, *Gandhi before India*, Penguin Books, London, 2013, p. 331.
8  David Nicholls, *The Lost Prime Minister: A Life of Sir Charles Dilke*, Hambledon Press, London, 1995.
9  Ibid., p. 298. He attended a Labour Party conference in 1906 and was offered the chair of the meeting in the absence of Ramsay MacDonald.
10 Olive Schreiner to W.P. Schreiner, 13 September 1892, UCT Manuscripts and Archives, BC16 Box 1 File 1/1892/12.
11 Nicholls, *The Lost Prime Minister*, p. 299.
12 Ibid., p. 308.
13 Stephen Gwynn and Gertrude Tuckwell, *The Life of the Rt. Hon. Sir Charles W. Dilke*, John Murray, London, 1918, p. 374.
14 Byles was Sir William Pollard Byles, a liberal MP and pacifist, who had opposed the Boer War. See ibid., p. 374.
15 Nicholls, *The Lost Prime Minister*, p. 308.
16 Ibid., pp. 308–309.
17 Hudson (Dilke's secretary) to Schreiner, 16 February 1909, UCT Manuscripts and Archives, BC12 File 11 (730).
18 This is dealt with in chapter 4.
19 C.P. Lucas, *Native Races in the British Empire*, 31 December 1907, MSS Mottistone 10/1–18, Nuffield College, Oxford.
20 Ibid., p. 10.
21 Ibid., p. 11 (emphasis added).
22 Dilke to Seely, 26 May 1909, MSS Mottistone 9/396, Nuffield College.
23 MacDonald to Schreiner, 18 June 1909, UCT Manuscripts and Archives, BC112 File 12 (10.1).
24 Martin Plaut, 'Keir Hardie's visit to South Africa, 1908', *Bulletin of the National Library of South Africa*, 68, 1 (June 2014), pp. 89–106.
25 Ramsay MacDonald, 'What I saw in South Africa, September and October, 1902', *The Echo*, London, 1902, pp. 118–119.
26 Jonathan Hyslop, 'The world voyage of James Keir Hardie: Indian nationalism, Zulu insurgency and the British labour diaspora 1907–1908', *Journal of Global History*, 1, 3 (November 2006), pp. 343–362.
27 Dilke to Schreiner, 24 May 1909, UCT Manuscripts and Archives, BC12 File 11 (7.1).
28 Dilke to Schreiner, 20 May 1909, British National Archives, PRO CO417/478.

29 Hansard, 13 May 1908, vol. 188, cols. 1215–1259.

30 Dilke to Schreiner, May 1909, British National Archives, PRO CO417/478.

31 Crewe to Dilke, May 1909, British National Archives, PRO 417/478, 17977.

32 Dilke to Schreiner, 24 May 1909, UCT Manuscripts and Archives, BC12 File 11 (7.1): 'the private deputation produced in our minds certainty that some amendments in the Protectorates schedule and provisions will be made by the home Government.'

33 The question of the centre versus the imperial periphery, and white colonial unity against London, is explored at length in Marilyn Lake and Henry Reynolds, *Drawing the Global Colour Line: White Men's Countries and the Question of Racial Equality*, Cambridge University Press, Cambridge, 2008.

34 Dilke to Schreiner, 24 May 1909, UCT Manuscripts and Archives, BC12 File 11 (7.1).

35 F.G. Gardiner, 'The South African Constitution and the native vote', *Socialist Review*, 3 (March–August 1909).

36 James Heartfield, *The Aborigines' Protection Society: Humanist Imperialism in Australia, New Zealand, Fiji, Canada, South Africa and the Congo, 1836–1909*, Hurst, London, 2011, pp. 233ff.

37 'Time and again, the Aborigines' Protection Society called on Britain to defend native territory against Boer encroachment.' Ibid., p. 235.

38 Ibid., p. 280.

39 The meeting called for the British government to 'prevent resort to any form of compulsion, by excessive taxation or otherwise, and to ensure for the natives of British South Africa the freedom in disposing of their labour, and the immunity from any approach to slavery to which they are entitled as subjects of the British Crown'. *Native Labour in South Africa: Report of a Public Meeting Jointly Convened by the Aborigines Protection Society and the British and Foreign Anti-Slavery Society, which was held at Caxton Hall, Westminster, 29 April 1903*, P.S. King and Son, London, 1903, p. 6.

40 H.R. Fox Bourne, *Blacks and Whites in South Africa*, P.S. King and Son, London, 1900, p. 93.

41 Jabavu to Fox Bourne, 28 March 1887 and 2 July 1887, Aborigines' Protection Society Correspondence, Bodleian Library, MSS Brit. Empire S18 C153.

42 Soga to Fox Bourne, 16 January 1906, Aborigines' Protection Society Correspondence, Bodleian Library, MSS Brit. Empire S18 C152.

43 Hardie introduction to Soga book, Aborigines' Protection Society Correspondence, Bodleian Library, MSS Brit. Empire S22 G198.

44 Abdurahman to Society, 13 July 1906, Aborigines' Protection Society Correspondence, Bodleian Library, MSS Brit. Empire S22 G198.

45 *The Aborigines' Friend*, March 1906, p. 484.

46 Ibid., p. 188.

47 Heartfield, *The Aborigines' Protection Society*, p. 285.

48 APS Minutes, 3 December 1908, Aborigines' Protection Society Correspondence, Bodleian Library, MSS Brit. Empire S20 E5/10.

49 As the minutes of the Society of 8 February 1909 record: 'Letters of sympathy with the Society on the sudden death, at Torquay on 2nd instant of its Secretary, Mr H.R. Fox Bourne, were read by Mr Bryant.' APS Minutes, 9 February 1909, Bodleian Library, MSS Brit. Empire S20 E5/10.

50 Dilke to Schreiner, 20 May 1909, UCT Manuscripts and Archives, BC112 File 11 (7.1).

## Chapter 6

1 Sadly, the primary material remaining from the rest of the deputation is thin. The activities of men like Dr Abdurahman or Jabavu, who deserve much fuller treatment, can mostly be read in the letters that remain in the official archives, in the UK and

South Africa, or in the papers of white politicians like Dilke or Schreiner, which were preserved.

2 Schreiner to Dilke, 5 July 1909, Dilke Papers, British Library, Add MSS 43941 (153).

3 *The Times*, 6 July 1909; *Manchester Guardian*, 6 July 1909.

4 A copy of the appeal is in the Cape Archives, as part of the correspondence between the Cape Prime Minister, John X. Merriman, and the Governor, Sir Walter Hely-Hutchinson, Enclosure no. 1, in Dispatch no. 131 of 16 June 1909, Cape Archives, P1020711.

5 Ibid.

6 Theophilus Lyndall Schreiner, in C.J. Beyers (ed.), *Dictionary of South African Biography*, vol. 4, Human Sciences Research Council, Pretoria, 1981, p. 546.

7 *Evening Standard and St James's Gazette*, 5 July 1909.

8 www.royalnavalmuseum.org/info_sheets_navy_league.htm.

9 Philip Magnus, *King Edward the Seventh*, John Murray, London, 1964, p. 527.

10 Merriman to Hely-Hutchinson, Enclosure no. 2, Dispatch no. 131, 16 June 1909, Cape Archives, P1020711.

11 The most insightful biography of Percy Molteno is an unpublished manuscript by Francis Hirst, *A Man of Principle: The Life of Percy Alport Molteno, M.P.* This is to be found on the Molteno Family Archive website, which also contains a useful introduction to this work; see www.moltenofamily.net/wp-content/uploads/2013/12/Introduction-selected-chapters.pdf.

12 This website provides a useful brief profile of Betty Molteno, http://feministssa.com/2011/01/03/herstory-profile-betty-molteno/. I am indebted to Catherine Corder, who is writing a biography of Betty Molteno, for sharing her letters with me and enlightening me about her.

13 Catherine Corder, private correspondence.

14 Alice Greene was the novelist Grahame Greene's aunt.

15 All the Betty Molteno letters are in UCT Manuscripts and Archives, a collection that consists of around 70 boxes of poorly catalogued material: see Molteno Murray Family Papers, BC 330.

16 Hirst, *A Man of Principle*, p. 162.

17 Quoted in *The Times*, 8 July 1909.

18 Basil Williams to Schreiner, 12 July 1909, UCT BC112 File 11 (24.3). To anyone who has worked in the media, this explanation, although apparently contradictory, is entirely understandable. Material delayed is often overlooked until it is too old to use.

19 *The Times*, 27 July 1909.

20 Schreiner to Davidson, 24 July 1909, Archbishop of Canterbury Papers, vol. 486, Lambeth Palace Archive.

21 Ibid.

22 Davidson to Schreiner, 28 July 1909, Archbishop of Canterbury Papers.

23 Davidson to Charles Bruce, 3 August 1909, Archbishop of Canterbury Papers.

24 *Royal Cornwall Gazette*, Truro, 15 July 1909.

25 *Mafeking Mail and Protectorate Guardian*, 'The late Mr Joseph Gerrans', 3 June 1915.

26 The gun, now in the Royal Artillery Museum in Woolwich, South London, is captured in a photograph in the National Army Museum, London. This shows a group around the weapon, with this caption: 'The Wolf Gun was a 4.5 inch howitzer made by British engineers from a drainpipe during the Siege of Mafeking. The weapon fired cannonballs made at an improvised blast furnace in the town. From an album of 48 photographs compiled for Lord Roberts.' National Army Museum, Accession no. 1971-01-36-1-33.

27 *Mafeking Mail, Special Siege Slip*, 20 February 1900; *Sydney Morning Herald*, 24 January 1900.

28 *Mafeking Mail and Protectorate Guardian*, 3 June 1915.

29 Paramount Chiefs Sebele and Bathoen and three other Headmen to Gerrans, 24 March 1909, High Commission for South Africa, Original Correspondence, British National Archives, PRO CO417/479.

30 Plaatje to Schreiner, 13 April 1909, National Library of South Africa, MSC27 Box 8 Letter 1430 1.

31 Jeff Ramsay, 'A child that does not cry dies in the cradle: the 1908–1910 campaign to keep Bechuanaland Protectorate out of the Union of South Africa', *Botswana Notes and Record*s, 27 (1995), pp. 85–96.

32 Ibid., p. 88.

33 Ibid., p. 89.

34 Ibid., p. 90.

35 Ronald Hyam and Peter Henshaw, *The Lion and the Springbok: Britain and South Africa since the Boer War*, Cambridge University Press, Cambridge, 2003, p. 95.

36 H.W. Just, *Natives in South Africa*, MSS Mottistone 9/236, Nuffield College.

37 General Metheun to Governor Walter Hely-Hutchinson, 6 November 1908, British National Archives, PRO CO48/602.

38 Ibid.

39 Ibid.; Ramsay, 'A child that does not cry'.

40 Ramsay, 'A child that does not cry', p. 88.

41 Agnes Merriman to Julia Merriman, 19 July 1909, emphasis in the original, quoted in L.M. Thompson, *The Unification of South Africa, 1902–1910*, Clarendon Press, Oxford, 1960, p. 402.

42 *The Observer*, 25 July 1909; J.C. Smuts, *Jan Christian Smuts*, Cassell, London, 1952, p. 117.

43 South Africa Bill, Conference Between Delegates from South Africa and the Secretary of State for the Colonies, 20 July 1909, British National Archives, PRO CO879 102.

44 *Daily Mail*, 19 July 1909.

45 There was a longer-standing antagonism between Germany and Britain over imperial possessions in Africa. Bismarck had pushed for the establishment of German colonies since the mid-1880s, causing considerable friction with Britain. See Paul Kennedy, *The Rise of Anglo-German Antagonism, 1860–1914*, George Allen and Unwin, London, 1980, pp. 167ff.

46 Robert K. Massie, *Dreadnought: Britain, Germany and the Coming of the Great War*, Jonathan Cape, London, 1992, p. 221.

47 Jean van der Poel, *The Jameson Raid*, Oxford University Press, London, 1951, p. 135.

48 The Kaiser was described as 'absolutely blazing and ready to fight England' by his military staff. See Massie, *Dreadnought*, p. 222.

49 Ibid., p. 226.

50 Holger H. Herwig, *'Luxury' Fleet: The Imperial German Navy, 1888–1918*, George Allen and Unwin, London, 1980, p. 50.

51 Christopher Clark, *The Sleepwalkers: How Europe Went to War in 1914*, Allen Lane, London, 2012, p. 149.

52 Roger Parkinson, *Dreadnought: The Ship That Changed the World*, I.B. Tauris, London, 2015, p. 110.

53 Massie, *Dreadnought*, p. 231.

54 John C.G. Röhl, 'Goodbye to all that (again?): The Fischer thesis, the new revisionism and the meaning of the First World War', *International Affairs*, 91, 1 (2015), pp. 153–166.

55 See, for example, John Kendle, *The Round Table Movement and Imperial Union*,

University of Toronto Press, Toronto, 1975.

56 Philip Kerr, 'Foreign affairs: Anglo-German rivalry', *Round Table*, November 1910, pp. 7–40, quoted in Kendle, *The Round Table Movement*, p. 108.

57 John Kendle, *The Colonial and Imperial Conferences, 1887–1911*, Longmans, London, 1967, pp. 94–97.

58 *Cape Times*, 16 June 1909.

59 Cd 4948, *Imperial Conference, Correspondence and Papers Relating to a Conference with Representatives of the Self-governing Dominions on the Naval and Military Defence of the Empire, 1909*, HMSO, London, 1909, p. 17. The South Africans representing the colonies were Merriman (Cape), Greene (Natal), Smuts (Transvaal) and Fischer (Orange Free State). The urgent need for a unified South African military to face potential threats, including from German South West Africa, was discussed in detail by a member of the Natal Legislative Assembly, P.A. Silburn, in *The Colonies and Imperial Defence*, Longman, Green, London, 1909.

60 Cd 4948, p. 44.

61 *Imperial Conference on the Subject of the Defence of the Empire 1909*, Imperial Conference Secretariat, October 1909, British National Archives, CO886/2.

62 Ibid., p. 24.

63 Ibid., p. 28.

64 Ibid., pp. 80–81.

65 *The Graphic*, 21 August 1909.

66 The three European powers and their colonies were Germany: South West Africa and Tanganyika; Portugal: Mozambique and Angola; and Belgium: Congo.

67 *The Times*, 29 July 1909.

68 *Guardian*, 29 July 1909.

69 *In and Against the State* was the title of a pamphlet published by the Conference of Socialist Economists in 1979; https://libcom.org/library/against-state-1979.

70 Earle to Schreiner, 8 July 1909, UCT Manuscripts and Archives, BC112 File 11 (9.3).

71 This is to be found in the Dilke papers in the British Library, as well as the Schreiner papers in the University of Cape Town and the National Library of South Africa, Cape Town. These are to be found at several locations including British Library (Dilke Papers Add MSS 43921, Add MSS 43941), UCT (BC317, BC112) and National Library (MSC27, Box 8).

72 Schreiner to Dilke, 6 July 1909, Dilke Papers, British Library, Add MSS 43941 (155).

73 Schreiner to Dilke, Dilke Papers, British Library, Add MSS 43941 (167).

74 *Cape Times*, 8 July 1909.

75 Betty Molteno to Alice Greene, 13 July 1909, UCT Manuscripts and Archives, BC330.

76 National Library of South Africa, MSC27, Box 8 Letter 1502 1.

77 *The Times*, 23 July 1909.

78 South African Native Races Committee (eds.), *The South African Natives, Their Progress and Present Condition*, John Murray, London, 1909; Alfred F. Fox, South African Native Races Committee to Schreiner, 24 July 1909, National Library of South Africa, MSC27, Box 8 Letter 1504 1.

79 J.H. Levy to Lord Crewe, 27 July 1909, National Library of South Africa, MSC27, Box 8 Letter 1509 1.

80 Dilke to Schreiner, 7 July 1909, UCT Manuscripts and Archives, BC112 File 12 (7.28).

81 Travers Buxton to Schreiner, 15 July 1909, UCT Manuscripts and Archives, BC27 Box 8 Letter 1492 1; *The Scotsman*, 28 July 1909.

82 *South Africa*, 31 July 1909, p. 275.

83 *The Times*, 28 July 1909.

84 *The Scotsman*, 28 July 1909.

85 *South Africa*, 31 July 1909, p. 275.

86 *The Times*, 28 July 1909.

87 Stead to Schreiner, 26 July 1909, UCT Manuscripts and Archives, BC112 File 12 (19.5).

88 Lady Violet Cecil to Schreiner, 18 July 1909, UCT Manuscripts and Archives, BC112 File 11 (4.9). Lady Violet referred to herself as 'Lady Edward Cecil' – her husband's name, as was customary at the time. For clarity I have referred to her as Lady Violet.

89 Julia Bush, *Edwardian Ladies and Imperial Power*, Leicester University Press, Leicester, 2000, pp. 46–47.

90 The League was the result of a visit to London by Katie Stuart, a niece of Olive Schreiner, who came on behalf of the South African Guild of Loyal Women, which served as the League's blueprint. The inaugural meeting was held on 2 April 1901 at the Prime Minister's residence, 10 Downing Street. It was hosted by Alice Balfour and attended by 25 upper-class or aristocratic women. See Eliza Riedi, 'Women, gender and the promotion of empire: the Victoria League, 1901–1914', *Historical Journal*, 45, 3 (September 2000), pp. 569–599.

91 Lady Violet Cecil to Schreiner, 21 July 1909, UCT Manuscripts and Archives, BC112 File 11 (4.8).

92 Charles Bruce to Davidson, 27 July 1909, Archbishop of Canterbury Papers, Lambeth Palace Archive.

93 Lady Violet Cecil to Lord Northcliffe, 26 July 1909, UCT Manuscripts and Archives, BC112 File 11 (4.4).

94 Abdurahman to Schreiner, 2 August 1909, National Library of South Africa, MSC27, Box 8 Letter 1522 1.

## Chapter 7

1 Hansard, 27 July 1909, vol. 2, cols. 753–97, http://hansard.millbanksystems.com/lords/1909/jul/27/south-africa-bill-hl.

2 *Morning Post*, 27 July 1909.

3 *Westminster Gazette*, 28 July 1909.

4 *Morning Post*, 28 July 1909.

5 *Midland Evening Post*, 28 July 1909.

6 Deborah Lavin (ed.), *Friendship and Union: The South African Letters of Patrick Duncan and Maud Selborne, 1907–1943*, Van Riebeeck Society, Cape Town, 2010, p. 33.

7 These letters are to be found in UCT Manuscripts and Archives, BC112 File 11.

8 Henry Wilson to Schreiner, 23 July 1909, National Library of South Africa, MSC27, Box 8 Letter 1503 2.

9 *The Times*, 30 July 1909.

10 This point referred to the fact that in Natal and the Cape black men had been allowed to stand for Parliament in the past.

11 Letter dated 29 July 1909, *APO*, 11 September 1909.

12 Lionel Earle to Schreiner, 2 August 1909, UCT Manuscripts and Archives, BC112 File 11 (9.1).

13 UCT Manuscripts and Archives, BC506 File A1.2

14 Petition, UCT Manuscripts and Archives, BC112 File 11 (7.24). *The Times*, 19 August 1909.

15 Betty Molteno to Alice Greene, 22 July 1909, Molteno Murray Family Papers, UCT Manuscripts and Archives, BC330.

16 Mangena was actually Xhosa. David Killingray, 'Significant black South Africans in Britain before 1912: pan-African organisations and the emergence of South Africa's first black lawyers', *South African Historical Journal*, 64 (2012), pp. 393–417; Chris Saunders, 'Pixley Seme: towards a biography', *South African Historical Journal*, 26 (1991), pp. 196–217.

17 Killingray, 'Significant black South Africans', p. 27.

18 www.sahistory.org.za/topic/african-national-congress-timeline-1866-1909; André Odendaal, *The Founders: The Origins of the ANC and the Struggle for Democracy in South Africa*, Jacana Media, Auckland Park, 2012, p. 417.

19 Menu of meal at House of Commons, undated, National Library of South Africa, MSC27 Box 8 Letter 1521A 1.

20 Molteno was probably staying at what was officially known as University Hall, Gordon Square, a university residence built in 1849.

21 *Review of Reviews*, August 1909.

22 *The Nation*, 14 August 1909.

23 Betty Molteno's writing is notoriously difficult to read. I am indebted to Catherine Corder for her attempt to decipher the letters.

24 MacDonald to Schreiner, 21 July 1909, UCT Manuscripts and Archives, BC112 File 12 (10.2).

25 Hardie to Schreiner, 6 August 1909, National Library of South Africa, MSC27 Box 8 Letter 1529 1.

26 *Daily Mail*, 11 August 1909.

27 Menu of meal at House of Commons, undated, National Library of South Africa, MSC27 Box 8 Letter 1521A 1.

28 www.historicopera.com/xearly/dupont5.htm.

29 See South African History Online, for a partial list of the delegates to the South African Native National Congress (which was renamed the African National Congress in 1923): www.sahistory.org.za/topic/delegates-attendance-sannc-founding -conference-1912.

30 See Odendaal, *The Founders*, pp. 424–434 for Dube's role in the deputation and their campaigning during their time in London.

31 Hansard, 16 August 1909, http://hansard.millbanksystems.com/commons/1909/ aug/16/south-africa-bill-lords.

32 Ibid.

33 *Daily Mail* and *The Times*, 18 August 1909.

34 *The Times*, 18 August 1909.

35 Hansard, 19 August 1909, http://hansard.millbanksystems.com/commons/1909/ aug/19/clause-35-qualifications-of-voters.

36 Hansard, 16 August 1909, http://hansard.millbanksystems.com/commons/1909/ aug/16/south-africa-bill-lords.

37 Ibid.

38 Hansard, 19 August 1909, http://hansard.millbanksystems.com/commons/1909/ aug/19/clause-26-qualifications-of-senators.

39 Ibid.

40 Ibid.

41 *APO*, 28 August 1909.

42 *The Times*, 20 August 1909.

43 *Manchester Guardian*, 30 August 1909.

## Chapter 8

1 *The Collected Works of Mahatma Gandhi*, Indian Government, New Delhi, 1999, vol. 9, www.gandhiheritageportal.org/cwmg_volume_thumbview/OQ== #page/400/mode/2up.

2   It was sent to Dr Abdurahman's residence, at 36 Longbridge Road, Earls Court.
3   *Indian Opinion*, 18 September 1909.
4   Raymond Suttner, *Recovering Democracy in South Africa*, Jacana Media, Auckland Park, 2015, p. 186.
5   Odendaal, *The Founders*, p. 479.
6   The Youth League Manifesto of 1944 accepted that many of the ANC's critics had a point when they attacked the organisation for 'being an unconscious police'.
7   Thomas Karis and Gwendolen Carter, *From Protest to Challenge: A Documentary History of African Politics in South Africa, 1882–1964*, vol. 2, Hoover Institution Press, Stanford, 1973, 'Congress Youth League Manifesto', p. 305.
8   Ramachandra Guha, *Gandhi before India*, Penguin Books, London, 2014, p. 330.
9   Ibid., pp. 300ff.
10  Ibid., p. 330.
11  Harish P. Kaushik, *Indian National Congress in England*, Friends Publications, Delhi, 1991, p. 25.
12  Nicholas Owen, *The British Left and India: Metropolitan Anti-Imperialism, 1885–1947*, Oxford University Press, Oxford, 2007, pp. 49ff.
13  Ibid., p. 67.
14  Ibid., pp. 72–73.
15  Richard James Popplewell, *Intelligence and Imperial Defence: British Intelligence and the Defence of the Indian Empire, 1904–1924*, Frank Cass, London, 1995, p. 130.
16  Jonathan Hyslop, 'An "eventful" history of Hind Swaraj: Gandhi between the Battle of Tsushima and the Union of South Africa', *Popular Culture*, 23, 2 (2011), p. 300.
17  Popplewell, *Intelligence*, p. 143.
18  Guha, *Gandhi before India*, p. 332.
19  Ibid., pp. 332–333.
20  A.J. Parel, 'The origins of Hind Swaraj', in Judith Brown and Martin Prozesky (eds.), *Gandhi and South Africa: Principles and Politics*, University of Natal Press, Pietermaritzburg, 1996, p. 43.
21  Guha, *Gandhi before India*, p. 333.
22  Rajmohan Gandhi, *Gandhi: The Man, His People and the Empire*, Haus Books, London, 2007, p. 139.
23  Ibid.
24  Guha, *Gandhi before India*, pp. 164–165.
25  Ibid., p. 327. In fact, Gandhi's South African campaign had already received world-wide publicity. *The Times*, for example, covered the events in 1908 in detail.
26  Guha, *Gandhi before India*, p. 344.
27  Ibid., p. 347.
28  Judith Brown, *Gandhi: Prisoner of Hope*, Yale University Press, New Haven, 1989, p. 51.
29  James D. Hunt, *Gandhi in London*, Promilla, New Delhi, 1978, pp. 117–118.
30  Ibid.
31  Parliamentary Question, 15 March 1909, British Library, India Office Records, IOR/L/PJ/6/937, File 1702.
32  'I am in entire agreement with the general policy that His Majesty's Government should interfere as little as possible with work of Union Government,' the High Commissioner, Lord Selborne, telegraphed the Colonial Secretary, Lord Crewe. British Library, India Office Records, IOR/L/PJ/6/937, File 1702, Telegram 26 April 1909.
33  Guha, *Gandhi before India*, p. 302. Interestingly, W.P. Schreiner refused to back Gandhi's cause. In an article on 'Deputation Notes' published in *Indian Opinion*

(Gujarati) on 18 September 1909, Gandhi wrote of a meeting with W.P. Schreiner: 'We met Mr Schreiner, and had a long talk. The gentleman also feels that there should be no objection to the entry of six Indians as a matter of favour, but that they cannot enter as a matter of right. He is honest in his opinions. But, having been convinced over a long time that we are an inferior people, he cannot see that it is insulting to propose that Indians may enter as a matter of favour.' (*Collected Works*, vol. 9, p. 365.) Despite this, Gandhi's relationship with Schreiner remained cordial and Schreiner chaired the meeting in Cape Town on 12 October 1912 to receive the Congress leader, Gokhale, at the beginning of his trip to South Africa. Gokhale, Gandhi and party left Cape Town for Kimberley on 24 October. The next day, Olive Schreiner came to see them at De Aar. W.P. Schreiner was the principal speaker at the Kimberley meeting for Gokhale on 25 October 1912. In his farewell speech at Cape Town, before leaving South Africa in July 1914, Gandhi said: 'One need not despair of a land which had produced an Olive Schreiner – *cheers* – W.P. Schreiner and a John X. Merriman. (*Cheers.*) These noble men and women would live when they had gone, and a land which had produced these noble men and women was a land that had a great future. Continuing, he said he would carry away with him happy recollections of many European friendships that would last when he had gone from South Africa.' (*Collected Works*, vol. 12, p. 504.) I am grateful to E.S. Reddy for these references.

34 Guha, *Gandhi before India*, p. 336.
35 Ibid., pp. 360–361.
36 Ibid., p. 362.
37 Gandhi, *Collected Works*, vol. 10, p. 458.
38 Parel, 'Origins', p. 42.
39 Ibid., p. 41.
40 Gandhi, *Collected Works*, vol. 10, p. 455.
41 Hyslop, 'An "eventful" history', p. 317.

**Chapter 9**
1 Betty Molteno to Alice Greene, 4 September 1909, UCT Manuscripts and Archives, BC330.
2 John Dube to W.P. Schreiner, 10 September 1909, National Library of South Africa, MSC27 Box 8 Letter 1549 1.
3 André Odendaal, *The Founders: The Origins of the ANC and the Struggle for Democracy in South Africa*, Jacana, Auckland Park, 2012, p. 438.
4 Christopher Saunders, 'Pixley Seme: towards a biography', *South African Historical Journal*, 25 (1991), pp. 196–217.
5 Betty Molteno to Alice Greene, 20 and 22 July 1909, UCT Manuscripts and Archives, BC330.
6 David Killingray, 'Hands joined in brotherhood: the rise and decline of a movement for faith and social change, 1875–2000', in Anthony R. Cross, Peter J. Morden, and Ian M. Randall (eds.), *Pathways and Patterns in History: Essays on Baptists, Evangelicals, and the Modern World in Honour of David Bebbington*, Spurgeon's College and the Baptist Historical Society, Didcot, 2015, pp. 319–339.
7 It is not clear which members of the deputation went to attend the Cardiff conference.
8 *PSA Brotherhood Journal*, 12, 10 (October 1909), p. 338. I am grateful to David Killingray for this reference.
9 Odendaal, *The Founders*, p. 464.
10 Brian Willan, *Sol Plaatje: South African Nationalist, 1876–1932*, University of California Press, Berkeley, 1984, p. 179.
11 Killingray, 'Hands joined in brotherhood', pp. 319–339.

12 Brian Willan, 'Sol Plaatje, De Beers and an old tram shed: class relations and social control in a South African town, 1918–19', *Journal of Southern African Studies*, 4 (1978), pp. 195–215.

13 See Heather Hughes, *First President: A Life of John L. Dube, Founding President of the ANC*, Jacana Media, Auckland Park, 2011, pp. 146ff.

14 Ibid., p. 149.

15 Helen Clark Diary, Clark Archive, Street, Somerset, Mil 70, July 1909 (this diary contains entries that continue until November 1909).

16 Visitor's Books, Clark Archive, Mil 73/02.

17 Helen Clark Diary, Clark Archive, Mil 70, July 1909.

18 Jabavu to Clark, Clark Archive, Mil 63/01.

19 Killingray, 'Hands joined in brotherhood', pp. 319–339.

20 Jabavu to Clark, 25 November 1911, Clark Archive, Mil 63/01.

21 *Cape Times*, 21 September 1909.

22 *Cape Times*, 22 September 1909; *APO*, 25 September 1909. Those who arrived were Schreiner, Abdurahman, Fredericks, Lenders, Rubusana, Dwanya and Mapikela. Others, like Jabavu and Gerrans, were expected back within a fortnight.

23 *Cape Times*, 22 September 1909.

24 *Cape Times*, 22 September 1909.

25 *APO*, 25 September 1909.

26 *APO*, 9 October 1909.

27 Ibid.

28 *Imvo*, 31 August 1909, quoted in Odendaal, *The Founders*, p. 435.

29 Odendaal, *The Founders*, p. 443.

30 *APO*, 1 January 1910.

31 *APO*, 15 January 1910.

32 *APO*, 21 May 1910.

33 *APO*, 26 February 1910.

34 *APO*, 26 February 1910.

35 Quoted in Hermann Giliomee, *The Afrikaners: Biography of a People*, Hurst, London, 2003, p. 296.

36 Odendaal, *The Founders*, p. 455.

37 T.R.H. Davenport, *South Africa, a Modern History*, University of Toronto Press, Toronto, 1987, p. 258.

38 Willan, *Sol Plaatje*, p. 150.

39 *Imvo*, 31 August 1909, quoted in Odendaal, *The Founders*, p. 435.

40 *APO*, 9 April 1910.

41 *APO*, 9 April 1910.

42 *APO*, 23 April 1910.

43 Gavin Lewis, *Between the Wire and the Wall: A History of South African 'Coloured' Politics*, David Philip, Cape Town, 1987, p. 59.

44 Ibid., p. 81.

45 Odendaal, *The Founders*, pp. 447ff.

46 Ibid., p. 451.

47 *Manchester Guardian*, 2 September 1910.

48 Ramachandra Guha, *Gandhi before India*, Penguin Books, London, 2013. Seme's mother was a sister of John Dube.

49 Peter Walshe, *The Rise of African Nationalism in South Africa: The African National Congress, 1912–1952*, C. Hurst, London, 1970, pp. 31–35.

50 This had resulted in a libel case against him and a lengthy legal battle in the British courts to clear his name.

51 Mangena to Schreiner, 10 August 1909, National Library of South Africa. I am indebted to Brian Willan for this reference.

52 Odendaal, *The Founders*, p. 458.

53 Willan, *Sol Plaatje*, p. 151.

54 Odendaal, *The Founders*, p. 458.

55 Ibid., p. 461.

56 Ibid., p. 459.

57 Ibid., p. 459.

58 Willan, *Sol Plaatje*, p. 152.

59 Odendaal, *The Founders*, p. 469.

60 The conference founded the South African National Native Congress, which was renamed the African National Congress in 1923.

61 Willan, *Sol Plaatje*, p. 155.

62 Ibid., p. 155.

## Chapter 10

1 These include Ramachandra Guha, *Gandhi before India*, Penguin Books, London 2013; Ashwin Desai and Goolam Vahed, *Inside Indian Indenture: A South African Story, 1860–1914*, HSRC Press, Cape Town, 2010; Robert Huttenback, *Gandhi in South Africa: British Imperialism and the Indian Question, 1860–1914*, Cornell University Press, Ithaca, 1971; Maureen Swan, *Gandhi: The South African Experience*, Ravan Press, Johannesburg, 1985.

2 *Ilanga*, 15 December 1912, quoted in Ashwin Desai and Goolam Vahed, *The South African Gandhi: Stretcher-Bearer of Empire*, Stanford University Press, Stanford, 2016, p. 169.

3 Guha, *Gandhi before India*, p. 437.

4 Interestingly, the British Colonial Secretary believed that the truth was more on Gokhale's side than on that of the South African government. He wrote in 1914 to the Viceroy, Lord Hardinge, saying: 'My kinsman, Colonel Crewe, who is one of the Opposition leaders there, though very friendly with Botha, writes to me that "when Mr Gokhale was out here he was not definitely promised the repeal of the £3 tax, but I think there can be no doubt that Smuts did lead him to think that the tax would be withdrawn."' Crewe to Hardinge, New Year's Day, 1914, British Library, India Office Records, MSS EUR Photo 471.

5 This argument is made in Desai and Vahed, *Inside Indian Indenture*, pp. 417–418.

6 M.K. Gandhi, *Satyagraha in South Africa*, p. 227, www.gandhiserve.org/cwmg/VOL034.PDF.

7 Guha, *Gandhi before India*, p. 448.

8 Ibid., p. 449.

9 For a description of Gandhi's mobilisation of his allies, see ibid., pp. 450ff.

10 His chief critic was the journalist P.S. Aiyar, who described Gandhi as the 'leader of a reactionary group' among Indians. See Guha, *Gandhi before India*, pp. 441–442.

11 Surendra Bhana and Goolam Vahed, *The Making of a Political Reformer: Gandhi in South Africa, 1893–1914*, Manohar Publishers, Delhi, 2005, p. 118.

12 Ibid., pp. 120–121.

13 Swan, *Gandhi*, p. 117.

14 Huttenback, *Gandhi in South Africa*, p. 303.

15 Guha, *Gandhi before India*, p. 470.

16 The Governor-General, Viscount Herbert Gladstone, remarked coolly to the Secretary of State: 'I do not think that any further concessions will be obtainable this session.' See Huttenback, *Gandhi in South Africa*, p. 310.

17 Ibid., pp. 310–311.

18 *Indian Opinion*, 13 September 1913.

19 Huttenback, *Gandhi in South Africa*, p. 315.

20 Rajmohan Gandhi, *Gandhi: The Man, His People and the Empire*, Haus Books, London, 2007, p. 161.

21 Desai and Vahed, *Inside Indian Indenture*, p. 383.

22 Swan, *Gandhi*, p. 244.

23 Desai and Vahed, *Inside Indian Indenture*, p. 379.

24 Maureen Swan argues that this change of stance came about because of the weakness of Gandhi's position and the lack of support from what she terms the 'new Indian elite' among the shopkeepers and businessmen who had previously been the bedrock of his campaigns. '[The] course of events between mid-September and mid-October suggests that Gandhi hoped to avoid an attempt to mobilize the underclass, with whom he had no direct contact, and that he relied on an elite campaign, supported by the threat of mass mobilization which was implied in the inclusion of the £3 tax question, to put pressure on the government.' Swan, *Gandhi*, p. 244.

25 Ibid., p. 235.

26 Kalpana Hiralal, 'Satyagraha on Natal's coal mines', *Journal of Natal and Zulu History*, 31 (2013), p. 43.

27 Swan, *Gandhi*, p. 244.

28 Shimon Lev, *Soulmates: The Story of Mahatma Gandhi and Hermann Kallenbach*, Orient BlackSwan, Hyderabad, 2012, p. 88.

29 Ibid., p. 89.

30 Gandhi to Kallenbach, 22 October 1913, *Collected Works*, www.gandhiserve.org/cwmg/VOL013.PDF.

31 Huttenback, *Gandhi in South Africa*, p. 316.

32 Swan, *Gandhi*, p. 249.

33 Joseph Lelyveld, *Great Soul: Mahatma Gandhi and his Struggle with India*, Vintage Books, New York, 2012, p. 118.

34 Hiralal, 'Satyagraha', p. 43.

35 Ibid., p. 46.

36 Ibid., p. 47.

37 Ibid., p. 49.

38 Huttenback, *Gandhi in South Africa*, p. 317.

39 Bhana and Vahed, *The Making of a Political Reformer*, p. 125.

40 Rajmohan, *Gandhi*, p. 165. Smuts was playing a clever game. He knew the marchers were short of supplies and was unwilling to 'relieve' Gandhi of being responsible for their needs. In the event a white baker agreed to provide bread for the marchers at every stop.

41 Huttenback, *Gandhi in South Africa*, p. 317.

42 Ibid., p. 318.

43 Swan, *Gandhi*, p. 254.

44 Desai and Vahed, *Inside Indian Indenture*, p. 415.

45 Lelyveld, *Great Soul*, p. 119.

46 Hiralal, 'Satyagraha', p. 51; Lelyveld, *Great Soul*, p. 119.

47 Guha, *Gandhi before India*, p. 492.

48 Maureen Swan, 'The 1913 Natal Indian strike', *Journal of Southern African Studies*, 10, 2 (April 1984), p. 239.

49 Chandrika Kaul, *Reporting the Raj: The British Press and India, c. 1880–1922*, Manchester University Press, Manchester, 2003, p. 101. Gandhi himself commented on the power of the media and of *Indian Opinion*'s role in bringing an end to British rule.

50 *Madras Times*, 25 November 1913.

51 Crewe to Hardinge, 27 November 1913, British Library, India Office Records, MSS EUR Photo 471.

52 Hardinge to Crewe, 27 November 1913, British Library, India Office Records, MSS EUR Photo 471.

53 Guha, *Gandhi before India*, pp. 487–492.

54 Crewe to Hardinge, 11 December 1913, British Library, India Office Records, MSS EUR Photo 471.

55 Huttenback, *Gandhi in South Africa*, pp. 321–322.

56 Swan, *Gandhi*, p. 255.

57 Huttenback, *Gandhi in South Africa*, p. 322.

58 Swan, *Gandhi*, p. 254.

59 Huttenback, *Gandhi in South Africa*, p. 323.

60 Betty Molteno's role in the 1913–1914 protests is drawn from Catherine Corder and Martin Plaut, 'Gandhi's decisive South African 1913 campaign: a personal perspective from the letters of Betty Molteno', *South African Historical Journal*, 66, 1 (2014). Catherine Corder's research into the letters between Betty Molteno and Alice Greene provided me with a unique insight into their relationship and the importance of Emily Hobhouse.

61 Her writings and her report on conditions at the camps, entitled 'Report of a Visit to the Camps of Women and Children in the Cape and Orange River Colonies', was delivered to the British government in June 1901. E. Hobhouse, *Report of a Visit to the Camps of Women and Children in the Cape and Orange River Colonies*, Friars Printing Association, London, 1901.

62 Rykie van Reenen, *Emily Hobhouse: Boer War Letters*, Human and Rousseau, Cape Town, 1984, p. 166.

63 G.P. Gooch, *Life of Lord Courtney*, Macmillan, London, 1920, p. 480.

64 Van Reenen, *Emily Hobhouse*, p. 225.

65 W.K. Hancock, *Smuts, the Sanguine Years, 1870–1911*, Cambridge University Press, Cambridge, 1962, p. 181.

66 Gandhi, *Indian Opinion*: Delegation Notes, before 11 September 1909, *Collected Works*, vol. 10, www.gandhiserve.org/cwmg/VOL010.PDF.

67 This is the monument to the Boer women who died in the concentration camps.

68 W.K. Hancock, and Jean van der Poel (eds.), *Selections from the Smuts Papers, vol. 3, June 1910 – Nov. 1918*, Cambridge University Press, Cambridge, 1966, p. 137.

69 Greene to Molteno, 27 December 1913, Molteno Murray Family Papers, UCT Manuscripts and Archives, BC330.

70 Guha, *Gandhi before India*, p. 496.

71 E.S. Reddy *Gandhiji's Vision of a Free South Africa*, Sanchar Publishing House, New Delhi, 1995, p. 78.

72 Hancock and Van der Poel, *Selections from the Smuts Papers*, pp. 152–156 (emphasis in the original).

73 Greene to Molteno, 30 December 1913, Molteno Murray Family Papers, UCT Manuscripts and Archives, BC330.

74 Molteno to Greene, 29 December 1913, Molteno Murray Family Papers, UCT Manuscripts and Archives, BC330.

75 Molteno to Greene, 2 January 1914, Molteno Murray Family Papers, UCT Manuscripts and Archives, BC330.

76 Hardinge to Crewe, 25 December 1913, British Library, India Office Records, MSS EUR Photo 471.

77 Guha, *Gandhi before India*, pp. 500ff for a description of the role both men played.

78 From a typed manuscript entitled 'Extracts from the Writings of "C.F. Andrews" volume xvi, p. 421', p. 4, in the Molteno Murray Family Papers, UCT Manuscripts and Archives, BC330.

79 Reddy, *Gandhiji's Vision*, p. 79.

80 Smuts had, in mid-1913, confronted a major strike by white miners on the Rand, which ended with the British army shooting 20 protesters. By early 1914 Smuts believed there was a syndicalist conspiracy to overthrow the government and was planning to crush the unions. Jonathan Hyslop, 'Gandhi 1869–1915: the transnational emergence of a public figure', in Judith Brown and Anthony Parel (eds.), *The Cambridge Companion to Gandhi*, Cambridge University Press, Cambridge, 2011, p. 48.

81 W.P. Visser, 'The South African labour movement's responses to declarations of martial law, 1913–1922', Paper presented at the War and Society in Africa Conference, South African Military Academy, Saldanha Bay, 12–14 September 2001.

82 See Jonathan Hyslop, *J.T. Bain: A Scottish Rebel in Colonial South Africa*, Jacana Media, Johannesburg, 2004, for a detailed treatment of the strikes and the deportations.

83 Bill Schwarz, *Memories of Empire, vol. 1, The White Man's World*, Oxford University Press, Oxford, 2011, p. 156.

84 Crewe to Hardinge, 30 January 1914, British Library, India Office Records, MSS EUR Photo 471.

85 Huttenback, *Gandhi in South Africa*, p. 324.

86 Hardinge to Sir Thomas Holderness, Under Sec. of State for India, 19 January 1914, British Library, India Office Records, MSS EUR Photo 471.

87 Guha, *Gandhi before India*, p. 513; Lelyveld, *Great Soul*, p. 129.

88 Guha, *Gandhi before India*, p. 506.

89 In reality, Gandhi was forced to drop his demands for inter-provincial migration for Indians within South Africa and concede an end to large-scale migration from India.

90 Desai and Vahed, *Inside Indian Indenture*, p. 418.

91 Ibid., p. 419.

92 Huttenback, *Gandhi in South Africa*, p. 330.

93 F.S. Crafford, *Jan Smuts: A Biography*, George Allen and Unwin, London, 1945, p. 78.

94 Guha, *Gandhi before India*, p. 529.

## Chapter 11

1 Phil Bonner, 'South African society and culture, 1910–1918', in Robert Ross, Anne Mager and Bill Nasson (eds.), *The Cambridge History of South Africa, vol. 2, 1885–1994*, Cambridge University Press, Cambridge, 2012, pp. 254–255.

2 Ibid., pp. 256–259.

3 Hermann Giliomee, *The Afrikaners: Biography of a People*, Hurst, London, 2003, pp. 301–310.

4 E. Walker, *W.P. Schreiner, A South African*, Central News Agency, Johannesburg, 1937, p. 177.

5 Giliomee, *The Afrikaners*, p. 300.

6 S.T. Plaatje, *Native Life in South Africa*, Ravan Press, Johannesburg, 1986 [1916], p. 21.

7 Brian Willan, *Sol Plaatje: South African Nationalist, 1872–1932*, University of California Press, Berkeley, 1984, p. 163.

8 Heather Hughes, *First President: A Life of John L. Dube, Founding President of the ANC*, Jacana Media, Auckland Park, 2011, p. 183. In taking this stand the Society was reflecting views of some missionaries who argued that for the first time the right of occupation in 'native reserves' was recognised in law. William Manning Marable, 'African nationalist: the life of John Langalibalele Dube', PhD thesis, University of Maryland, 1976, p. 252.

9 Hughes, *First President*, p. 177.

10 Dube came close to cancelling the visit, but feared his status as ANC leader would be irrevocably damaged if he did. Ibid., p. 185.

11 Willan, *Sol Plaatje*, p. 172.

12 Hughes, *First President*, p. 185.

13 Willan, *Sol Plaatje*, p. 173.

14 Ibid., p. 176.

15 Ibid., p. 178.

16 The pamphlet was *The Zulu Appeal*, and was published in June 1914.

17 Hughes, *First President*, p. 186; Willan, *Sol Plaatje*, p. 186.

18 Hughes, *First President*, pp. 187–189. It is also possible that Dube was returning early to try to deal with a scandal, which had been uncovered by Betty Molteno and Alice Greene – the fact that he had had an affair with a female student at Ohlange and that she had borne him a child.

19 Willan, *Sol Plaatje*, p. 196.

20 Johannes Meintjes, *General Louis Botha: A Biography*, Cassell, London, 1970, p. 205.

21 S.B. Spies, 'The outbreak of the First World War and the Botha government', *South African Historical Journal*, 1 (1969), pp. 47–48.

22 Ibid., pp. 47–48.

23 Ibid., p. 52.

24 www.navy.mil.za/newnavy/mendi_history/mendi_hist.htm.

25 See Timothy C. Winegard, *Indigenous Peoples of the British Dominions and the First World War*, Cambridge University Press, Cambridge, 2012.

26 Bill Nasson, *WWI and the People of South Africa*, Tafelberg, Cape Town, 2014, p. 42.

27 Albert Grundlingh, *Fighting Their Own War: South African Blacks and the First World War*, Ravan Press, Johannesburg, 1987, p. 39.

28 Ibid., p. 57.

29 Nasson, *WWI and the People of South Africa*, p. 46.

30 Ibid., p. 50.

31 Grundlingh, *Fighting Their Own War*, p. 129.

## Chapter 12

1 There were more parties than are listed here: this is just a summary.

2 Marilyn Lake and Henry Reynolds, *Drawing the Global Colour Line: White Men's Countries and the Question of Racial Equality*, Cambridge University Press, Cambridge, 2008, p. 185; Charles Lucas, 'Suggestions as to Coloured Immigration into the Self-Governing Dominions', no. 2, British National Archives, CO886/1/1, p. 2.

3 Hardinge to Crewe, 27 November 1913, British Library, India Office Records, MSS EUR Photo 471.

4 Deborah Mutch, '"Are we Christians?" W.T. Stead, Keir Hardie and the Boer War', in Laurel Brake, Ed King, Roger Luckhurst and James Mussell (ed.), *W.T. Stead, Newspaper Revolutionary*, British Library, London, 2012, p. 143.

5 *Morning Leader*, 10 April 1901.

6 Freda Troup, *South Africa: An Historical Introduction*, Penguin Books, Harmondsworth, 1972, p. 211.

7 Bill Schwarz, *Memories of Empire, vol. 1: The White Man's World*, Oxford University Press, Oxford, 2011, pp. 308–314.

8 Ibid.

9 Robert MacGregor Dawson (ed.), *The Development of Dominion Status, 1900–1936*, Frank Cass, London, 1937, p. 25.

10 Ibid., p. 112.

11 Sheridan Johns, *From Protest to Challenge: A Documentary History of African Politics in South Africa, 1882–1990*, vol. 1, Jacana Media, Auckland Park, 2014, p. 319.

12 *APO*, 9 April 1910.

13 *APO*, 23 April 1910.

14 Hermann Giliomee, *The Afrikaners: Biography of a People*, Hurst, London, 2003, p. 412.

15 African National Congress, *A Brief History of the African National Congress*, www.anc.org.za/show.php?id=206.

16 Brian Willan, *Sol Plaatje: South African Nationalist, 1876–1932*, University of California Press, Berkeley, 1984, pp. 156–157.

17 Ibid., p. 156.

18 *Indian Opinion*, 10 February 1912.

19 Ashwin Desai and Goolam Vahed argue that Gandhi alone 'made no effort to reach out to other oppressed groups'. Ashwin Desai and Goolam Vahed, *The South African Gandhi: Stretcher-Bearer of Empire*, Stanford University Press, Stanford, 2016, p. 305. As I have indicated, this is not correct: all black movements of this period took this position to a greater or lesser degree.

20 I am grateful to Brian Willan for this insight.

21 Gavin Lewis, *Between the Wire and the Wall: A History of South African 'Coloured' Politics*, David Philip, Cape Town, 1987, p. 78.

22 *Indian Opinion*, 10 February 1912.

23 Lewis, *Between the Wire and the Wall*, p. 79.

24 *Indian Opinion*, 18 September 1909, www.gandhiheritageportal.org/cwmg_volume_thumbview/OQ==#page/400/mode/2up.

25 Joseph Lelyveld, *Great Soul: Mahatma Gandhi and His Struggle with India*, Vintage Books, New York, 2012, p. 114.

26 Heather Hughes, *First President: A Life of John L. Dube, Founding President of the ANC*, Jacana Media, Auckland Park, 2011, p. 179. The visitor was William Pearson.

27 Ibid., p. 179.

28 Vivian Bickford-Smith, *Ethnic Pride and Racial Prejudice in Victorian Cape Town: Group Identity and Social Practice, 1875–1902*, Cambridge University Press, Cambridge, 1995, pp. 183–209.

29 M.A. du Toit, *South African Trade Unions: History, Legislation, Policy*, McGraw-Hill, Johannesburg, 1976, p. 34.

30 Peter van Duin, 'Artisans and trade unions in the Cape Town building industry, 1900–1924', in Wilmot James and Mary Simons (eds.), *Class, Caste and Color: A Social and Economic History of the South African Western Cape*, Transaction Publishers, London, 2009, pp. 97–98.

31 Ibid., pp. 104–105.

32 Johns, *From Protest to Challenge*, p. 37.

33 Ibid., p. 40.

34 Ibid.

35 Ramachandra Guha, *Gandhi before India*, Penguin Books, London, 2013, p. 433.

36 Lewis, *Between the Wire and the Wall*, p. 78.

37 Heather Hughes, '"The coolies will elbow us out of the country": African reactions to Indian immigration in the colony of Natal, South Africa', *Labour History Review*, 72, 2 (August 2007), p. 163. Sol Plaatje took a similar position, tending to treat Indians as sojourners in South Africa who had taken land at the expense of Africans. Private communication from Brian Willan.

38 It is worth noting that as early as 1910 Nokutela Dube (John's wife) was probably the 'Mrs Dube' who was among the people who backed Gandhi's passive resistance campaign, collecting eight signatures and 6s 6d for its fund. See Hughes, *First President*, p. 154.

39 Neil Parsons, '"No longer rare birds": Zulu, Ndebele, Gaza, and Swazi envoys to England, 1882–1894', in Gretchen Gerzina (ed.), *Black Victorians/Black Victoriana*, Rutgers University Press, New Brunswick, 2003, pp. 110–144. I am grateful to the author for a copy.

40 Peter Limb, 'The Empire writes back: African challenges to the British (South African) Empire in the early 20th century', *Journal of Southern African Studies*, 41, 3 (2015).

41 http://hansard.millbanksystems.com/commons/1909/aug/16/south-africa-bill-lords#S5CV0009P0_19090816_HOC_57.

42 Testimony of Professor D.D.T. Jabavu, Walter Rubusana, and the Rev. Abner Mtimkulu of the Cape Native Voters' Convention and Meshach Pelem of the Bantu Union, before the Select Committee on the Subject of Native Bills, 30 May 1927, www.sahistory.org.za/archive/native-disabilities-south-africa-pamphlet-professor-d-d-t-jabavu-july-1932.

43 The librarian at the Royal Archives advised me that there is nothing to suggest that the matter was even raised with the King in 1937, when the legislation was being discussed in South Africa. The royal prerogative is always used on the advice of the government concerned. So in Australia or Canada the Crown is advised by their respective governments and not by the British government. See W.P.M. Kennedy and H.J. Schlosberg, *The Law and Custom of the South African Constitution*, Oxford University Press, London, 1935; Donald B. Molteno, *The Betrayal of 'Native Representation'*, South African Institute of Race Relations, Johannesburg, 1959.

44 T.R.H. Davenport, *South Africa, a Modern History*, University of Toronto Press, Toronto, 1987, p. 313.

45 Olive Schreiner, *Closer Union: A Letter on the South African Union and the Principles of Government*, 22 December 1908, http://webapp1.dlib.indiana.edu/vwwp/view?docId=VAB7036&doc.view=print.

# Select bibliography

Adhikari, Mohamed, *Not White Enough, Not Black Enough; Racial Identity in the South African Coloured Community*, Ohio University Press, Athens, Ohio, 2005

Bhana, Surendra and Vahed, Goolam, *The Making of a Political Reformer: Gandhi in South Africa, 1893–1914*, Manohar Publishers, Delhi, 2005

Bickford-Smith, Vivian, *Ethnic Pride and Racial Prejudice in Victorian Cape Town: Group Identity and Social Practice, 1875–1902*, Cambridge University Press, Cambridge, 1995

Bickford-Smith, Vivian, Van Heyningen, Elizabeth and Worden, Nigel, *Cape Town in the Twentieth Century*, David Philip, Cape Town, 1999

Boehmer, Elleke, *Empire, the National, and the Postcolonial, 1890–1920*, Oxford University Press, Oxford 2002

Bozzoli, Belinda, *The Political Nature of a Ruling Class: Capital and Ideology in South Africa, 1890-1933*, Routledge and Kegan Paul, London, 1981

Bridgman, F. Brainerd, 'The Native Franchise in the Union of South Africa', PhD, Yale University, 1939

Bright, Rachel, *Chinese Labour in South Africa, 1902–1910*, Palgrave Macmillan, Basingstoke, 2013

Brown, Judith M., *Gandhi: Prisoner of Hope*, Yale University Press, New Haven and London, 1989

Brown, Judith M. and Parle, Anthony (eds.), *The Cambridge Companion to Gandhi*, Cambridge University Press, Cambridge, 2011

Brown, Judith M. and Prozesky, Martin (eds.), *Gandhi and South Africa: Principles and Politics*, University of Natal Press, Pietermaritzburg, 1996

Bundy, Colin, *The Rise and Fall of the South African Peasantry*, Heinemann, London, 1979

Bush, Julia, *Edwardian Ladies and Imperial Power*, Leicester University Press, Leicester, 2000

Cartwright, A.P., *The Corner House: The Early History of Johannesburg*, Purnell and Sons, Cape Town and Johannesburg, 1965

Cecil, Hugh and Mirabel, *Imperial Marriage: An Edwardian War and Peace*, John Murray, London, 2002

Cruise, Adam, *Louis Botha's War: The Campaign in German South-West Africa, 1914–1915*, Zebra Press, Century City, 2015

Davey, Arthur, *The British Pro-Boers, 1877–1902*, Tafelberg, Cape Town, 1978

Dawson, Robert MacGregor (ed.), *The Development of Dominion Status, 1900–1936*, Frank Cass, London, 1937

Desai, Ashwin and Vahed, Goolam, *Inside Indian Indenture: A South African Story, 1860–1914*, HSRC Press, Cape Town, 2010

Drew, Allison (ed.), *South Africa's Radical Tradition: A Documentary History*, UCT Press, Cape Town, 1996

Drew, Allison, *Discordant Comrades: Identities and Loyalties on the South African Left*, Ashgate, Aldershot, 2000

Dube, John L., *The Zulu's Appeal for Light and England's Duty*, Unwin Brothers, London, 1909

Etherington, Norman, Harries, Patrick and Mbenga, Bernard, 'From imperial hegemonies to imperial conquest, 1840–1880', in *The Cambridge History of South Africa*, vol. 1, Cambridge University Press, Cambridge, 2010

Evatt, Herbert Vere, *The King and His Dominion Governors: A Study of the Reserve Powers of the Crown in Great Britain and the Dominions*, Oxford University Press, London, 1936

Eybers, G.W., *Selected Constitutional Documents Illustrating South African History, 1795–1910*, George Routledge and Sons, London, 1918

Fox Bourne, H.R., *Blacks and Whites in South Africa*, P.S. King and Son, London, 1900

Gandhi, Rajmohan, *Gandhi: The Man, His People, and the Empire*, University of California Press, Berkeley, 2007

Giliomee, Hermann, *The Afrikaners: Biography of a People*, Hurst, London, 2003

Giliomee, Hermann and Mbenga Bernard, *New History of South Africa*, Tafelberg Publishers, Cape Town, 2007

Goldin, Ian, *Making Race: The Politics and Economics of Coloured Identity in South Africa*, Longman, London, 1987

Gooch, G.P., *Life of Lord Courtney*, Macmillan, London, 1920

Green, Jeffrey, *Black Edwardians: Black People in Britain 1901–1914*, Frank Cass, London, 1998

Grundlingh, Albert, *Fighting Their Own War: South African Blacks and the First World War*, Ravan Press, Johannesburg, 1987

Guest, Bill, 'Indians in Natal and Southern Africa in the 1890s', in Judith Brown and Martin Prozesky (eds.), *Gandhi and South Africa: Principles and Politics*, University of Natal Press, Pietermaritzburg, 1996

Guha, Ramachandra, *Gandhi before India*, Penguin Books, London, 2013

Guy, Jeff, *The View across the River: Harriet Colenso and the Zulu Struggle against Imperialism*, James Currey, Oxford, 2002

Hale, Frederick, 'Socialist agitator, traitor to the British Empire or angel of peace? Keir Hardie's visit to Natal in 1908', *Journal of Natal and Zulu History*, 14 (1992)

Hale, Frederick, 'James Keir Hardie in South Africa: the politics of race in a working class colonial setting', *Quarterly Bulletin of the National Library of South Africa*, 56, 4 (June 2002)

Hale, Frederick, 'Public issues perceived from the theological left flank: the social ethics of Ramsden Balmforth in the Union of South Africa', *Studia Historiae Ecclesiasticae*, 38, 1 (2012)

Hancock, W.K., *Smuts, the Sanguine Years: 1870–1919*, Cambridge University Press, Cambridge, 1962

Hancock, W.K. and Van der Poel, Jean, *Selections from the Smuts Papers, vol. 2, June 1902–May 1910*, Cambridge University Press, Cambridge, 1966

Heartfield, James, *The Aborigines' Protection Society: Humanist Imperialism in Australia, New Zealand, Fiji, Canada, South Africa and the Congo, 1836–1909*, Hurst and Company, London, 2011

Hewison, Hope Hay, *Hedge of Wild Almonds; South Africa, the Pro-Boers and the Quaker Conscience, 1890–1910*, James Currey, London, 1989

Higgs, Catherine, *The Ghost of Equality: The Public Lives of D.D.T. Jabavu of South Africa, 1885–1959*, Ohio University Press, Athens, 1997

Howe, Stephen, *Anticolonialism in British Politics: The Left and the End of Empire, 1918–1964*, Clarendon Press, Oxford, 1993

Hughes, Heather, *First President: A Life of John L. Dube, Founding President of the ANC*, Jacana Media, Auckland Park, 2011

Hunt, James D., *Gandhi and the Nonconformists: Encounters in South Africa*, Promilla, New Delhi, 1986

Hunt, James D., *An American Looks at Gandhi: Essays in Satyagraha, Civil Rights and Peace*, Promilla, New Delhi, 2005

Huttenback, Robert, *Gandhi in South Africa: British Imperialism and the Indian Question, 1860–1914*, Cornell University Press, Ithaca, 1971

Hyam, Ronald, *Elgin and Churchill at the Colonial Office: The Watershed of the Empire-Commonwealth*, Macmillan, London, 1968

Hyslop, Jonathan, 'The world voyage of James Keir Hardie: Indian nationalism, Zulu insurgency and the British labour diaspora 1907–1908', *Journal of Global History*, 1, 3 (November 2006)

Innes, Duncan, *Anglo-American and the Rise of Modern South Africa*, Heinemann Educational Books, London, 1984

Jabavu, D.D.T., *The Findings of the All African Convention*, Alice, 1935

Jebb, Richard, *The Imperial Conference: A History and Study*, Longman Green, London, 1911

Jenkins, Roy, *Sir Charles Dilke: A Victorian Tragedy*, Collins, London, 1958

Johns, Sheridan, *Raising the Red Flag: The International Socialist League and the Communist Party of South Africa, 1914–1932*, Mayibuye Books, Bellville, 1995

Johns, Sheridan, *From Protest to Challenge: A Documentary History of African Politics in South Africa, 1882–1990*, vol. 1, Jacana Media, Auckland Park, 2014

Judd, Dennis and Surridge, Keith, *The Boer War*, John Murray, London, 2002

Kaushik, Harish P., *Indian National Congress in England*, Friends Publications, Delhi, 1991

Kendle, John Edward, *The Colonial and Imperial Conferences, 1877–1911*, Longmans, London, 1967

Killingray, David, 'Feminine discord, racial equality, and the Universal Brotherhood of Man, 1887–1913', unpublished

Killingray, David, 'Hands joined in Brotherhood: the rise and decline of a movement for faith and social change, 1875–2000', unpublished

Killingray, David, 'Rights, land, and labour: black British critics of South African policies before 1948', *Journal of Southern African Studies*, 35, 2 (June 2009)

Killingray, David, 'Significant black South Africans in Britain before 1912: Pan African organisations and the emergence of South Africa's first black lawyers', *South African Historical Journal*, 64, 3 (September 2012)

Lake, Marilyn and Reynolds, Henry, *Drawing the Global Colour Line: White Men's Countries and the Question of Racial Equality*, Cambridge University Press, Cambridge, 2008

Lake, Marilyn, 'The white man under siege: new histories of race in the nineteenth century and the advent of White Australia', *History Workshop Journal*, 58 (2004)

Le May, H.L., *British Supremacy in South Africa, 1899–1907*, Clarendon Press, Oxford, 1965

Legassick, Martin and Ross, Robert, *From Slave Economy to Settler Capitalism: the Cape Colony and its extensions, 1800–1854*, in *The Cambridge History of South Africa*, vol. 1, Cambridge University Press, Cambridge, 2010

Lelyveld, Joseph, *Great Soul: Mahatma Gandhi and His Struggle with India*, Vintage Books, New York, 2012

Levy, Shimon, *Soulmates: The Story of Mahatma Gandhi and Hermann Kallenbach*, Orient Black Swan, Hyderabad, 2012

Lewis, Gavin, *Between the Wire and the Wall: A History of South African 'Coloured' Politics*, David Philip, Cape Town, 1987

Lewsen, Phyllis (ed.), *Selections from the Correspondence of John X Merriman, 1905–1924*, Van Riebeeck Society, Cape Town, 1969

Limb, Peter, *The ANC's Early Years; Nation, Class and Place in South Africa before 1940*, University of South Africa Press, Pretoria, 2010

Limb, Peter, 'The Empire writes back: African challenges to the British (South African) Empire in the early 20th century', *Journal of Southern African Studies*, 41, 3 (2015)

Lorimer, Douglas A., *Science, Race Relations and Resistance: Britain, 1870–1914*, Manchester University Press, Manchester, 2013

Lowe, Cedric James, *The Reluctant Imperialists: British Foreign Policy 1878–1902*, Routledge and Kegan Paul, London, 1967

Lowe, C.J. and Dockrill, M.L., *The Mirage of Power, British Foreign Policy 1902–14*, Routledge and Kegan Paul, London, 1972

MacDonald, Ramsay, *Labour and Empire*, Routledge, London, 1907

Marais, J.S., *The Cape Coloured People, 1652–1937*, Longmans, London, 1939

Marks, Shula, *Reluctant Rebellion: The 1906–1908 Disturbances in Natal*, Clarendon Press, Oxford, 1970

Marks, Shula and Rathbone, Richard, *Industrialisation and Social Change in South Africa: African Class Formation, Culture and Consciousness, 1870–1930*, Longman, London, 1982

Marks, Shula, 'Southern Africa', in Judith M. Brown and Wm. Robert Louis (eds.), *The Oxford History of the British Empire*, vol. 4, Oxford University Press, Oxford, 1999

Marlowe, John, *Milner, Apostle of Empire*, Hamish Hamilton, London, 1976

Marquand, David, *Ramsay MacDonald*, Richard Cohen Books, London, 1997

Massie, Robert K., *Dreadnought: Britain, Germany and the Coming of the Great War*, Jonathan Cape, London, 1992

Mehrotra, S.R., *The Mahatma and the Doctor: The Untold Story of Dr Panjivan Mehta, Gandhi's Greatest Friend and Benefactor, 1864–1932*, Vakils, Feffer and Simons, Mumbai, 2014

Meredith, Martin, *Diamonds, Gold and War: The Making of South Africa*, Simon and Schuster, London, 2007

Morgan, Kenneth O., *Keir Hardie: Radical and Socialist*, Phoenix, London, 1997

Morgan, Kenneth O., 'Lloyd George, Keir Hardie and the importance of the Pro-Boers', *South African Historical Journal*, 41 (November 1999)

Narain, Iqbal, *The Politics of Racism: A Study of the Indian Minority in South Africa down to the Gandhi-Smuts Agreement*, Shiv Lal Agrawal, Delhi, 1962

Nasson, Bill, *Abraham Esau's War: A Black South African in the Cape, 1899–1902*, Cambridge University Press, Cambridge, 1991

Nasson, Bill, *WWI and the People of South Africa*, Tafelberg, Cape Town, 2014

Nauriya, Anil, *The African Element in Gandhi*, National Gandhi Museum in association with Gyan, New Delhi, 2006

Nicholls, David, *The Lost Prime Minister: A Life of Sir Charles Dilke*, Hambledon Press, London, 1995

Nimocks, Walter, *Milner's Young Men: The 'Kindergarten' in Edwardian Imperial Affairs*, Hodder and Stoughton, London, 1970

Odendaal, André, *The Founders: The Origins of the ANC and the Struggle for Democracy in South Africa*, Jacana Media, Auckland Park, 2012

Orpen, Joseph Millerd, *The Native Question in Connection with the South Africa Bill or Union Constitution Act. Including Remarks upon Lord Selborne's Address before the Cape University on the 27th of February, 1909*, Dispatch Printers, East London, 1909

Owen, Nicholas, *The British Left and India: Metropolitan Anti-Imperialism, 1885–1947*, Oxford University Press, Oxford, 2007

Owen, Nicholas, 'The soft heart of the British Empire: Indian radicals in Edwardian London', *Past and Present*, 220 (August 2013)

Pakenham, Thomas, *The Boer War*, Abacus, 1992

Parkinson, Roger, *Dreadnought: The Ship That Changed the World*, I.B. Tauris, London, 2015

Parsons, Neil, 'No longer rare birds in London', in Gretchen Gerizina (ed.), *Black Victorians/Black Victoriana*, Rutgers University Press, New Brunswick, 2003

Patel, A.J., 'The origins of Hind Swaraj', in Judith M. Brown and Martin Prozesky (eds.), *Gandhi and South Africa: Principles and Politics*, University of Natal Press, Pietermaritzburg, 1996

Power, Paul F., 'Gandhi in South Africa', *Journal of Modern African Studies*, 7, 3 (October 1969)

Price, Richard, *An Imperial War and the British Working Class: Working Class Attitudes and Reactions to the Boer War 1899–1902*, Routledge and Kegan Paul, London, 1972

Pyrah, G.B., *Imperial Policy and South Africa, 1902–1910*, Oxford University Press, London, 1955

Riedi, Eliza, 'Women, gender and the promotion of Empire: the Victorian League, 1901–1914', *Historical Journal*, 45, 3 (September 2000)

Rive, Richard and Couzens, Tim, *Seme: The Founder of the ANC*, Skotaville Publishers, Johannesburg, 1991

Röhl, John C.G., 'Goodbye to all that (again?): The Fischer thesis, the new revisionism and the meaning of the First World War', *International Affairs*, 91, 1 (January 2015)

Rose-Innes, Sir James, *The Native Franchise Question, A Speech Read at the Opening Meeting of the Non-racial Franchise Association*, Cape Town, 1929

Ross, Robert, Mager, Anne Kelk and Nasson, Bill, *The Cambridge History of South Africa, vol. 2, 1885–1994*, Cambridge University Press, Cambridge, 2011

Saunders, Christopher, 'F.Z.S. Peregrino and the South African Spectator', *Quarterly Bulletin of the South African Library*, 32 (1977–78)

Schneer, Jonathan, *London 1900: The Imperial Metropolis*, Yale University Press, New Haven, 1999

Schneer, Jonathan, 'The Pan-African Conference of 1900', in Gretchen Holbrook Gerizina (ed.), *Black Victorians/Black Victoriana*, Rutgers University Press, New Brunswick, 2003

Schoeman, Karel, *Only an Anguish to Live Here: Olive Schreiner and the Anglo-Boer War, 1899–1902*, Human and Rousseau, Cape Town, 1992

Schreiner, Olive, *Closer Union*, The Constitutional Reform Association, Cape Town, 1908

Selborne, Lord, *Address Delivered by Lord Selborne before the Congregation of the University of the Cape of Good Hope, on Saturday, 27th Feb., 1909*, R.L. Esson, Johannesburg, 1909

Sherwood, Marika, *Origins of Pan-Africanism: Henry Sylvester Williams, Africa, and the African Diaspora*, Routledge, Abingdon, 2011

Strachan, Hew, *The First World War in Africa*, Oxford University Press, Oxford, 2004

Swan, Maureen, *Gandhi: The South African Experience*, Ravan Press, Johannesburg, 1985

Tatz, C.M., *Shadow and Substance in South Africa: A Study of Land and Franchise Policies Affecting Africans, 1910–1960*, University of Natal Press, Pietermaritzburg, 1962

Thema, R.V. Selope, *In Defence of the Cape Native Franchise*, Lovedale Institution Press, Alice, 1928

Thompson, Andrew, *The Empire Strikes Back? The Impact of Imperialism on Britain from the Mid-Nineteenth Century*, Pearson Education, Harlow, 2005

Thompson, Leonard M., *The Unification of South Africa, 1902–1910*, Oxford University Press, London, 1960

Thompson, Leonard, *A History of South Africa*, 4th edn, revised and updated by Lynn Berat, Yale University Press, New Haven, 2014

Torrance, David E., *The Strange Death of the Liberal Empire: Lord Selborne in South Africa*, Liverpool University Press, Liverpool, 1996

Trapido, Stanley, 'The emergence of liberalism and the making of 'Hottentot nationalism', 1815–1834', Collected Seminar Papers, Institute of Commonwealth Studies, 42

Troup, Freda, *South Africa: An Historical Introduction*, Penguin Books, Harmondsworth, 1972

Van der Ross, Richard, 'A political and social history of the Cape Coloured people, 1880–1970', PhD, University of Cape Town, 1973

Van der Ross, Richard, 'The founding of the African People's Organisation in 1903 and the role of Dr Abdurahman', *Munger Africana Library Notes*, 28 (February 1975)

Van Reenen, Rykie, *Emily Hobhouse: Boer War Letters*, Human and Rousseau, Cape Town, 1984

Vickers, Rhiannon, *The Labour Party and the World, vol. 1: The Evolution* of *Labour's Foreign Policy, 1900–1951*, Manchester University Press, Manchester, 2003

Walker, Eric, *W.P. Schreiner: A South African*, Oxford University Press, Oxford, 1969

Wessels, André (ed.), *Lord Kitchener and the War in South Africa, 1899–1902*, Sutton Publishing for the Army Records Society, Stroud, 2006

Whyte, Frederick, *The Life of W.T. Stead*, Jonathan Cape, London, 1925

Willan, Brian, *Sol Plaatje: South African Nationalist, 1876–1932*, University of California Press, Berkeley, 1984

Willan, Brian (ed.), *Sol Plaatje, Selected Writings*, Witwatersrand University Press, Johannesburg, 1996

Willan, Brian, 'De Beers and an old tram shed: class relations and social control in a South African town, 1918–1919', Journal of Southern African Studies, 4, 2 (April 1978)

Williams, H. Sylvester, *The British Negro: A Factor in the Empire*, W.T. Moulton, Brighton, 1902

Winegard, Timothy C., *Indigenous Peoples of the British Dominions and the First World War*, Cambridge University Press, Cambridge, 2012

Wolpert, Simon, 'The Indian National Congress in nationalist perspective', in Richard Sisson and Stanley Wolpert (eds.), *Congress and Indian Nationalism*, University of California Press, Berkeley, 1988

Yap, Melanie and Man, Dianne Leong, *Colour, Confusion and Concessions: The History of the Chinese in South Africa*, Hong Kong University Press, Hong Kong, 1996

# Index

*References in bold indicate illustrations.*